# Sexual Fascism

**Garry Otton**
**Sexual Fascism**
*Sex in the Scottish Media*

**Published by**
**Ganymede Books Ltd**

First published in 2001
by Ganymede Books Limited
78 Montgomery Street, Edinburgh EH7 5JA

Cover illustration by Garry Otton

Printed in Scotland

British Library Cataloguing in Publication Data
A catalogue record for this book is available from the British Library
ISBN 0-9541131-0-1 (paperback)

# Contents

# Foreword
## *by Peter Tatchell*

In decades to come, historians will look back in utter disbelief at the way homosexual people and issues were reported in the media in the late twentieth and early twenty-first centuries. They will find it hard to comprehend that a minority community was so mercilessly vilified and scapegoated in a supposedly civilised, democratic, multicultural society.

The title of this book, **Sexual Fascism**, is no exaggeration. Fascistic is the only word appropriate to describe the witch-hunting homophobia of much of the media – particularly the tabloid press – with its casual, routine baiting of queers as perverts, plague-carriers, pædophiles and porn-peddlers. When we are not bad, mad and dangerous to know, we are sick, sad and sinful. Moreover, one moment faggots and dykes are denounced as an irrelevant, insignificant minority on the outer fringes of society, and the next we are part of a sinister pink freemasonry that has a disproportionate, unwarranted influence at the heart of public life.

Not since the demonisation of Jews in Nazi Germany has any minority in Western Europe suffered such sustained, overt, unapologetic press hostility – with the full connivance of many in the political and religious establishment.

For those who doubt such claims, Garry Otton has provided the evidence, documenting in meticulous detail the homophobic excesses of the Scottish media, both explicit and subtle. His book bears witness to an ugly, intolerant period in media history, citing almost unbelievable examples of ignorance and bigotry. There are some honourable exceptions, but not many.

Sexual Fascism is, to its credit, much more than an exposé of media homophobia. It reveals the diverse moral panics – both homosexual and heterosexual – which have blighted the Scottish press and diminished public debate. Puritanism and narrow-mindedness in all their forms are the enemy of reason, compassion and justice. Whatever our sexuality, we all suffer when calm, dispassionate debate on sexual matters is silenced by media hysteria.

Although Garry Otton mostly confines his documentation and analysis to reporters and broadcasters in Scotland, my own research on the coverage of lesbian and gay issues by the UK-wide media corroborates his findings. Homophobia may not be as explicit as it once was. But far from disappearing, it has merely become more subtle and insidious.

Take, for example, the bombing of the Admiral Duncan, a gay bar in Soho, London, in April 1999. It provoked unprecedented condemnation of anti-gay hatred by all sections of the media. Even the tabloid press - despite its long history of queer-bashing - was quick to express solidarity with the lesbian and gay community. The Sun declared: *"There is a huge tide of sympathy towards the minorities. An attack on THEM is an attack on each and every one of US"*.

But it is The Sun – through its columnists Garry Bushell, Richard Littlejohn and Norman Tebbit – that for decades stirred up the prejudice it suddenly claimed to deplore.

The right-wing broadsheets exhibited similar breath-taking hypocrisy. The Daily Telegraph thundered against the *"stupefying evil"* of the attack on the Admiral Duncan pub. Only a few months earlier, however, it condemned the vote by MPs to equalise the age of consent, justifying its support for discrimination with homophobic slurs that were not a million miles from the bigotry that motivated the Soho bomber.

While the opponents of gay equality vigorously deny any link, there is undoubtedly a continuity of hatred between the demonisation of homosexuals by the media and acts of violence against the gay community. The tabloids, in particular, have blood on their hands. With headlines such as *"Poofters on parade"* (Daily Star) and *"Poofs in the pulpit"* (Sunday People), they help legitimate the homophobic hatred that inspired the Soho bomb, and many lesser queer-bashing attacks.

Peter Hitchens denies any such connection, no matter how slight and indirect, between homophobic attitudes and hate crimes. Writing in The Express immediately after the bomb, he defended the right of newspapers to be homophobic: *"I am wor-*

*ried that there will now be attempts to suppress certain attitudes and opinions, on the grounds that they may 'lead to' incidents like these bombings. That would be wrong... If we really want to stamp on the idea that you can blow up people you do not like, then attacks on 'homophobia' are not the answer".*

Despite the media's supposedly new gay-friendly attitude following the Soho bomb, the reality is more ambiguous. Even the reporting of the bombing contained a mixture of sympathy and insult. The Sun could not resist describing the pub where the bomb exploded as a *"gay haunt"*.

As soon as it became known that not all the victims of the blast were gay, much of the media suddenly de-gayed its coverage by focusing almost exclusively on the heterosexual victims. The News of the World led with *"Pregnant wife killed"*, and The Sun reassured its readers that *"the victims were certainly not all gay"*. Nik Moore, the gay man who died, was not even mentioned in The Mail on Sunday, and he was relegated to a footnote in The Mirror.

Has press coverage of gay people and issues really changed since the Soho bomb? There is, undoubtedly, a new mood of media tolerance. But is it genuine and permanent? The coming out of Boyzone singer Stephen Gately, just months later, was clouded by accusations that he declared his sexuality under duress, fearing he was about to be outed by the tabloids. Whatever the reason for Gately's coming out, his press treatment was remarkably supportive.

Media coverage of Ron Davies MP was, alas, quite different. Although he mishandled the exposure of his *"moment of madness"*, when he was robbed after a dalliance with a man on Clapham Common, nothing justifies his subsequent hounding by the tabloids, especially the honey-trap tactics of the News of the World. Davies voted for an equal age of consent. He was not hypocritical. There were no public interest grounds for outing him. His subsequent revelation that he is bisexual and receiving psychiatric treatment for risk-taking behaviour was honest and brave. Yet Davies's candour was reported with little sympathy. Nearly all the published quotes were from critics arguing that these revelations make him unfit to hold public office.

Was the mistreatment of Davies the last gasp of media homophobia? Or has press prejudice merely become less blatant and more devious?

The Times obituary of the distinguished composer Sir Michael Tippett insultingly dismissed him as unmarried, ignoring his 30-year openly gay relationship with Meirion Bowen. Given that much of the media readily depicts gay men as universally promiscuous, this failure to acknowledge a loving, enduring homosexual relationship was deeply offensive.

When a would-be assailant stalked film director Steven Spielberg, most of the press – including The Guardian – gratuitously dubbed the man a *"homosexual stalker"*. Straight men who stalk women are, in contrast, never labelled *"heterosexual stalkers"*. The Mirror went further, denouncing Spielberg's stalker as a *"gay pervert"*. Had the stalker been black, would The Mirror have dared call him a *"black pervert"*?

More double standards were evident during reporting of the murder of fashion designer Gianni Versace. Nearly all the press branded his murderer, Andrew Cunanan, a *"gay serial killer"*. Heterosexual mass slayers like Peter Sutcliffe are, of course, never described as *"straight serial killers"*.

Journalists who always rush to condemn anti-Semitism said nothing when The Daily Mail denounced as a *"perversion"* a life-saving AIDS prevention campaign for gay men, and when the home of an elderly gay murder victim was pejoratively referred to by The Daily Telegraph as his *"lair"*.

Similar insidious homophobia featured in the Sunday Telegraph last year, when it alleged that the *"life expectancy of a practising male homosexual is about 30 years less than that of heterosexual men"*, and that *"80 per cent of the victims of pædophilia are boys molested by adult males"*. No reputable research endorses either claim, yet both allegations were printed as undisputed fact.

The limits of tolerance are also evident by the lack of press outcry against the system of "sexual apartheid" that denies lesbians and gay men legal equality. If black people were banned from getting married and their relationships denied legal recognition there would be uproar from all sections of the media. Most newspapers would throw their weight behind campaigns to overturn the racist ban. But when lesbians and gays are denied the right o marry – or to any alternative system of partnership rights - there are no howls of indignation. Much of press endorses this exclusion, with the liberal minority confining their response to barely audible murmurs of disapproval.

This differential treatment in the reporting of racism and homophobia is equally apparent with regard to hate-motivated murders. While the racist killing of Stephen Lawrence has received massive news coverage, the murder of gay actor Michael Boothe by queer-bashers in west London in 1990 was given perfunctory attention. Both were horrific hate crimes. Why the different treatment by the media? To add insult to injury, the campaign to reopen the bungled police investigation into the slaying of Boothe was largely ignored by the press. It seems that the murders of gay men are still deemed unworthy of media sympathy.

These criticisms apply to virtually all sections of the media in all parts of the UK. The great strength of Garry Otton's book is that it offers a much more detailed, concentrated account of homophobia and sexphobia by focussing on one specific part of Britain – Scotland – which is, broadly speaking, a microcosm of press and broadcasting malaise throughout the UK. Unique, insightful and truly shocking, **Sexual Fascism** is a must-read for everyone concerned with journalistic ethics, public opinion formation, sexual morality, and the state of the queer nation.

*Peter Tatchell,*
*July 2001.*

# Introduction

In the summer of 1995, 35-year-old Michael Doran was violently murdered in Queen's Park in Glasgow when a gang of three lads and a 14-year-old girl went on a 'queerbashing' rampage, putting a hammer through one man's head, beating another so badly he was unable to walk and, finally, murdering Michael Doran. Michael received 83 blows to his body. They stabbed him several times in the groin, stamped on his face until they had broken every bone in his head and left him in the bushes, choking to death in his own blood. With their clothes still bloodstained, the gang then joined friends at a nearby party, bragging about what they had just done. The inadequate reports that followed, including a whole column begging sympathy for the female member of the gang helped launch the Scottish Media Monitor, an acerbic monthly column that appeared first in **Gay Scotland** and later in **ScotsGay** magazine, examining the treatment of sexuality in the Scottish media.

Weeks after Michael's tragic murder - a chilling copycat of a killing in Queen's Park that led to the last hanging at Barlinnie prison in the sixties - Thomas Hamilton gunned down a classroom of children and their teacher in Dunblane Primary School. Gays were soon swept up in a tidal wave of moral panic.

Scoutmasters and gym teachers, boys' club managers and priests were dragged across the pages of the Scottish press in frenzy. One 'sex beast' after another was 'caged'. A 24-year-old was jailed for three months after being found on school grounds in Paisley; a 77-year-old man was sentenced to four years for taking pictures of kids at the seaside in Ayrshire; a drunken 37-year-old priest faced shame and retribution after allegedly groping a 16-year-old; and Iain Macdonald was jailed for 18 years for the 'rape' of Charles Kumar. (Charles denied he was gay - but went on to work in a gay sauna and win a heat in the Mr Gay UK contest). Public toilets, saunas, parks and swimming-pool changing areas throughout Scotland became flash points of moral warfare. A 29-year-old man was sentenced for peeking at two 14-year-old boys in one swimming-pool changing area, and at another, a 34-year-old scoutmaster faced indecency charges after filming boys with a video camera. A swimming-pool attendant warned parents "all your children are at risk", and was reported in a tabloid begging for more staff to patrol open changing-rooms. "The only way to clampdown on this kind of thing is by fitting screens to the top and bottom of cubicles and security guards watching at all times", he said.

The final five years of the 20th century can be seen as a period of unusual sexual repression. Not only was there a failed attempt to equalise the age of consent for homosexual men, but there was also the failed campaign to wreck the repeal of Section 28 (2a in Scotland) - a Thatcherite law designed to discriminate against young gays in the classroom - by militant religionists. By contrast, in the world of entertainment, this was also a time when unemployed men stripped for 'The Full Monty' and radio stations banned the 'Bloodhound Gang' for doing it like they do on the Discovery Channel.

Much of the Scottish media both protects and excludes readers in a process of restraint, contraction and limitation on sexual issues. A perceived threat to children from 'perverts' was trumpeted by tabloid campaigns such as the **Record**'s 'PervertWatch' and the **News of the World**'s 'Name and Shame'. The press attach a sense of shame and fuel moral outrage to any legitimate means of sexual expression. Most prominent amongst these campaigns has been the 'Channel Filth' attack on Channel 5's late night depiction of erotica and the **Daily Record**'s SmutWatch campaign. An increasingly politicised church, fearful of moral decay and advances in liberty and expression, succoured these campaigns. One of the victories 'won' by the Church and their media cronies was the banning of an exhibition of erotica in Glasgow. Such campaigns, however, paled into insignificance to what the fledgling Scottish parliament faced when they were caught unawares by the longest political debate in its history; the bankrolling of a campaign by Scottish business tycoon, Brian Souter to prevent the repeal of Section 2a, (known as Clause 28 in England and Wales), which forbade the so-called 'promotion' of homosexuality in schools.

When any issue of sexuality has appeared in the Scottish media - as it does on an almost daily basis - it is rarely the academics that the journalists turn to, but instead a string of religious and conservative 'spokespersons'. In Scotland it has been Mrs Ann Allen of the Kirk's ridiculously-named Board of Social Responsibility; the notorious 'Sexfinder General', the late Monsignor Tom Connolly for the Catholic Church; Phil Gallie, a deposed Tory MP; and any number of partisan organisations like the Christian Institute and Family and Youth Concern. This laziness on the part of journalists to latch on to sound bites or PR machines attached to religious organisations has both distorted and misrepresented Scotland's sexuality. In colluding with moral conservatives; throwing up a regular diet of propaganda and misinformation on sexual issues, the Scottish press have failed the public they are supposed to serve; thus contributing to Scotland's appalling record of sexual repression - Scotland has Europe's highest rate of teenage pregnancy (some *seven times* higher than the Netherlands) whilst sexual pathology, crime, ignorance and disease are rife. In the Netherlands, sex education begins at Primary level and the age of consent is 12. Nonetheless, children start having sex *later* than their Scottish counterparts and don't wait for years before crying foul when the sex is wrong!

In support of the morally conservative sexual propaganda issued by churches, there has been an abundance of equally conservative columnists operating within almost every major newspaper in Scotland. Best known of these was Jack Irvine, a former editor of Scottish editions of the **Sun**, whose column in the **Scottish Mirror** regularly carried his rabid homophobia, inspiring Brian Souter to enlist his support for a £2million campaign backing the Church's influence on sex education in schools. One of Irvine's most controversial remarks was his reference to *"slobbering queers"*. There were plenty more of his ilk. Jim Sillars, a former SNP MP, wrote weekly in the **Scottish Sun** and advised readers that homosexuals need to get the homosexual age of consent *"as low as possible to ensure a continuous supply of sexual partners"*. In the **Daily Record**, they had Tom Brown whose comments on gays' *"sad, seedy perversions"* border frequently on obsession. He was later asked to be the First

Minister's speechwriter. It is his expressed opinion that *"only sexually inadequate adults buy dirty magazines"*, an opinion apparently shared by the **Daily Record**'s matronly agony aunt Joan Burnie - or 'Old Mother Burnie' as she is known to some - who evoked the ire of many of her readers by describing erotic videos as *"filthy"*. She once advised a woman whose husband enjoyed erotica to *"burn anything you find"*. She has written: *"If my sons grew up to think porn was harmless, then I'd know I'd failed as a mum..."* The **Sunday Mail** had Gary Keown. Never mind the *"pansies"*, his opinion of women was equally suspect. *"The drunker they are, the better... Give me two slappers pulling at each other's cheap perms... Mini skirts riding up flabby thighs..."* The **Scottish Daily Mail** is the most favoured tabloid of the morally conservative. In 1933, an editorial suggested: *"I urge all British young men and women to study closely the progress of the Nazi regime in Germany. They must not be misled by the misrepresentations of its opponents"*. It was reported Hitler wrote to owner Lord Rothermere on 20 May 1937: *"Your leader articles published in recent weeks, which I have read with great interest, contain everything that is within my own thoughts"*. 55-years after the Allied Forces declared victory against Nazism, during the campaign to repeal Section 2a in Scotland, the **Scottish Daily Mail** ran anatomical drawings showing how to distinguish gay people from 'straight' and reported what was, in reality, a benign group of a dozen protesters from the Scottish Socialist Party handing out leaflets to the congregation outside homophobic multi-millionaire Brian Souter's church in Perth as a *"50 strong... gay law mob"* with their *"leaders"*. No such gay 'leaders' attended. Katie Grant was also used by the **Scottish Daily Mail** to spout a morally conservative agenda behind the benign persona of a 'concerned parent'. Before Section 2a was repealed, she sent a siren call to readers, warning them how the government was about to remove legislation that would ensure schools would be awash with gay propaganda. **The Scotsman**, once a more liberal broadsheet, boasted Linda Watson-Brown, who believed all men are potential rapists and is a virulent anti-porn campaigner. The **Daily Telegraph** had Alan Cochrane who led this paper's campaign against the repeal of Section 2a in Scotland. Even **The Herald**, despite its support for ditching this Tory-backed legislation, rode with one foot on the brake and a string of religionists in the back seat. Stewart Lamont wrote of his disgust of gay men's apparent love of public conveniences; Michael Fry thought the repeal of Section 2a would give children AIDS; and 'wee free' John Macleod who - before he was himself 'outed' - used to think gays *"simply not equipped to live"*. **Scotland on Sunday**, gave the **Mail**'s Katie Grant and Gerald Warner a Sunday voice. Warner, a speechwriter to the former Tory Scottish Secretary, Michael Forsyth, once wrote that condoms offer no protection against AIDS and continually propagated the myth that there was a powerful gay clique undermining the Government. (With such powerful friends in Government, it's surprising how difficult it has been for them to pass laws guaranteeing gay equality). Warner believed teenage mothers created a *"social blight"* and giving council houses to them was simply a *"reward for promiscuity"*. He once warned in his column: *"We cannot sit idly by and watch minority pressure groups and their allies secure an absurdly disproportionate profile in the media..."* Without one 'out' gay columnist batting against this surfeit of sexually regulating writers, what Scottish newspapers did he read?

With just one percent attending church, Scotland's sexual liberals deserve a better voice. But whatever you think of sexual politics in the new Scotland: lesbians, gays, bisexuals and people of transgender are on their own. Each day, individuals work to regulate and control the definition of sexuality within a narrow boundary defined by a personal morality fed by the church. This forest of deadwood has taken many years to grow. But not until a red top, a red frock and a pair of red shoes – that is to say, the red top tabloid, the **Daily Record**, the red-frocked Cardinal Winning and that Scottish businessman with his penchant for red shoes, Brian Souter - swished through Scotland in a blaze of intolerance and bigotry, was the people of Scotland exposed to a moral debate that spilled over into the 21st Century.

This book, covering a period of five years, provides a snapshot of the sexual attitudes that existed in Scotland at the end of the old millennium and at the start of the new. If, as studies have shown, Scotland is more liberal today than it ever has been before, then the newspapers have clearly failed to keep up with those changes.

# Acknowledgments

*This is an opportunity to extend a special thanks to some of those who had a part to play in making this book possible, be it pure inspiration or practical help. Alienation Design for care of www.scottish-mediamonitor.com, Christopher Brookmyre, Ann Coltart, Susan Craig, Douglas Bingham and Melvin Donaldson of The Control Panel, Dominic d'Angelo, Brian T Deans, Wayne Easton, Gordon Gosnell, Catherine Halliwell, John Hein, Karen Hetherington, Dr Richard Hillman, Tim Hopkins, Terry Sanderson, SubCity Radio, Peter Tatchell and the Glasgow Women's Library.*

*For Nan*

# Chapter One
## *The Church, the Sex Show and Bashing the Bishop*

"*It's a sin.*
*Everything I've ever done,*
*Everything I ever do,*
*Every place I've ever been,*
*Everywhere I'm going to,*
*It's a sin...*"
**Pet Shop Boys**

There's too much sex in the media. So we are told. Too much sex on the telly, too much sex in school, too much sex in the papers: Just too much sex. But what we learn about sex - like the odd infection - is largely picked up, if not in the school playground, in this case, from the media itself. The media shrugs its shoulders and claims it just *reflects* public opinion. Or does it...?

In 1997, there was a rush up the crinoline of the Scottish media after they were informed plans were afoot to hold an exhibition of erotica at Glasgow's Scottish Exhibition and Conference Centre. When this fair - already successfully held in several European cities, including London - was first mooted, one of Scotland's most sexually-inhibited tabloids the Glasgow-based **Daily Record** announced: "*Sex show flops... 1700 protests flood in to stop erotic carnival*". From the **Scottish Daily Mail** there were "*red faces at sex shop show of 'depravity'*." The organisers of the exhibition soon found themselves up against, not only a prohibitive media, eager to add their voice to the outrage, but also well-organised religionists and old-fashioned Labour councillors banging their fists on the table. And it seemed virtually *any* voice of outrage would do, including the Scottish director of Youth for Christ and the Scottish manager of Christian Action Research and Education (CARE). There were the usual favourites, familiar to the readers of Scottish newspapers. Monsignor Tom Connelly, a moral spokesman for the Catholic Church, so opinionated on sexual issues, his appearances in the press earned him the title 'Sexfinder General'. He thundered: *"The motto of the city is 'Let Glasgow flourish by the praising of God's name and the preaching of his word'. Erotica has no place in that. We have enough problems in this city without importing this depravity"*. It was suggested that if the exhibition went ahead, others would label Glasgow *"a capital of sleaze"*. Reverend David Anderson, general secretary of the Evangelical Alliance frothed: *"It is going back to an uncivilised state of savagery"* and Ali Syed, chairman of the Pakistani Media Relations Committee said: *"These people are capitalising on human weakness and frailty"*. The **Scottish Daily Mail** gave the Erotica chairman, David Wiseman only a few lines to protest. A campaign to rubbish the exhibition was soon underway with the tabloid's tones becoming more and more hysterical. Readers learnt that Wiseman's group were planning to turn the Scottish Exhibition and Conference Centre *"into the biggest sex shop in Europe for three days...!"* John Young, a former Tory councillor in the Labour-led Glasgow City Council warned readers of the **Mail**: *"A large section of the population will find this totally offensive but, given the track record of the Labour administration here, they will probably find a way of giving it a grant"*.

The issue didn't come to a head until the following summer. Out went the crotchless knickers and satin codpieces and in came whalebone corsets and firm trusses, lining-up to sabotage Scotland's first ever fair of erotica. Glasgow City Council's licensing applications sub-committee had apparently bowed under the weight of *"4,000 letters of protest"*, orchestrated, of course, by the Church and media. *"Moral victory as city sex festival is banned"*, crowed the **Scottish Daily Express**. *"No Erotica please, it's so insulting to our city"*, sniffed the **Scottish Daily Mail**. Little effort was made by the media to seek the opinion of the liberal majority who were left reeling from the announcement. Most people hadn't even been aware an erotica fair was being planned; let alone the work going on behind the scenes to ban it! In case anyone rumbled the concerted campaign of Bible-thumping religionists, the **Scottish Daily Mail** found Isobel Wilkie of Glasgow Women's Aid, which helps battered women, to lend her support to their moral vigilantism by adding: *"Most women who are sexually abused say it came from a man acting out a depraved fantasy he had seen in pornographic films"*. Her comments only reflected deep divisions within the women's movement. Feminist writers Catherine McKinnon and Andrea Dworkin, having spoken in Glasgow, were international players. They worked hard during the eighties trying to secure legal judgements in America that were based on the assumption that soft-core pornography caused harm. Groups like Women Against Violence Against Women (WAVAW) and Scottish Women Against Pornography (SWAP) bought this twaddle wholesale and even turned on lesbian groups exploring fetishes and women's fantasies, dividing the women's movement throughout the eighties with unsuccessful bids to link sex with violence. Their half-baked truths were served up to the councillors on the licensing sub-committee and they swallowed it hook, line and sinker.

As if expecting the *"4,000"* protesters to turn up all at once, Glasgow City Council moved the meeting to Shettleston Town Hall, but only about 100 shuffled along, mostly retired, apparently intent on nannying anyone not offering sex as a sacrament to God. The 12 protesters who spoke all claimed the event was dangerous to children, demeaning to women, and damaging to the city. The late Cardinal Thomas Winning sent one of his advisors, ex-TV presenter and former member of the extreme Catholic right-wing faction Opus Dei, Ronnie Convery to add: *"Glasgow has been spared an insult to its good name"*. A promotional video was shown at the hearing that the **Scottish Daily Mail** suggested *"featured graphic examples of naked women, body piercing, leather-clad models and various sex aids"*. And, if that wasn't bad enough, the organisers tried to calm the outrage by suggesting the fair might be held later in the year, perhaps just before Christmas. Councillor Martin Lee gasped: *"I would be concerned about taking my grandchildren to an event at the SECC before Christmas and seeing adverts for this…"* The committee's convenor, John Moyne announced crisply that after *"careful consideration"* the erotic fair would not be held in Glasgow. Moyne had already gained some notoriety in Glasgow after going on record to say the City had "no problem" with prostitutes. Following the brutal murders of seven women, he was forced to admit on the documentary, BBC 'Frontline Scotland' that he might have been wrong! There is a noticeable consistency in John Moyne's conservative approach to sexual issues, particularly after both Glasgow Sheriff Court and the Court of Session threw out Glasgow Licensing Board's efforts (of which Moyne was chairman) to refuse an entertainment licence for 'table dancing' over their expressed fears that it was sleazy, attracted the wrong sort of people and promoted *"violent conduct of a sexual nature against women"*. Glasgow did have one lap-dancing club at the time, called Truffles, highly regulated and permitting only topless girls but no naked acts. With another application in the offing, the Board stubbornly sought an opinion from Senior Counsel, with a view to taking the matter before the House of Lords, before good sense - and some thought toward the restrictions of the public purse - prevailed.

Over the decision to ban the exhibition of erotica in Glasgow, **The Herald** noted, *"the objectors applauded enthusiastically as the sound of councillors' minds shutting was almost audible"*. A story in the **Scottish Daily Express** bore the sub-heading: *"'Sinful' Erotica exhibition was a real turn-off to too many Scots"*, but **The Herald** just sniggered: *"No sex please, we're from Glasgow"*. The **Daily Record**'s agony aunt, Joan Burnie scolded: *"In my experience, anyone who wants that sort of knowledge has absolutely no difficulty in hunting it out, no matter how young or old they might be... Like the top shelf of any newsagent"*. That was, presumably, when the media weren't orchestrating campaigns to remove them!

Another licensing chief, Jim Coleman demonstrated in the **Scottish Sun** how he intended to run the city with an iron hand. *"No one messes with Glasgow and if you break the rules the result is simple - we'll shut you down! Call me Mary Whitehouse if you want...* (She) *played an important rôle in keeping filth off the telly where it could be watched by kids or anyone. I've raised standards in Glasgow and aim to keep them that way"*. The effect of his censorious opinions stretched further than just lap-dancing club applications, as the organisers of Glasgow's gay festival, Glasgay! knew only too well. He told the **Scottish Sun**: *"Glasgay was becoming too in your face and the public couldn't accept it. It was becoming offensive with guys all kissing each other dressed as nuns. I found it distasteful and so did the public who were going mental and I'm glad to see the organisers seem to have wrapped* *it up"*. Of Divally's, Glasgow's only licensed erotic cinema, he said: *"Their application came up on an extremely rare occasion when I couldn't be present... But Divally's hasn't got much to boast about cause they can't show anything hardcore. If they do they're busted and out of business... Every licence holder in Glasgow now knows that if they step out of line I will shut them down"*.

The Licensing Board must have had its work cut out after the **Sunday Mail** sniffed: *"a live sex show is planned to introduce teenagers to student life"* at gay club entrepreneur, Stefan King's Archaos nightclub in Glasgow. This was organised by *"sleazy DJ Neil Mackay"* who was promptly demonised for not towing the **Sunday Mail**'s sex-repressive line. *"He shrugs off a growing storm of protest about his seedy show in university and college Freshers' Week - just days after the youngsters leave their family homes"*. He protested to the Mail that all he wanted to show them was "how open-minded the city really was", which - considering the levels of intolerance often found in the City - was exemplary. The **Sunday Mail** accused him of *"bragging"* and reported that he even *"smirked"* when he spoke to them!

The **Daily Record**'s pages have been filled with censorship and condemnation. Regularly whinging and squealing their moral rectitude they were delighted to assist Jim Coleman after discovering *"sordid acts of gay girl group"* Rock Bitches, performing at Glasgow's RatTrap club. The **Daily Record** stormed out in high dudgeon. *"Sick... the band members cavorted naked onstage before inviting fans to join an orgy... The vile scenes were photographed by the* **Record***..."* and promptly *"handed... to the police"*. A black strip marked *"censored"* covered a girl's breast. Worse! The **Daily Record** saw one dressed in a nun's habit, holding a crucifix! The Scottish Catholic Church's spokesman, Tom Connelly, the notorious 'Sexfinder General', was *"disappointed the licensing courts allowed such an act to take place"* and as chairman of the Licensing Board, Jim Coleman promised to have *"a word"* with the RatTrap. Despite no complaints from members of the public buying tickets for the performance, he was able to assure readers of the **Daily Record** that he didn't expect to see the band performing in Glasgow again. Within a few years, no one saw the RatTrap again either. It closed down.

Because 'Sexfinder General', Monsignor Tom Connelly, spokesman for the Catholic Church in Scotland on all matters sexual didn't like director, Robert Wainwright's film, 'Stigmata', he didn't feel anyone else should either! The self-appointed moral regulator *"called for Glasgow City Council's licensing board to set an example by banning the film from city cinemas"*. The board were renowned for their strict stance on film censorship. They had already banned Martin Scorsese's controversial 1988 movie 'The Last Temptation of Christ' and Monty Python's religious spoof, 'The Life of Brian'. The 'Sexfinder General' decided: *"Glasgow people in the past have shown themselves far too sensible and they don't go to films like this"*. It didn't appear they had much choice in the matter! Sections of the media gave him a voice. The 'Sexfinder General' told the **Daily Record** *"a film like this encourages and excites violence from the type of people who do want to go and see it. I have every faith that the licensing authority will be much too sensible to let this film be shown"*.

At the seaside town of Ayr, Margaret McCracken attempted to open a sex shop in Burns' Statue Arcade. South Ayrshire Council received 283 written objections and was faced with a wildcat protest from hundreds of protesters organised by several churches storming their meeting as they decided whether or not they should issue a licence. Despite assurances that goods requiring a licence would be kept at the back, that no entry would be given to anyone under 21 and the windows, as required by law, would be completely blacked out, the Licensing Board refused to give a licence. One tearful woman claimed her son had become addicted to pornography, changing and distorting his personality until he had become "sinful". A minister advised that sex was God's gift to loving couples and allowed them to express their love in a caring way within marriage. An elderly lady, describing herself as a born-again Christian, lectured the Board for five minutes on the state of their "immortal souls" before promising them: "I'll pray for you. I'll pray that you'll be saved from this evil".

The religionist tones of the **Daily Record** have been familiar. When former "madam", Josie Daly, a disabled pensioner who made several millions running brothels, was pictured in the **Record** in her wheelchair outside court, the caption appearing under her picture read: *"WAGES OF SIN"*.

Whether such religionist-inspired repression achieved the

results required by the Church is doubtful. In 1996, a specially commissioned poll for **Scotland on Sunday** revealed that double the number of people in the North said they had more than 10 sexual partners compared to the South of Scotland. Highland Health Board manager, Gordon Stone, working in an area where religion often had a vice-like grip, told **Scotland on Sunday**: *"The activities of the Highland population suggest the church influence is less in practice than the column inches and air time they get indicates"*.

Any religionist daring to step out of line with the intention of promoting sex as something positive, recreational, healthy and fun was soon slapped down by the Scottish media as the Right Reverend Richard Holloway, Episcopalian Bishop of Edinburgh found to his cost. His support for homosexuals unleashed a campaign of vilification in the press as religious factions sought to have him removed. *"He is to give his support to gays within the church"*, they squealed. The **Scottish Daily Mail** saw it as a *"'one-track mind' of gay campaign bishop"* drawing attention to the fact he was being *"criticised from within his own church... for talking about sex too much"*. Rev William Ward of St Mary the Virgin in Arbroath told The **Scottish Daily Mail**: *"All he seems to talk about is sex. The issue of homosexuality within the priesthood has been dealt with for centuries in a sympathetic way"*. (Largely burning, hanging, torture and of course, more recently, the sexual abuse of children). The **Scottish Daily Mail** added darkly that the Bishop *"was forced to apologise... when he described opponents of women priests as 'miserable buggers'."* Over his calls to ordain gays, Scottish editions of the **Daily Express** headlined: *"DO NOT REWRITE THE BIBLE BISHOP"*. The paper underlined how they had been met *"with outrage from Scots Church leaders"*. The 'Sexfinder General', Father Tom Connelly was summoned to warn in tones of moral certainty: *"As far as we are concerned, homosexuality is neither right nor wrong, but homosexual acts are..."* Mrs Ann Allen, convenor of the Church of Scotland's ridiculously-named Board of Social Responsibility, said: *"I don't think anything in Christian doctrine substantiates what the Bishop says. If he wants to rewrite the Bible then I think he may find his comments substantiated"*.

*"He champions homosexual rights"*, scoffed the **Scottish Daily Mail** before discovering, to their horror, Bishop Richard

Holloway also *"confesses to having smoked cannabis"*! Holloway's call for the legalisation of cannabis set fire to their pages. *"RESIGN PLEA TO DRUGS BOAST BISHOP"*, they barked. The **Scottish Daily Mail** press-ganged anyone they could find to badmouth him: Mothers Against Drugs, Locals Against Drugs, a Tory law and order spokeswoman, the Chief Constable of Strathclyde police and, of course, someone from the Kirk. Too bad, when a few days later, Wee Free, Professor Donald Macleod - certainly no liberal - added cannabis was no more harmful than alcohol. But - as the **Scottish Daily Mail** pointed out impatiently - *"Prof Macleod – a controversial figure even within his own church – was acquitted at Edinburgh Sheriff Court in May 1996 on charges alleging he molested five women"*. Another religionist commentator and declaring himself *"once friends"* with the Bishop, A N Wilson – leapt in to catalogue *"the risks to civilisation if we follow his moral path"*. (This is a friend)? Wilson bitched how Bishop Holloway had intended to stand as a Member of the Scottish Parliament but ditched the idea *"to stay in the church and fight the gays' corner"*. This came about after the rank homophobia he witnessed at a church conference in Lambeth. A N Wilson was peeved Holloway saw *"very little wrong with... homosexuality"* and *"the trivial and ultimately silly question of 'gay rights'"*. He thought sex outside marriage was both bad behaviour and immoral and sniffed: *"Richard Holloway has had an unusual career in the Church – not that of the conventional Anglican vicar, educated at minor public school... His upbringing had been more Rab C Nesbitt than Barchester Towers"*. He added: *"No wonder Islam is the only world religion which is growing apace, to judge, and ultimately to consume our filthy, corrupt society"*. For all his moral rectitude, A N Wilson was no saint. Not only did he leave the faith, he even divorced his wife!

The **Scottish Daily Mail**'s regular columnist, Colette Douglas Home, wife of *The Herald* editor, Mark Douglas Home, described Bishop Holloway as *"a trendy bishop grabbing the headlines"*. She begrudged having to *"run the gauntlet of unpopularity with our youngsters because we know that in the long run they will benefit from the strictures we impose... Then along comes a populist bishop and contradicts all we've been saying"*. (Pity. For as long as this *"populist"* Bishop has to *"run the gauntlet of unpopularity"* in the Scottish media, we know that in the long run readers will benefit from some of the strictures he imposes. Then along comes the **Scottish Daily Mail** and contradicts all he's been saying)! They were not the only ones. The **Daily Record**'s dickey-bowed Tom Brown, otherwise known as 'pop Brown' or the 'Brigadier' to readers of **ScotsGay** magazine, heaved himself up out of his fireside chair to moan: *"Bishop Richard Holloway, has for years specialised in sermons of spectacular silliness... Ignorance, anything-goes libertarianism and a happy-clappy carefree blindness to the consequences were to blame... We are now paying the penalty for our 'harmless' pursuits of the 60s".* And, after confessing having once partaken of a smattering of the weed on his All-Bran, sighed: *"These days, the only thing I take on my All-Bran is a banana..."* This is a message that is consistently voiced amongst religionists. That it is not lack of sex education that is responsible for Scotland's poor record of sexual health, but permissiveness rooted in the sixties and 'too much' sex education. This doesn't add up. Despite a reported 75% increase in cases of chlamydia in five years, three-quarters of 16 to 25-year-olds have never heard of it! Which begs the question: What prolific sex education could they be talking about?

Almost anything the Most (Right-on) Reverend Richard Holloway said appeared to evoke outrage. The illiberal **Scottish News of the World** described him as *"renegade"* and *"controversial"* after he sparked a *"holy war"* by claiming youngsters who slept together didn't necessarily lack sexual ethics. Scots bishop. David Easton, vice-convenor of the Church of Scotland's Board of Social Responsibility droned how *"a Christian ideal is chastity before marriage and fidelity within marriage. We see sex as God's gift to be expressed in marriage. Many will find his comments insulting... I am astonished... I think it is a pathetic attempt by an ageing bishop to be 'with it'."*

It was in the face of his media assassination that Bishop Holloway light-heartedly quipped at a re-hab centre in Possilpark: *"Has anyone got a joint?"* Quite apart from bringing the house down, it brought the **Daily Record** down on him like a ton of bricks! A good dose of hot air, pompous drivel and moral finger wagging was in order. Their comic reporter Steve Martin whipped up a *"fury over dopey bishop's drug joke at rehab clinic..."* He reckoned that: *"The blundering Bishop of Edinburgh provoked anger... by asking at a drugs unit: 'Has anyone got a* *joint'?"* Professional impartiality was 'oot the windae' for this report as the Bish discovered his *"latest gaffe was greeted with outrage by anti-drug campaigners – especially as he made the daft remark in heroin-ravaged Possilpark, Glasgow"*. The **Daily Record** lined-up a host of representatives of organisations only too happy to bash the Bishop: Mothers Against Drugs, Scotland Against Drugs, Scottish Drugs Forum and wee Willie Thornton, a **Record** photographer who dutifully gasped: *"People were cringing"*. I should think so! The alleged remark was made in front of the Archbishop of Canterbury and 70 senior churchmen. The **Daily Record** went on to mention, in the same tenor, how Bishop Holloway *"advocates tolerance of gays and lesbians"*. The **Scottish Sun** soon joined in the campaign to have *"the Bishop, who has been married to wife Jean for 34 years and has three grown-up children"*, booted out. A *"shocked Rev Mike Parker"*, and *"Alistair Ramsay, of Scotland Against Drugs"* helped him on his way. Under the heading: *"Shocked"*, we learnt how *"he supported the rights of homosexuals – even attacking the Anglican Church for claiming gay sex was incompatible with the Bible…"* Also, how he *"supports gay marriages… and approves of couples having sex before they tie the knot…"* The **Scottish Sun** decided his support for homosexuality actually caused the most controversy.

Bishop Holloway recognised another life-long pacifist and human rights campaigner who had been vilified by the media: Peter Tatchell. He called him a prophet. The **Daily Record** expressed their contempt and once again, there were *"fresh calls to resign…"* They found anti-drugs campaigner Maxie Richards to support them when she sagely advised the Bishop to *"…go by the authority of the Scriptures. If he does not want to do that then it is up to him to go off and grow daisies…"*

Not until the Most Rev Dr George Carey was up in Dundee did he pick his moment to put the boot up the Bishop's backside. Of course, the **Scottish Daily Mail** *had* to be there! *"Carey throws the book at Holloway's Godless morality"*, they rejoiced.

Under Cardinal Winning, former leader of the Catholic Church in Scotland, moral certainty was never in doubt. Hugh Farmer, Scottish correspondent for Catholic newspaper, **The Universe**, wrote a piece in **The Scotsman** justifying why Pope John Paul II, 80-years-old and in failing health, attacked the estimated 200,000 who turned up for Gay Pride in Rome in

2000. Farmer showed *"no surprise"* and felt the Pope, (who carefully picks a college of cardinals to carry his own extreme views) spoke *"for all Christians and those of other faiths and beliefs who cherish Christian values"*. This immediately outlawed moderate Christians from a sinister new alliance of extremists. Farmer was able to rescue the Church from the inevitable results of this intolerance by resting the blame on 'the Word of God'. On homosexuality, Farmer believed: *"The act is wrong because it can never be procreative"*. He turned everything on its head to explain: *"The Church, in rejecting erroneous opinions regarding homosexuality, does not limit but rather defends personal freedom and dignity realistically and authentically"*. The **Daily Record** concentrated on the *"VATICAN ANGER OVER GERI'S SICK POPE JIBE"* when *"controversial singer"* Geri Halliwell took to the stage in Rome and 'cavorted' with a dancer dressed as the Pope. At one point during the performance, 'the Pope' was seen to kiss the former Ginger Spice's bare stomach. The Catholic Church in Scotland found it *"horrifying"*. Little attention was given to the fact that at the celebrations, a gay couple were attacked as far-right groups attempted to hijack the event. Furza Nuova, an Italian far-right group staged a 700-strong rally on the opening night and later, religious leaders teamed up with the far-right National Alliance Party for a torch-led procession in the city.

Religious sexual repression also includes 'curing' homosexuality. The 'curing' of homosexuals centres on the mistaken belief that it is a disorder. In the case of Father Sean McAulay it resulted in his internment in a 'clinic'. He left St Columba's Cathedral, Oban for Washington's St Luke's Institute in the US, which specialised *"in treating priests with addictions and sexual problems"*. The **Daily Record** gossiped: *"Concerns were raised within the church after Father McAulay was seen regularly in a bar next to St Columba's drinking with a young man he claimed was his nephew. A local, who did not wish to be named, said: 'Tongues were wagging…The young man often wandered around in tight shorts and it didn't seem appropriate in the company of a priest'."* Readers were furnished with a description of what awaited the recalcitrant priest. *"Inside the building, visitors are greeted by a smiling female receptionist… Treatment includes giving priests the drug Depo-Provera to quell sex drive… Priests have to sign a contract agreeing* *to be monitored for years to come"*. St Luke's president, Rev Canice Connors assured the **Daily Record**: *"It is a recoverable disorder"* and a senior churchman told the **Scottish News of the World**: *"We are praying for his recovery"*.

Not all religionists escaped sexual repression with their lives as the case of footballer Justin Fashanu demonstrated. He found himself on a teenage gay assault charge and hanged himself in a garage. It wasn't just that Fashanu was gay: he was black, cut off from his family, a professional in one of the most homophobic of occupations and, according to the **Daily Record**, was promising *"to return to America and enter a Christian programme, Exodus International, which 'cures' sex addictions and homosexual lifestyles"*. If only the Church had been there with the same kind of support they offered one *"sex shame minister"* who resigned after having an affair with a 17-year-old schoolgirl. Reverend Terry Morgan, of Arthurlie Parish Church in Barrhead, quit after teachers at her school exposed his relationship with the teenager. The girl had originally gone to the 37-year-old for counselling after bereavement in her family. The Church of Scotland gave Rev Morgan £1,300 to help start a new life.

Behind the Church's powerful autocracy lurked other tawdry secrets. A string of allegations against the Poor Sisters of Nazareth brought about judgement day in the High Court in Aberdeen for Sister Alphonso, alias Marie Docherty. Former children from the orphanage lined up to provide testimonies of daily beatings, sexual abuse from visiting priests, the force-feeding of a little girl with her own vomit, the wrapping of bed-wetters in their urine-soaked sheets, the forcing of a little girl into a cold bath in the middle of an epileptic fit which Sister Alphonso was supposed to have described as *"the work of the devil"*, lads being dropped into scalding baths and the 'cleansing' of menstruating girls by immersing them in baths filled with Jeyes disinfectant. One woman claimed Sister Alphonso had dragged her by her hair and beat it against a wall so hard it broke her front teeth leaving only the stumps. Helen Cuister told a court that when she began menstruating, Sister Alphonso told her that it was 'God's punishment' for girls who did not behave and that her punishment would go on until midnight when she would die for being so dirty. Louise Clark told the same court how she had been beaten mercilessly simply for not attending church. Sister Alphonso told the court how, as a child she had pulled down her knickers and asked her father to hit her and, when as a sister in the Aberdeen home, she had given the girls a good talking to after she caught them watching forbidden TV programme, 'Top of the Pops'.

The church stood by Sister Alphonso. A Scottish Catholic Church source told the press: "The view within the church is that she deserves sympathy, not more punishment. The church will rally round her." In a prepared statement, the Rt Rev Mario Conti, the Catholic Bishop of Aberdeen and Orkney explained: "Some practices which, today seem excessive and even cruel, would not have been viewed in this light years ago. These convictions do not, moreover, invalidate the great good, which was done by Sister Marie and the Church, in caring competently and appropriately for many thousands of children over the last 100 years". The Catholic Church appointed a team of leading lawyers, including former Solicitor General Paul Cullen, QC. Still dressed in her nun's habit, Marie Docherty was found guilty of just four counts of cruelty and unnatural practices. Former care assistant Helen Howie, 75, was angry that she was not called as a witness. "She has made all these children out to be liars", she said, "but everything they said was true. A couple of times when my husband came to collect me from his work he had to pull her off to stop her beating the children. I called him many a time to take her away from the children". Docherty's age, state of health, lack of previous convictions and the time that had passed since the crimes took place were all taken into consideration. After whispering a polite 'thank you' to Sheriff Colin Harris, Marie Theresa Docherty was free to walk away. The **Scottish Daily Mail** tried to *"put this case in perspective"* and commented that what Sister Alphonso did *"was not in the same category as the more sordid offences involving paedophile priests and social workers"* assuring readers *"there was no sexual element involved"*. It was around this time that Frances Edmonds, a 35-year-old mother was jailed for 12 months and placed on the sex offenders' register for 10 years for having consensual sex with two 14-year-old boys. The **Scottish Sun** called her a *"blonde... seductress"*.

More scandals were to follow. After lodging papers at the

Court of Session in Edinburgh containing allegations by 11 former pupils who claimed to have been brutalised by an order of Catholic monks, solicitor Cameron Fyfe claimed he was handling the biggest abuse case Scotland had ever seen. Allegations from former pupils of St Ninian's List D School in Gartmore, Stirlingshire included electric shocks administered from a device described as a type of generator kept in a boot room where boys had to hold on to a pair of wires leading from the machine. Central Scotland Police were involved in compiling a report for the Procurator Fiscal that also included complaints of regular thrashings, being forced to eat vomit, sexual fondling and serious physical abuse.

The Catholic Church's chief apologist Katie Grant wrote with some certainty in **Scotland on Sunday**. She was dismissive of the allegations made against the Catholic Church - *"...many, let us not forget, turning out to be completely false and unsubstantiated... fertile territory for ingenious headline writers"*. She recommended the Church *"keep its head"* and solidly advised they respond to *"unfair headlines"* by modelling itself on Christ. She believed there was *"a kind of hysteria abroad"* and cried: *"Soon... Catholic priests will be accused not only of abusing children but eating them too. All nuns will be branded monsters and anybody voluntarily taking a vow of chastity a potential pervert..."*

The **Big Issue in Scotland** told a particularly harrowing tale by resident John McCorry of the behaviour of the nuns from the Smyllum Park Orphanage near Lanark. *"They warped our sexualities. We were told that the toilet - and even using the word toilet - was evil. We couldn't refer to any part of our body between the neck and knees as anything other than 'our front'. But as a result kids would get beaten for talking about their fronts. We would get beaten for asking to go to the toilet. It was institutionalised insanity... Boys who wet the bed were beaten all the time... They were forced to drink Epsom salts over and over again. But that ended up making them doubly incontinent. Most of the boys who suffered this ended up soiling themselves a few hours later. The most disgraceful thing I ever saw was one boy who was forced to walk up and down all day in the dining hall with his wet sheet under his arm. The sister who made him do this was shouting at us, saying, 'Why aren't you laughing at him?' There was the sound of forced laughter everywhere. The boy was crying. It was sadistic, sick, mental torture"*. The Catholic Church's spokesman, the 'Sexfinder General', not usually reluctant to offer a sound bite to the press decided to leave it to his secretary to explain to the **Big Issue in Scotland**: *"It's nothing to do with us any longer"*.

Father Desmond Lynagh was a priest and teacher at the old junior seminary Blair's College, near Aberdeen; he was found guilty of abuse and jailed for three years. Cardinal Joseph Gray failed to take action despite being approached by Father John Fitzsimmons after a trainee priest broke a 17-year silence. Once again, the 'Sexfinder General' refused to comment.

Following the sudden death at 66 of the 'Sexfinder General', Monsignor Tom Connolly of liver cancer in the autumn of 2000, Hugh Farmer wrote in his obituary: *"...Just as when he was handling the good news, Fr Tom made himself available to the media and didn't hide the facts"*. **The Scotsman** wrote that he was *"privately on the church's more liberal wing... he was nonetheless accepted by all sections and managed to weave a diplomatic course when asked to comment on potentially divisive issues"*. Connolly was the first priest to be put in charge of the Church's Media Office. Skilled in expounding the Church's views, the 'Sexfinder General' was sufficiently respected by the Pope to be appointed to the Pontifical Commission for Social Communication. In 1998, he was made a Prelate of Honour with the title of Monsignor. His deft handling of the media ensured the Church's propaganda gained a high profile. Benefiting from government licences handed out to new commercial stations, he helped form the Catholic Broadcasting Centre under the guidance of BBC broadcaster Bishop Angelus Andrew. He was also a member of the International Association for Catholic Broadcasters (UNDA), the Vatican's worldwide organisation for Catholic broadcasters, and was a member of the consultative committee of the Media and Theological Education course at Edinburgh University. In his office, he left a framed photograph of himself with Pope John Paul II, and - although he never discussed football - one of handsome former Rangers football star, Ally McCoist.

More scandals continued to hit the Catholic Church. The leader of the Catholic Church in England and Wales, Archbishop Cormac Murphy-O'Connor, faced controversy after he admitted he had let "pædophile" priest Michael Hill carry on working despite allegations of child abuse. By the summer of 2001, men who worked at the De La Salle Scottish residential homes run by a Catholic order of monks were charged with offences dating back to the 1950s. Victims claimed they had been subjected to electric shock punishments, beaten with whips, punched and kicked.

The liberal **Sunday Herald** attacked the Catholic Church and printed 'Liam's' story: *"The priest would sit the child on his knee, facing away from him, tell Liam to stare at some icon or votive picture such as the Sacred Heart on the wall of his chapel house and whisper in the boy's ear how much God loved him. Minutes later, the sexual assault would be over. Then the priest would turn Liam towards him and cuddle him, telling him he'd go to Heaven, sometimes adding: 'It wasn't that bad, was it, son?'"* The **Sunday Herald** challenged the 'Sexfinder General's' unusual silence, confronting him with a full affidavit from a Michael X who, after claiming to be sexually abused by Father Lynagh, also accused the late Father Kennedy, spiritual advisor at Blair's College. Connolly blasted: *"Michael X can talk to you all he likes, for us the matter is over. He may have made these allegations to you, but he never made them to me. Father Kennedy is dead and there ain't much I can do about that. So that is that"*.

In 1996, a BBC documentary revealed how an offshore insurance fund called Catholic National Mutual had been established 16 years earlier to safeguard the Church, amongst other things, against claims for sexual abuse.

There can be no question how powerful and well established the Church – not just the Catholic Church - is in Scotland. To raise money for new pews at a small Church of Scotland church on a housing estate in the spring of 2001, 180 parishioners from Glenrothes in Fife managed to put £4,500 on a plate passed round the congregation. Amongst a quite considerable portfolio of assets, one of the Kirk's more recent financial projects is a new £14million hotel in Tiberius in Israel.

It was not until 2001, in a report headed by Lord Nolan reviewing child protection in England and Wales that the Church was advised to put a watchdog in every parish to protect children from priests, have bishops set up teams in every diocese to combat child abuse, check all volunteers and would-be priests for criminal records, re-examine thousands of claims of sexual assault by clergy on young parishioners and "err on the side of caution" when considering doubtful candidates.

During the campaign against the repeal of Section 2a in Scotland, homosexuality was used as a tool to patch-up differences between different religious factions. New alliances were formed. More Muslim children were encouraged to attend Catholic schools. Over the acquisition of Bellahouston Academy by Muslims for a private school for girls in Glasgow, Bashir Mann told **The Herald**: *"In a true democracy people should be free to live as they please…"* But Mann was no patron of liberty, fighting against the westernisation of young Asians. *"The provision of halal meat, the acceptance of modest codes of dress, the right to prayer rooms, the separation of girls and boys in sports and recreation. Muslims want their children to learn their religion… They believe that in this secular and self-centred society only their religious values can save them from the evils of drugs, drink, promiscuity, and gambling… Muslims are holding firm to their religious identity and to a religious agenda for action. Indeed religion is central to the self-definition of Muslims…".*

The influence of religion over the world is wide ranging. In February 2000, Christian TV and radio broadcasters, writers, publishers, producers and Internet providers gathered for four days of dinners, awards and workshops for the 57th annual convention of National Religious Broadcasters in the USA. Gratefully accepted by the recipients, awards went to homophobic broadcaster, Dr Laura Schlessinger who received a standing ovation for "serving the Christian community in a distinguished and exemplary manner" and Federal Communications Commission (FCC) Chief of Media, Roy Stewart. The US broadcasting regulator said they had no control over employees receiving awards. Attorney Jay Sekulow who heads Pat Robertson's American Center for Law and Justice told the conference: "I don't think it is time for disarmament by the Religious Right. We must be politically involved. I don't think there is anything wrong with motivating literally millions of people to deal with these issues".

Any liberalisation of attitudes to sex within the church has always met with fierce opposition in the media. The suggestion that forward-thinking Dr Ruth Page, a woman, might be selected as Moderator of the Church of Scotland, had columnist

Gerald Warner frothing at the mouth in the **Scottish Daily Mail**. Labelling her a 'trendy' he barked: *"It is happy-clappy, nice-to-be-nice, candyfloss religion that has emptied the churches. The Christian denominations, if they are to survive, must preach certainty, not compromise"*. He begged for *"a return to doctrine, dignified worship and spirituality"*. Warner was already getting impatient with the Catholic Church and its *"mindless instinct for the soft option"*. Turning on Bishop Holloway, Warner chastised him for *"championing homosexuality (in the Christian tradition, one of the Four Sins Crying to Heaven for Vengeance) and undermining the fight against drugs"*. Gerald Warner is a particularly unpleasant militant, right wing, extreme religionist favoured by not just one, but *two* popular Scottish newspapers. Of course, such fanatics have always found their home in the heart of religion. Tempted by a world of total certainty and control, they display contempt for the mind and uncritical acceptance of authority from above. Their words betray a belief that the world is decaying and must be rescued from nihilism and rootlessness. Their words portray an appeal for tradition and an emphasis on inequality, stern laws, and warfare against decadence. Heroism, nationalism and patriotism are all held in high their esteem. In such a world, security and stability is a currency that is easily exchanged for freedom and justice.

Today, on issues of sexuality, the media betrays a nation that is otherwise sexually confident and at ease with itself. Instead, it portrays Scotland as guilt-ridden, homophobic and sexually repressed. Behind the copy are people at the mercy of a minority of powerful and influential people attempting to confine, railroad and limit the nation's moral agenda for their own benefit, and, ostensibly everyone else's too. Opening the pages of the Scottish press in the year 2000, only one thing dominated the agenda for a full six months. Gay sex. More precisely, the repeal of Section 28 - or Section 2a in Scotland - a pernicious piece of legislation inserted by Margaret Thatcher's Conservative Government to prevent the so-called 'promotion' of homosexuality in schools. In 1999, the biggest-selling Scottish newspapers were united to protect the public from homosexuality while, one hundred years ago; they simply pretended it wasn't there!

As the twentieth century breathed its last, the Scottish

papers were taken up with the gruesome story of the alleged *"Gay Ripper"*, 'Ian' Beggs. The news story centred on a head found on an Ayrshire beach, limbs in Loch Lomond and a torso no one could find. Police were blamed for incompetence when Beggs, a man with a violent past, slipped through their net and fled to Amsterdam. He was labelled an Ulsterman, a member of the National Front and a self-hating queer. He was jailed for the murder of a gay man and had a record of violent assaults. His assault on a young gay man he met in Glasgow gay nightclub Bennets resulted in the victim launching his naked body out of the window of Beggs' Kilmarnock home after he was attacked with a razor blade. Beggs attended a Quaker school in Northern Ireland, but was still won over by the forces of moral and political conservatism. The Loyalist Ulster Volunteer Force in County Down threatened him after locals complained he had been involved in an alleged homosexual scandal. A senior UVF commander in the town at the time told the **Scottish Sun**: *"We put a gun to his head and told him to leave at once and never show his face if he wanted to stay alive"*. A lad the **Daily Record** called 'Hugh' described sex with Beggs. *"I think it was dirty to him. He couldn't come to terms with it as if it was against everything he been taught and so it was all your fault"*. The **Daily Record** explained: *"Hugh was just 14-year-old when he met Beggs in the sauna at the Galleon Centre in Kilmarnock – a favourite haunt for the town's gay community"*. And *"neighbours said Beggs regularly went to the gay haunt* - referring to Bennets, another venue gays apparently only 'haunt' - *and was often seen returning with young men"*. Before it was known Beggs had fled to Amsterdam and might have been on the loose, the **Daily Record** printed advice to locals in Kilmarnock. *"Police in Kilmarnock have urged Christmas revellers in the town to make sure they do not become separated from friends and to avoid contact with strangers"*. Reporter Stephen Martin warned: *"Net love can be date with danger"*. He advised *"Beggs use of the Internet to trawl for gay sex is a chilling warning to e-daters... The web is littered with chat rooms"*. There was no caution for gays at all, only mention of Loveguide's astrology matches, Handidate's service for the disabled and the hetero-sexual market leader, Dateline. *"Some of the romance chat rooms turn out to be highly explicit..."*. The report warned: *"And women need to be especially careful. A female log-in name is likely to attract* *more attention, some of it inevitably unwelcome, than a male one".*

A century before, the word 'homosexuality' was comparatively new. It first appeared in Prussia in 1869 before gaining wider currency amongst the scientific community towards the turn of the nineteenth century. By 1900, Queen Victoria's reign was almost over and the Marquis of Salisbury led the Conservatives in government. The press were printing special war editions while 'Tommy' fought the Boers. In Scotland, city pubs were open from 10 am until 5 pm, and as 1899 turned into 1900, men were getting into tights for the pantomime season at the Royal Princess's Theatre in Glasgow for 'Sinbad the Sailor'. 'Aladdin' was on at The Grand while 'A Runaway Girl' was performed at The Metropole. The curtains were up for the 'Soldiers of the Queen' at the Lyceum in Govan, and 'Dick Whittington and his Cat' trod the boards in nearby Paisley. Hengler's Circus drew crowds at the Scottish Zoo and Sam Hagues' Minstrels did four performances a day at the Waterloo Rooms. If that was not enough, you could always see Macleod's waxworks or enjoy the military spectacular, 'Briton or Boer'. Oscar Wilde's novella, 'The Picture of Dorian Gray' - a wilful rebuke of Victorian manhood - had already been printed ten years earlier, in 1890. The **Scots Observer** then wrote: *"If he can write for none but outlawed noblemen and perverted telegraph boys, the sooner he takes to tailoring (or some other decent trade) the better for his own reputation and the public's morals".*

One of Scotland's most prudish and sexually repressed tabloids - as it was in the 1890s and was again in the 1990s under the editorships of Terry Quinn and Martin Clarke - was the **Daily Record**. It recently boasted how its *"loyalty to the people of Scotland and the cause of fairness and accuracy has never been in doubt…"* It has crowed how it has *"fought for the jobless, the deprived, the under-privileged and all those who have no voice".* If it were true! A century ago it was a broadsheet that described itself - as it does today - a tabloid *"full of reading suitable for every member of the family circle".* Both then and now, it knew how to flex a reactionary muscle. One hundred years ago, Mrs Alec Tweedie told readers of *"a seaside resort without a Jew… Although the Israelites are not legally forbidden, they are morally kept back by custom from setting foot on a certain little island… It cries with all its strength 'Jews prohibited!' Borkum is the name of this courageous* *little island"*. The **Daily Record** - even then boasting *"the largest sale in Scotland"* - permitted Tweedie to admire how the locals *"finish the day with this great anti-Jewish song. The 'Borkum Lied…' A wonderful performance. The audience all join in, most of them stand up; they wave their hats, sticks or handkerchiefs. …A good sprinkling of clergymen and Catholic priests, join vociferously in the refrain… Anti-Jewish postcards may be bought in every shop in Borkum; they represent the front door of an hotel, where the landlord is shrugging his shoulders with sarcastic regret that he has no room left for the party of Jewish travellers struggling, baggage in hand, up the hotel steps… Pictures of an anti-Semitic nature are to be found in the shops. An excellent one was a drawing in which faces were designed out of Jewish names – for instance, Moses written in a round and flowery hand would be transformed into a wonderful Israelite type… It was not actually cruel, the spirit was of fun and derision than of anger; but it was most unkind, for the fun carried a bitter dart, doubtless, to poor Jewry's heart"*.

A century ago, marriage was heavily promoted and violence was rife. Almost 500 men were arrested each week in Glasgow, half of those on drink-related charges. Life was very hard for its citizens. Based in Glasgow, the **Daily Record** reported how Alexander Preston, a miner from Calder *"was found guilty of pouring a kettleful of boiling water all over his wife's body, and afterwards pouring whisky on the scalds, and throwing a bread-knife and two pails at his daughter"*. He was jailed for 12 months. *"Archibald Maclellan, labourer, 61 Maclean Street was charged with having assaulted Mrs Maclellan by kicking her, and striking her with his fists, and further with brandishing an open knife. He was fined two guineas, or suffer 30 days imprisonment…"* A fine of £3 3s was imposed on *"James Storrie, a riveter for having on the Saturday night assaulted a labourer, living in his own neighbourhood, with a poker"*. By way of comparison, Glasgow's **Evening Times** revealed how *"Hugh Gornay painter, pleaded guilty at Port Glasgow Police Court of using obscene language in Church Street on Saturday night, and Baillie Leitch imposed the full penalty – 40 shillings or 20 days in jail"*.

The good womenfolk of Glasgow were placated by the soothing tones of Gwendoline. Addressing the wives of wealthy merchants in her column *"Mems. For Madam"*, in Glasgow's **Evening Times**, she spoilt readers with recipes like marrow-bones on toast and bestowed on them *"toilet hints"* like her *"excellent tooth and mouth wash"* mixed with Eau de Cologne and French rose water. Fashion was Gwendoline's forté: Her advice clearly carried some weight with the ladies. *"Still is the glace silk blouse or shirt an object of importance in the toilette..."* she recommended. And: *"For deep mournings a great deal of crepe is to be worn"*. In 'Woman's Realm,' a similar column in the **Daily Record**, Janet revealed a *"toilet trade secret"* that answered every lady's burning question: *"How to keep beautiful over the holidays"*. Janet had standards to impart in her regular column, once remarking: *"It makes me shudder to see women bite thread or silk with her teeth"*. She even demonstrated an ability to face difficult questions of sexuality, asking: *"Should servants be allowed followers?"* To this question, she advised the lady of the house to confront domestic staff with a pertinent question: *"Now what did I tell you about having followers?"* Giving ground, she suggested they might then be permitted to invite a member of the opposite sex round for tea. Only once a fortnight, mind! Janet was on hand to offer words of wisdom *"to fat people"* or, imparted behind the fanciful notion of 'courting', to *"mothers who wreck children's lives"*. In this case Janet advised: *"When son John goes a-courting, or some young man surprises you by paying attention to the little girl you have always thought of as 'Little Fannie,' pause awhile before you decide on opposing their desires and thwarting their hopes"*.

The **Daily Record** was able to reveal the *"girls who have the best chance of marrying... Actresses stand the best chance of marriage, domestic servants come a good second, and the typewriters are well up in the list. Governesses are almost the last in the ranks..."* The reason *"why some girls remain unmarried"* was a deserving case for Janet's pen. First she offered some condolences to those spinsters who were prevented from marrying because others were dependent on their earnings - brothers and sisters perhaps - before cheerily observing, *"there is much to admire in the life of an unselfish old maid"*. But the pressure was not just on women to marry. The **Daily Telegraph** advised men that marriage was a cure for baldness! The question arose in the **Glasgow Herald** as to who lived the longest: Single or married men? *"Dr. Carper, of Berlin, has calculated that the mortality among bachelors, from the age of thirty to forty-five years is 27 per cent,* *whilst among married men of the same age it is only 18 per cent".* In Janet's column, she tackled this great issue of the time, listing *"nine reasons for spinsterhood".*

*Because he might not be an orphan.*

*Because he might like tidies.* (A child's pinafore).

*Because he might be fond of using 'pet' names.*

*Because he might part his hair in the middle of his head.*

*Because he might demand an itemised account of household expenditures.*

*Because dinner would have to be taken with the same person each day.*

*Because marriage would necessitate daily letter writing when either he or she might be away.*

*Because all the good men seem to be married already.*

*Because he has not proposed.*

Then, as now, there were always those who despised anyone challenging the *status quo*. In Glasgow's **Evening Times**, a college lecturer advised readers in his regular column: *"'A Young Man's Fancies' ...I have no sympathy for a women who goes about shrieking for her rights – whatever they may be: but for the woman who busies herself, quietly and steadily, to obtain her minds desire".* It was in the face of such obstinacy that women suffragettes turned to violence and wrested some semblance of social and political emancipation from the hands of conservative men and women. It is a struggle that continues today. In 1995, Janet's successor on the **Daily Record**, agony aunt, Joan Burnie told **ScotsGay** magazine - where she is more popularly known as 'Old Mother Burnie' - how she found International Woman's Day *"patronising, appalling and awful".*

One woman asked in the **Daily Record**, a century ago, *"whether the woman warrior can properly be held up as an example for the imitation of her sex",* adding that this *"may be a question open to debate".* The writer was keen to promote the feminine traits of women who behaved like men. Of these 'women warriors': *"What is certain is that she has seldom, if ever, shown herself unfeminine in the sense of being unattractive to man, or indifferent to his affectionate regard. ...Almost all the woman warriors about which history is eloquent were married. ...Student of their careers is constantly rewarded by the discovery of distinctly feminine traits".* Her argument was backed by the story of French heroine, Jeanne

Hachette whose attempted rape was halted by delivering a crashing blow to the head of one of her assailants. Even so, the writer pointed out that Hachette bravely resisted all temptation to join in the revengeful fighting and was satisfied to merely carry a banner for the men. *"A very feminine thing to do; and ones heart goes out to Jeanne Hachette for doing it"*. For most women, of course, life was just a daily struggle to survive and not one that offered much opportunity for political emancipation as advertisements placed in Glasgow's **Evening Times** demonstrated: *"GIRL (respectable) Wanted for Fish Shop; one with some experience preferred – Address 2478 Evening Times office"*.

Searching for gay men and women in century-old Scottish newspapers is disappointing. There were ubiquitous adverts for *"Dr Williams' Pink Pills for Pale People"* and a headline in the **Daily Record** that wrote of *"a reverend gentlemen offering to toss"*. This turned out to be a gentleman winning some goods in a toss of coins. There was a *"Dundee man's outness"* which turned out to be a theft of a waterproof coat and a story headed *"Hawick policeman abused"*; an unfortunate incident where a constable was severely kicked in the legs. In a small report from Govan Police Court, four boys aged between 12 and 14 stole, amongst other things *"six dolls and a pound of tobacco"*.

On that great British tradition of homosexual rôle-play, the old **Daily Record** had wise words to impart on the subject of *"fags and fagmasters"*. The writer advised, *"the system of fagging plays such an important part in teaching a young boy to know 'where he are…' A boy of ordinary brains, who goes to Eton at fourteen, will be a fag for about his first year and half, and have a fag his last year and a half. As to the position in the school which makes a boy able to fag others, or to be fagged himself, the top eight or nine divisions in the school can fag the 'lower boys', who are in the bottom twelve divisions or so… When the list of fagmasters and fags has been arranged, the fags have to come and ATTEND TO THEIR MASTERS' wants at breakfast and tea, and make themselves generally useful"*. Amongst other things, we are told; they have to *"cook sausage"* and *"at luncheon, or dinner one should rather say, the whole house meet together so that no mess-fagging goes on; but the fagmaster's bath must be emptied and his room tidied up after football, and the same duties may have to be performed for anyone else who has a right to demand it. Besides there is some general fagging, which they are* *liable to perform for anyone who is in the position to fag there".*

Organisations like the Boy Scouts were another hotbed of homosexuality, surviving in a litany of militaristic drill. In 1900, Lord Meath was chairman of the Lads' Brigade Association. His 'old school' endeavours were reported in the **Daily Record**: *"In furtherance of a scheme for the promotion of a more general teaching of military drill, to lads of a certain age, he has been in correspondence with the War Office with the view of enlisting the assistance of the authorities".* The 'old school' has been well represented on the **Daily Record**. Tom Brown, described as a *"voice of authority"* scorned the *"new, pink badges in political correctness"*, clicking his heels to recall how *"...we Boys' Brigaders goose-stepped to our drill hall, we always regarded the rival youth army as 'cissies...' none of that nonsense for your decidedly butch Boys' Brigade members. Our uniform was... spit-and-polish boots, a belt and sparkling buckle... In Kirkcaldy we were so manly we refused to wear the pansy little pillbox hat. Nothing nancy-boy there. And DEFINITELY no hanky-panky in the well-drilled ranks - or out of them".* Tom Brown, or 'Brigadier' Brown as readers of **ScotsGay** knew him, played a pivotal rôle in denouncing the free expression of sexuality in Scotland. In a century, the **Daily Record** has made few advances in eliminating bigotry and intolerance within its pages. One hundred years ago, such attitudes were manifest, such as this article on Africans - or *"kaffirs"* demonstrates, purporting to show a black man's weakness for lying. *"A whole race with no knowledge of truthfulness. ...The native mind is totally unable to form a conception of what we understand by truthfulness... Suppose you catch a 'boy' admitting a misdemeanour. Ask him what he has been doing and he'll look up in your face, a picture of innocence, and reply, 'Ikona, baas' – a plump denial. ...You proceed to administer reproof – with the foot. What does he do? ...If he is used to it, he retires precipitately with a satisfied smile, not necessarily because he got the thrashing, but because he no longer has it to look forward to".* Resisting charges of racism one hundred years later over some sensational reports on asylum seekers, the **Daily Record** insisted: *"The worthwhile campaign to extend the Scottish hand of friendship to asylum-seekers was immediately devalued by a hysterical - and wrong - attack on the **Daily Record**. No paper is more ANTI-racist than the **Record**".* That claim was challenged when a Turkish Kurd, Firsat Dag. was murdered in a racist attack in Glasgow. The **Daily Record** implied he was a scrounger and a cheat.

Appearing different in Scotland, a century ago, meant leaving you open to ridicule and torment from the moral arbiters from a higher class. In a court report headed: *"Different Ideas of Decency"*, the reporter amused readers with what he had witnessed in the courtroom. *"'Call the witness, David Jones', ordered the lawyer. 'David Jones!' Shouted the constable. A little man, wearing a huge white apron that reached to the ground before and behind, like a woman's skirt, shuffled into the court and the witness-box. The magistrate eyed the apron with evident disfavour, and said: - 'Why do you wear such an article of dress in this place? Don't you know that persons coming to court of law are expected to appear properly and decently dressed?' 'That's just it, my lord', stammered the witness: 'You see, sir, my pants ain't as good as they ought to be, and, in fact, you Worship, there's holes in 'em, and I had to wear this apron for the sake of decency'"*.

In Glasgow, homosexuals mingled with hookers in the theatres, a relationship that continues today. The Tron theatre bar in Glasgow has been a discreet meeting-place for gays for many years and it is not unusual to see female sex workers come off the streets to warm up in the Waterloo Bar, a gay bar that skirts the red-light district of Glasgow. But where there is licence; there are the constraints of religion. *"Ought Christians go to the theatre?"* asked **The Puritan** and repeated by the **Daily Record**. Mr Samuel Smith wrote: *"It is too true that the stage today is a large extent a teacher of vice. I expect it is lower than it has been since the evil days of Charles II..."* Rev. Dr. R F Horton wrote: *"To point out the character of such a play as 'The Gay Lord Quex' will not have the effect of deterring, but rather of alluring. The theatre lives by playing on those dangerous chords"*. The Rev. Dr Monro Gibson told the paper he considered it his duty *not* to go to the theatre. And Rev. Dr. John Smith of Edinburgh wrote: *"You refer, and justly, to the highly dubious situation of many plays. Why should clean livers immerse themselves, and still more their children, in these polluted atmospheres..."* of *"nauseous morality"*.

But if religion has been at the root of Scotland's repressed attitudes to sex, the exclusiveness of marriage now dressed the Church's shop window. Marriage was the cause over which Scotland's longest-running political battle was fought over the repeal of Section 2a, a redundant law forbidding the so-called 'promotion' of homosexuality in schools. The blame for the decline of marriage was laid at the feet of a moral decay that was threatening the Church and had their media cronies on the attack in a war that took to the streets in a spiteful poster campaign not witnessed in Scotland since the Nazis seized power in Germany.

The **Scottish Daily Mail** marked *"the decline of the tradition-al family…"* with its front page apparently chucking in the towel, screetching: *"GIVING UP ON FAMILY VALUES…"* To their disgust, new statistics showed 40% of children were now born to unmarried mothers. In Glasgow and Dundee, it amounted to over half the babies born. The 'Sexfinder General' seized the opportunity to promote the Church. He believed *"…the trend could be reversed if school children were educated on family values in the curriculum"*. Hugh Brown, spokesman for the Kirk confessed: *"One of the problems is that there are not enough incentives for getting married…"* He blamed governments for having *"…failed to provide any financial carrots to couples thinking about making that commitment"*. Barbara Littlewood, a lecturer in sociology at Glasgow University tried to make clear that the figures didn't necessarily show that fewer children were being born into stable relationships. She had looked at the registrations of births. They demonstrated that the majority were still in the father and mothers' name suggesting that even if they were not married, they were most probably in a stable relationship.

Marriage was exclusive, a church-owned tradition gays only ventured into at their peril. 'Old Mother (Joan) Burnie' in the **Daily Record** was up in arms over the liberal Richard Holloway, the Bishop of Edinburgh's support for gay marriage. It is *"the prerogative of heterosexuals"*, she sniffed, while the **Daily Record**'s editorial begged: *"Has the Bishop gone over the edge?"* Neither was there any sympathy from Burnie for a young gay man who became involved and sought emotional commitment from a married man: *"It's wrong to have an affair with a married man"*, she snapped. With her mind firmly set on *"tradition"*, she had little patience left for a gay guy whose sister was getting married. *"…Climb off your moral hobby horse"*, she exploded after he shared with her his grief over being separated from his boyfriend in the seating arrangements. Over a woman who discovered her husband had been to a gay bar, she sniffed: *"If he had doubts about his sexuality he should have done something about it before he married"*. Then, to a woman who's old school pal turned up, someone she was ashamed to confess to having had sex with at Guide camp. *"You've got this way out of proportion... It doesn't mean you or your friend ever was, and far less is, gay... Like you, she is married"*.

For a guy who *"did all the guy things..."* before he met another guy in the States and discovered what he'd been missing, 'Old Mother Burnie' was unsympathetic. *"What do you want me to say?"* she snapped. *"Give you permission to do the dirty on your wife and kids and to swan off into the moonlight with lover boy?"* Never mind the pressures that existed in Scottish society for him to conform to a heterosexual ideal. It was a wonder her 'advice' wasn't enough to send him toppling over the Forth suspension bridge in paroxysms of guilt. *"...What you don't do is to ditch everything on the strength of a couple of nights of illicit sex"*. And if that wasn't enough to make him feel thoroughly wretched... *"I hope you used protection. If you didn't and are sleeping with your wife, you are guilty of criminal negligence and before you do one other thing, get yourself tested for all the STDs"*. No helpline number appeared. She summed up the only avenue open to him in just two words: *"Get counselling"*.

Joan Burnie's view of marriage sometimes took on a fairytale hue, like her off-the-cuff advice to Sophie Rees-Jones on her engagement to Prince Edward. *"So you have finally managed to fulfil every little girl's dream and captured your very own Prince Charming... But your task is even harder than Cinders' - she only had to place her pretty toes in a glass slipper..."* But the media harridan warned: *"If what journalists say gets to you, stop reading the papers. Don't play games with the media"*.

Anyone falling outside the institution of marriage was shown no mercy. *"The once-proud reputation of Grampian Police has slowly sunk under a tide of sleaze"*, warned the **Daily Record** after pointing to a *"party girl who has brought shame to a police force"*. Moira Scott underwent an internal enquiry at Grampian Police for *"claiming she had affairs with three senior officers"*. The **Daily Record** had photographs! *"They suggest that when the mother-of-one casts aside her uniform at the end of the day, her inhi-*

*bitions follow closely behind. ...They show a flamboyant woman, one who enjoys the physical attentions of men - and doesn't care who knows it".* What to some might have been pictures of a woman having a good time on a work's night out, to the **Daily Record** were *"explicit"* snaps, one of her in *"a black top and short skirt... flashing her frilly knickers and suspenders... pictured with two men, one of whom is trying to lift her skirt, while another caresses her feet".* And much worse, Moira *"likes sex"!* The **Daily Record** managed to find a colleague to gossip: *"She enjoys taking showers in the nude under the waterfalls".* The **Daily Record** lamented the loss of her virtue and reminded Moira: *"The portrayal of a sexually voracious woman is in sharp contrast to the smiling woman, in virginal white silk and lace, pictured 10 years ago on the day she married second husband Richard".*

The *"liberalisation"* of family law by the Scottish Justice Minister, Jim Wallace contained a promise to give unmarried fathers equal rights to their children as married fathers. Family values campaigners *"warned"* of trouble ahead. Dismissed as an *"anti-marriage charter"* by the Tories, they promised to launch a major campaign to show the Executive as weak on 'family values'.

Any erosion of the firm bed of morality had to be resisted. The inclusion of the European Convention of Human Rights into Scots Law pained the hapless Gerald Warner! He insisted they would attack our otherwise *"seamless constitution and social fabric..."*, he warned in the **Scottish Daily Mail**, *"all will be at its mercy"*, suggesting: *"The electorate may not accept homosexual marriage, but the Convention will enforce it. What lies beyond that? Legislation to legitimise paedophilia (it exists in Holland)? Children divorcing parents? Vasectomies for 12-year-olds? Legalised bestiality ('Man weds dog')?"*

With more than 800 Scottish 13 to 15-year-olds falling pregnant every year, getting four young mothers to address a conference called 'Teenage Mothers – Let Them Succeed,' organised by Fife Council and the National Association of Maternal and Child Welfare helped them gain a positive image of themselves. It provoked anger in the **Scottish Daily Mail**. 'Sexfinder General,' Monsignor Tom Connolly from the Catholic Church bellowed: *"It is not good for schoolgirls to be having sexual relationships because for the young man she is a play thing"* and Mrs

Anne Allen, from the Board of Social Responsibility restated the Kirk's position: *"Parenthood belongs within marriage and adulthood"*. Hidden in the text, kids expressed their fears over Tony Blair, the Labour leader's suggestion that young pregnant mothers might be sent to hostels. He had already stated a desire to see sex education, in and out of school, stressing the importance of marriage and had begged religious leaders to get involved. Scotland's 'Sexfinder General' agreed with the institutionalisation of pregnant teenagers. *"Any kind of help with parenting skills and with how to look after their money has to be an improvement…"* The **Scottish Daily Mail**'s so-called *"leading commentator"* - Gerald Warner, sneered at *"the Government's refusal to make the active promotion of marriage and family life central to its initiative"* and spat his disgust at teenage mothers and *"the social blight they create"*. Never passing an opportunity to get a bite at his favourite *bête noir: "political correctness"*, he dismissed the handing out of council houses to pregnant mothers as *"effectively a reward for promiscuity"* that would only encourage *"alternative lifestyles"* which he claimed the Labour government *"favour…"* Of Kay Ullrich, the SNP spokesman who *"claimed that there was no evidence to suggest that girls got pregnant to secure a council house"*. He scoffed: *"Does she also believe in the tooth fairy?"*

# Chapter Two
## *SmutWatch! Clearing the Shelves of Sin and Peddling Porn on TV*

*"We could use the cage*
*I've got a lot of rope*
*I'm not full of rage*
*I'm full of hope*
*This is not a crime and you're not on trial*
*Bend over baby, I'm gonna make you smile*
*Light the candles, 'til they're nice and soft*
*And when they start to drip, I'm gonna get you off"*
**Madonna**

Newspaper campaigns against 'pornography', like the promotion of marriage, are virulent. Shaking their fists from Rupert Murdoch's pulpit in Glasgow's Kinning Park, the **Scottish News of the World**, under its editor David Dinsmore, regularly launched scathing attacks on 'porn'. *"We get filthy porn magazines taken off shelves… Children have been exposed… Now - after action by your campaigning News of the World - the filth has been banned from the shelves. Disturbingly, the explicit sex mags were in the Sauchiehall Street branch of Alldays, the national convenience store chain used by families"*. It is hard to believe this was not the **War Cry**, but a popular paper read by working-class men already familiar with the 'soft porn' widely available in Britain. The tabloid warned: *"In an attempt to comply with decency laws, some parts of the male and female anatomies had been inked over with a black marker pen. But a number of pages had been completely missed"*. Instead of laughing off such utter tripe, Alldays promised to hold an enquiry and Strathclyde police said they would look into the matter. With its own pictures of young, topless models, the tabloid presents a mass of contradictions. They were back in the newsagents again a few years later crying: *"SCOTTISH NEWS OF THE WORLD CLEANS UP COMPUTER*

*PORN IN SWEET SHOPS"*. The tabloid had found an *"an evil scam to flood sweetshops with vile pornography"*. They claimed it had *"been smashed thanks to the News of the World"*. With pre-paid internet access cards sold to over-18s from Atlantic Marketing, they thought *"teenagers would have been able to watch every imaginable form of disgusting filth on their home computers... as well as gay sex scenes and many items too shocking to be mentioned in a family newspaper"*. There was an arrogant, swaggering tone to their moral policing. *"Shopkeepers in Scotland who agreed to stock the cards have been backing out in their hundreds after we exposed the evil scheme. One groaned: 'I don't want to end up in the News of the World'. Shopkeeper 'burly' John Crowley in Dumbarton Road, Glasgow quaked: 'I've been tipped off the News of the World are after me over this. I've stopped dealing in the cards altogether. I want nothing more to do with them. Word among the corner shops is, 'Get rid of them or you'll have the police round'."* The tabloid left satisfied that *"A day after we bought £3 cards at Mo's and B&K Stores in Glasgow's Great Western Road, the shops stopped dealing in them"*.

Another headline in Scottish editions of the **News of the World** - *"Zoo dirty perverts!"* - accompanied a picture of *"family fun"*: kiddies being lifted up by their parents to see the animals at Edinburgh Zoo. Readers were warned: *"Fiends shoot filth next to kiddies... under the noses of innocent bairns"*. The *"fiends"* were Curran and McDowall, *"shamelessly"* filming one of their 'Sex in Public Places' erotic videos using an ice cream van *"as the backdrop for the tawdry tape..."* You could smell the roses growing up around the cottage door of Tory councillor, Moira Knox spluttering: *"Appalling... Absolutely disgraceful. To think that this has been done in the same place where those lovely little smiling faces see the penguins walk"*. Without actually having seen it, the 'Sexfinder General' growled: *"Outrageous... From what I have been told it is clearly absolutely shocking"*. Zoo spokesperson, Amanda Alabaster was supposedly *"distressed and shocked"*.

The **Scottish News of the World** once again displayed its infantile response to sexuality with a predictable *"PORN DIARY SOLD BESIDE KIDS' BOOKS"* panic over 'Forbidden Erotica' stacked too close to football annuals at Glasgow's Bookworld store. Prudish reporter Graham McKendry gasped in horror at a *"collection of shocking hardcore porn... FILTH... 400 pages of perverted images... diary of depravity... startling collection* *of undiluted filth... so explicit that it is supposed to be shrink-wrapped to stop innocent eyes looking at it".* Goodness me! What was it that shrink-wrapped the rather powdered and trembling Graham McKendry so much? *"It includes lesbian and group sex and other depraved acts too shocking to be described in a family newspaper"*, he squealed. The Rotenberg collection is a superb collection of erotica spanning several decades from Victorian times. The tabloid suggested that the *"sex perv pics spark off fury"*, and called on Mrs Ann Allen of the Church of Scotland's Board of Social Responsibility to provide it for them. She *"stormed"* about kids being *"exposed"* and added her concerns for spoilt *"childhood innocence... Hopefully customers will be wise enough to give this book a wide berth"*. Margaret McKay of Children First who wanted children taught sex in a *"wholesome"* way backed her. A shop spokesperson told me someone had opened the cellophane wrapper on one of the books. Following their exposure in the Sunday tabloid, they erected a notice requesting shoppers ask to see a copy that was kept behind the counter. Eventually, all copies of the book were removed. The **Scottish News of the World**'s thirst to expose and condemn remained unquenched: *"DO YOU KNOW A SCANDAL? CALL 0141 420 5301"*, they added beneath the story.

Actively campaigning to combat 'sleaze' the **Scottish News of the World** even sent a reporter to attend a gay men's S&M training session in Glasgow. The reporter pretended to enjoy being tied up and shown the ropes while photographers waited outside to snap those attending. On another occasion, ever vigilant on matters of the flesh, they sent a couple of reporters to visit a sexy sauna. Park Grove House and Aquarius saunas were accused of placing *"sleazy brothel ads"* in a Rangers football club brochure. According to the **Scottish News of the World**, the football club had succumbed to the unlikely scenario of being *"duped by two disgusting sex parlours"*. Reporters Craig Jackson and David Leslie popped into the sauna to witness *"Dawn's grubby offers of sex extras..."* and *"the disgusting scene of sleazy men being offered seedy sexual favours..."* in a *"HOUSE OF ILL REPUTE"*. The pair ogled *"a leggy, attractive woman called Donna"*, and claimed: *"The blonde was wearing a figure-hugging gown with high heels – but when she bent over it was clear she had NOTHING on underneath"*. More surprises followed. When one of the poor lads was introduced to another girl, it became clear she also *"was not wearing knickers"*. After a five-minute massage, the tabloid journalist was offered sex: *"...Our man showed the red card to this filthy come-on, then made his excuses and left"*. The **Scottish News of the World** reported it as a *"RANGERS VICE DEN SHOCKER..."* and in a vigilant mood, begged: *"Do you know a scandal...? Help us to expose Scotland's seedy sex industry. Perhaps you worked in a brothel, or spotted a celebrity visiting a sauna? Whatever it was, we want to know about it"*.

It wouldn't be long before reporter David Leslie found *"shamed Kirk minister Alec Shuttleworth... copped in a seedy sauna by the vice squad. The 41-year-old probationary minister was collared in a bedroom with a tart. He had paid the hooker £60 but cops burst in before any sexual act took place"*. The **Scottish News of the World** once again begged hungrily: *"Do you know a saucy sex scandal? Perhaps you know a mucky minister who isn't practising what he preaches"*. A few years later, **The Scotsman** reported how he had been *"put in charge of a £38,000 local history project which involves working with children and visiting the elderly"*.

Even in otherwise sympathetic publications, the sexual subjects, like S&M were not always safe. Fetishist's Hellfire Club in Glasgow let *"gatecrasher"*, Jonathan Trew - wearing a *"woman's spangly top"* and painted nails - do a story on the club for Scotland's events magazine **The List**. He was left *"gingerly"* feeling his way round a *"rather unpleasant basement torture scene"*, prevaricating about his own *"innocence in these matters"*. His waspish comments were an insult to the good nature of his hosts. *"There's a wrinkled sexagenarian in a leather waistcoat... And most scary of all, a wide, short man in a dog collar and white T-shirt with the word 'slave' written across it"*.

Adult magazine, **Scottish Contacts** even offered S&M holidays, much to the disgust of Glasgow's **Evening Times**. *"Scots perverts are being invited to 'torture' sessions on the Continent"*, it sniffed. Space was made for the 'Sexfinder General' to spit: *"To say this is on the top shelf and not a danger to people is rubbish. It's vulgar, depraved, sick and dangerous"*. A spokesperson for the social services warned: *"'adult fun' can go wrong"* and stating the obvious, added: *"The problem replying to box numbers is that you don't know who you're making contact with"*. The report even warned: *"Mass killers Fred and Rosemary West had a similar 'tor-*

*ture dungeon' in their basement"*.

Readers were treated to a *"special investigation"* after reporter Norman Silvester captured Glasgow man, Andrew Wylie selling a few erotic videos in a sting operation organised by the **Sunday Mail**, another tabloid with a penchant for morality campaigns. *"We name the evil boss in filthy film scam"*, the report boasted. The pitch of the **Sunday Mail**'s manufactured hysteria was disturbing. *"Sick... seedy... scum... vile... filth... sleaze... degrading..."* were all the negatives they managed to squeeze into this one report. The pictures were of: *"King Porn... Scotland's Mr Sleaze... The man behind a wave of filth that's flooding the country... Plying his vile trade in hardcore porn. He sells his sick flicks from 'under the counter' in his shop, which also offers family movies for hire and sale"*. Seemingly ignorant of the illegal status of much erotica at this time, Silvester seemed surprised that *"films can change hands for up to THREE times the usual price"*. In another operation, the puritanical **Sunday Mail**'s journalist, Russell Findlay found *"SLEAZE ON WHEELS"*, when *"sleaze merchant"* and *"filthy video porn peddler..."* Ashok Srivastava advertised his mobile phone number in adverts for sex tapes. Despite the **Sunday Mail**'s assurances these were *"hard-core"*, all they managed to show was a woman in black stockings and a corset. Some of the best of the **Sunday Mail**'s venom was saved for *"smooth-talking Victor Shields"*. The price he paid for running an erotic video shop, a magazine distribution network and a sexy sauna was the label: *"Sleazy... sordid... in the shadows of Scotland's sickest industry... in a world of bogus names, anonymous box numbers and secret sex parties... in the frontline of a rising tide of filth... amongst Scotland's sleaziest, sickest and most depraved"*. Links with 'innocent children' or 'families' are usually sought and this story was no exception. *"In a strange irony, Shields also operates as a dealer in children's toys..."* As for the erotic videos he sold from his shops in Glasgow: *"The contents of the films are too disgusting to describe in a family newspaper"*. So, **Sunday Mail** readers must take their word for it, joining them in condemning Victor's *"unsavoury activities"* before passing the information over to the vice squad.

When **Sunday Mail** journalist, Derek Alexander found ex-featherweight-boxing champ David McHale's *"dingy video shop called Rox"*, on Glasgow's south side he described it as the boxer's *"seedy porn empire"*. The **Sunday Mail** boasted: *"We can reveal that the sleazy boxing hero is raking in the cash from selling hard-core PORN videos...* and referred to McHale's earnings as *"well below the belt"*. Not only did this reporter discover *"Mr Sleaze... peddles the filth from under the counter"* but he was doing it with *"a grin on his face"*. Not the way Mr Alexander likes to see shopkeepers greet customers when they walk in! After McHale *"plucked a tape from his sinful stock"*, the **Sunday Mail** warned smugly *"after today's knock-out blow, McHale will find his shady business on the ropes"*.

Destined only for a handful of 'arts' cinemas, Catherine Breillat's 'Romance' was another sort of movie the **Sunday Mail** disapproved. The **Sunday Mail** wanted to know: *"Is it just porn?"* and begged: *"Is Scotland ready for this French shocker?"* MP Gerald Howarth, chairman of the Commons Family and Child Protection Group said: *"Small wonder 12-year-old girls become pregnant when films like this are available"*. After witnessing *"full frontal nudity"* the **Scottish Sun** dragged out the 'Sexfinder General', to warn: *"Films such as this just encourage perverts and rapists..."*.

In Glasgow, the **Evening Times** had to cover their noses with lace hankies as they passed Soho Books in Glasgow's Gallowgate: *"SHUT DOWN THIS SLEAZY PORN DEN"* they screamed. Glasgow's **Evening Times** helped launch a police investigation after its censorial chief reporter Iain Duff strolled in to find *"sickening hard-core pornography... openly on sale..."* He breathlessly reported: *"Shocking videos and magazines are imported from Europe – and sold OVER the counter for up to £45 each"*. This was a *"SICK STORE"*, he gasped. A *"sleazy shop"*, with *"shocking videos"* dealing in a *"vile adult trade"* of *"every sick perversion and fetish imaginable... a mecca for the 'dirty mac brigade'"*. Of course, church leaders were called on to be *"disgusted"* and order the shop be *"closed down immediately"*. For the customary link with kiddies, a local resident was found to add; *"the porn could be seen by children..."*.

A *"catalogue of filth"* that *"features full-frontal shots of men and women wearing cut-away clothing"* so upset prudish reporter Allan Caldwell that Glasgow's **Evening Times** gave him the front page to vilify the *"SECRET OF SCOTLAND'S PORN KING"*. Even the **Milngavie and Bearsden Herald** joined in.

Russell Stirton's *"seedy sex business..."* gave **Evening Times'**s Caldwell a fit of the vapours. This was a *"vile trade in adult sex... Lust, perversion and masochism... Thousands of products for perverts, sadists and the sexually depraved..."* and a *"vile mail order trade..."* with *"all forms of lust to satisfy the perverts"*. Owner Russell Stirton tried to explain that those in the trade bought from the same people, therefore there was little difference between his business and Ann Summers or Lovecraft. But it would have taken more than a bottle of room odourisers to revive poor reporter Allan Caldwell who sniffed: *"Neither* (Ann Summer's or Lovecraft's catalogues) *contained any full-frontal shots..."* He presented the Loveboat catalogue to one of Stirton's neighbour's who promptly declared it: *"filthy and disgusting"*, helpfully adding: *"It is shocking that this business is being run from a house in our neighbourhood. There are children playing around here"*. Local East Dunbartonshire councillor Eric Gotts added: *"Hopefully this man will be shamed through the publicity into giving up running this business from his home"*. It was, of course, blatant hypocrisy, since elsewhere in the **Evening Times** they were running advertisements that invited readers to call *"bored housewives"* on premium-rate numbers.

The **Daily Record** induced a level of moral panic that bordered on the ridiculous. They declared, *"outrage as gay doll is put on sale"* and promptly exhumed the body of the 'Sexfinder General' to splutter: *"This is an obscenity and to promote it as a Christmas gift sickens me..."* The **Record** advised: *"The 12-inch doll, called Billy, comes in a sailor suit, leather and cowboy outfits, and boasts it is 'better endowed' than Barbie's mate, Ken"*. It was a big hoo-ha over a sexy doll on sale for £39.95 in an Edinburgh sex shop. Local council Tory leader, Daphne Sleigh tightened the reins on her corset to shriek: *"I am asking council lawyers to see if it can be banned"*. The **Daily Record** found no one with a good word to say about poor 'Billy'. When Billy's well-hung black friend, Tyson arrived in Scotland, the **Scottish News of the World** resuscitated former Tory MP Phil Gallie to blast: *"It's sick. Customers should give a wide berth to shops that stock it... Scots should rise above it"*.

'Billy' wasn't the only doll to cause such consternation in the red-tops after a po-faced mum was pictured with her young daughter Ashley holding a *"sex-swap dolly"*. The headline

erupted: *"SEX CHANGE STUNNER! MY DOLLY'S A BOY!"*
Seven-year-old Ashley Hennessy was undressing *"her pink-clad,
blonde-haired doll"* when the little girl discovered her *"freak toy"*
was really *"a BOY TOY ...with all the bits to prove it"*. After buying the doll from a John Moore catalogue, Ashley's mum told
the **Record**: *"It is enough to put a little girl off dolls for life. She got
a terrible fright and came running down the stairs screaming at me to
look. I was absolutely mortified when I saw it... It looks more like a
transvestite doll than a toy for a wee girl. Ashley just threw it to one
side and hasn't wanted to play with it since"*. A bewildered spokeswoman for Littlewoods told the **Daily Record**: *"We picked the
item believing it was a female doll and all the accessories are pink. A
full inquiry will be made... We want to apologise for any distress
caused"*.

The rather religious **Record**'s line on erotica could be summoned up by the opinion of its own columnist, Tom Brown
when he insisted: *"Only sexually inadequate adults buy dirty magazines"*. The editorial endorsed this opinion by admitting coyly
that *"porn publications... are an embarrassment..."*.

The **Daily Record** was appalled that *"it's as easy to buy hard-
core pornography as a loaf of bread"* following the British Board of
Film Classification's outgoing chief censor, James Ferman's call
for a relaxation of the law. Dropping the description of
'reporters' for a term more widely used in policing, the
**Record**'s *"investigators"* went on a search for *"sick sex video
films"* dressed for *"an innocent shopping trip"*. The 'investigators'
were shocked when the assistant serving behind the counter in
a shop selling erotic videos *"showed no surprise when we asked to
buy a porn movie and pulled out a drawer and three cardboard boxes
of the filthy films. He said: 'What do you fancy'?"* Stopping at
another fine purveyor of erotica *"a young man again showed no
signs of surprise when asked for a porn movie. He simply said: 'what
kind do you want'"*. Their agony aunt, 'Old Mother (Joan)
Burnie' was ushered in for some overtime. *"It's the usual crazy
logic of the bleeding heart liberal who worries only about the rights of
some half-baked minority without considering his responsibilities to
the rest of us... Ferman's freedoms put women in chains... We are
predominately porn's real victims... Sex is nice. Sex is natural. Sex is
normal. But hard core pornography is none of these things"*. But
James Ferman had already made a clear distinction between

sex and violence. The **Record**'s agony aunt had her own ideas about erotica. Answering a letter from a woman who thought her husband was *"addicted to pornography"*, Burnie wrote: *"…It's not some harmless hobby. …Burn anything you find"*. To another woman living with *"a porn mad husband"* Burnie simply insisted she: *"Move out and move on"*. And to a girl who discovered her dad had been accessing erotica on the Internet he was labelled a *"dirty old man"*. She recommended the daughter speak to him and *"tell him yourself that you don't like having this filth in your home, which might shame him into behaving himself"*. There was only one thing left for the morally vigilant tabloid to do. The **Daily Record** declared: *"We passed on the shop addresses to the Trading Standards Department and the police in Glasgow"*.

The subject of erotica never sat very easily with editor Martin Clarke's **Daily Record**. When a woman wrote to their agony aunt after finding *"a disgusting video"* in her hubby's car, she complained, *"…He started to ask me to do peculiar things in bed, like spanking…"* 'Old Mother Burnie' dived in on her broomstick to retort: *"You and I both know what caused him to suddenly discover this liking for spanking, don't we…? What happens when he decides that is no longer enough and wants something even more extreme? What happens, for instance, if he wants to be the one who spanks rather than the one who is spanked? The general problem with porn is that is invariably depicts women as being willing to do anything, no matter how depraved or degrading, to satisfy their men's fantasies…"* For a disabled man who thought he might be addicted to porn, she settled the matter swiftly. After calling him *"sad"*, he was admonished with the remark: *"Anyway, it's your life and if you want to waste it in this way, who am I to tell you otherwise, even if I think it is stopping you from having any sort of a real life at all"*.

With Martin Clarke as editor of the **Daily Record**, the religious-inspired prudery of Scotland's biggest circulation tabloid knew no bounds from its daily prayer to its virulent support for the retention of Section 2a. Reporting on a Russian programme where a young, naked female reporter interviewed personalities, the tabloid covered her breasts with the strip: *"Too Volga for a family newspaper"*. This appeared on the same day as a feature on the American launch of a new, lockable chastity bra, marketed to young women.

The **Daily Record** was clearly upset that *"BEEB PRODUC-
ER MADE CHILD PORN VIDEOS"* but only after reading the
small print did you learn Robert Bathgate was certainly no Jean
Daniel Cardinot. Far from 'making' them, he just *"copied tapes of
German and Dutch porn"* and *"to defray the costs he copied them and
sold them to friends..."* Not only was he portrayed as a *"pervert"*,
*"podgy"* and *"wig-wearing"*, but also the tabloid gave out his
address. Bathgate was *"caged"* for 15 months. In Germany,
where erotica is freely available, they have seen an 11 per cent
*fall* in sex crimes over a 10-year period. By way of contrast, in
Scotland over a period of 18 years, sex attacks have *increased* by
over 30 per cent. It has to be remembered of course, tabloids
have a vested interest in sex pathology and crime since it helps
sell more newspapers.

However acceptable exploring erotica on the Internet in the
privacy of your own homes might be, such practices in the
workplace soon presented the media with new opportunities
for demonstrating public shame and outrage. The North
Lanarkshire councillor who *"called up smutty pictures"* was only
one of many disgraced by the tabloids. Four Highland Council
employees, including a senior official resigned after being
found downloading pornographic material from the Internet. A
spokesman for the Council told the **Scottish Express**: *"It came to
our attention that four employees were using the computers for less
than pure reasons"*. In a separate case, the **Scottish News of the
World** reported that financial giants Scottish Widows had axed
three staff after bosses caught them trawling *"for filth"* on the
Internet. In a similar case, 86 workers were suspended from
West of Scotland Water. The **Sunday Mail** reported how officials at Highlands and Islands Enterprise suspended Sandy
Dingwall, a disabled man caught in a *"porn storm"* after he
accessed what the tabloid called: *"Internet sleaze"* and when
Kevin Fitzsimons, a 39-year-old lecturer at the Royal Scottish
Academy of Music and Drama in Glasgow was sacked for gross
misconduct, the **Scottish News of the World** gasped: This was
the academy *"whose patron is the Queen Mum"* before begging:
*"Do you know a shocking Internet story? Ring us on 0141 420 5301.
We'll call you back"*. The behaviour was widespread and was
being carried out at the highest levels. Six senior civil servants
in the Scottish Executive were sacked for gross misconduct and

many other members of staff face disciplinary action or dismissal after they were accused of viewing indecent websites on the Internet. A leaked document apparently revealed there had been some 128 cases of Internet misuse in the Executive in four months. The **Scottish Sun** reported how *"a shamed government worker"* had been suspended and *"frogmarched"* out for hacking into a gay site on his computer at the Scottish Executive. Otherwise described as the *"worker's porn shame"* the **Sun** gasped: *"It is believed he accessed a gay website NINE times in ONE day"*. After declaring how the Executive had already sacked six *"sleazy staff"* for looking up *"nookie sites"*, the **Sun** gasped: *"EIGHTY people have been surfing sex sites"*.

Investment bank Merrill Lynch sacked 15 traders and staff for swapping sexy pics. The **Daily Mail** called it a 'porn scandal' that *"sent shockwaves through the City"*. The employers were told to clear their desks and collect their personal possessions before being marched out by security guards. The company were using software to monitor 'porn'. The mobile phone company, Orange dismissed 45 of its staff in a similar crackdown. Royal and Sun Alliance sacked ten and suspended 80 staff after a cheeky e-mail was found featuring cartoon character Bart Simpson having sex with a donkey.

In Bedford, it was the Bishop of Bedford who was to have the casting vote on the future of four council employees who accessed erotica on the Internet whilst using works computers at home.

One council employee was hauled before his bosses to explain why he was sending smutty e-mails to employees. After vigorously protesting his innocence, a further investigation revealed that the council's IT people had included the word 'Willie', the employee's name, among words deemed offensive.

John Clark, 59 of Dundee was arrested and put on probation for 18 months after he reportedly *"shocked and disgusted"* a former colleague at the chicken factory where he worked by sending her a Valentines card containing an explicit poem.

**The Scotsman**, with Paisley-born former **Sunday Times** editor Andrew Neil as its executive editor, boasted a virulent anti-porn campaigner to occupy its 'opinion' columns on a regular basis. Linda Watson-Brown belonged to a school of thought that saw all men as potential rapists, particularly if their ardour was been fuelled by 'porn'. She wrote: *"Rape has always been at the heart of man's political power over woman. When second-wave feminists began to suggest that 'all men are rapists', they were referring often to the potential, not the actuality. They were right then, and they are right still"*. **The Scotsman** allowed her to comment on the Independent Television Commission's intention to review the regulatory requirements imposed on commercial broadcasters, which, *"...in the eyes of some, will promote prostitution and serve further to normalise pornography..."* a step she eyed with *"incredulity"*. Ms Watson-Brown saw none of the changes, subtleties or nuances in the expression of erotica; quite certain it was just *"the systematic practice of exploitation and subordination based on sex. It produces bigotry and contempt, it justifies hatred and aggression. It harms the opportunities and rights of women, children and men"*. The ITC's use of a consultative process brought about Ms Watson-Brown's sneers of derision for a practice *"not unknown to governments and others claiming adherence to the democratic process"*. The ITC was recommending that some erotica would be appropriate post-watershed material. Even escort agencies would be free to advertise. Suddenly, Ms Watson-Brown was *"a woman"* who was challenged by *"abusive, exploitative material"*. The extent to which she had been *"abused"* was demonstrated to readers by recounting her visit to Stansted Airport when she saw *"explicit magazines with clear genital photographs on the covers at the eye level of children"*. She thought the ITC wrong because *"the majority of four-year-olds have a television in their bedrooms"*; apparently forgetting only 30 per cent of UK households have children! The ITC wanted compelling arguments for the consultation process and warned those who shout the loudest were not going to get special treatment. Ms Watson-Brown wanted to *"prove them wrong..."* insisting *"there is still time to shout, and still time to be extremely loud about it"*. With the help of **The Scotsman**, her militant campaign was given added gusto. In another feature, she picked up an issue of the men's magazine, **GQ** to declare: *"This month's commodity was under age sex"*. She found: *"A ten-year-old boy suggests that she shows her breasts, and we are expected to snigger at the precocity of his early interest rather than be appalled"*. She squeezed in Catherine Harper of Scottish Women Against Pornography to scream: *"They are openly advocating abuse"*. Watson-Brown collected some comments from magazine retailers. A confused spokesman for supermarket giant Asda said: *"We will not censor magazine selection, but we will give customers what they want. We have boundaries, and we will act on anything people feel strongly about"*. Backed by a similar quote from Safeway stores, and clearly wanting to get the ball rolling, she was confident enough to remind readers that *"retailers say that only a few comments are enough"* to get magazines removed from shelves. Catherine Harper had her letter printed on the letters' page, thanking her, saying: *"We have a collective responsibility to object and challenge the availability of pornography, the aim of which is to desensitise us, and, ultimately, accept their message of hatred towards women"*.

Linda Watson-Brown deforms the expression of sexuality in both men and women, gay and 'straight'. Her regular column gives her the opportunity to parade 'facts' to denigrate male sexuality. She believed the portrayal of Sarah Payne in the media, a little girl found strangled in a field as innocent, sweet, pretty, trusting and in white socks was *"appropriated by abusers"*. The *"theft"* of Sarah's innocence was supposed to have been consumed unquestionably, perverting everything we read about the case and *"hijacked by mass pornographers"*. Her conclusion was: *"Pornography legitimises violence and sexualises children"*. How did she know this? In this instance, she declared it was because someone who had done *"many respected studies"* with male offenders said that the women in rape scenarios, that Watson-Brown insisted *"play such a large part"* in *"porn"*, end up thanking their attacker in 97 per cent of cases. So therefore: *"The research is clear, the links obvious…"* In fact, independent studies over links between 'pornography' and violence are anything but clear. Studies have shown erotica to actually reduce the levels of aggression in some men. Heinrich Pommerenke was a mass murderer who considered it his duty to punish all women, believing them to be the source of all evil. He attacked his first victim in a local park after seeing Cecil B De Mille's 'The Ten Commandments'. To suggest erotic pictures in a magazine are responsible for men going on to rape women is just nonsense. Many men will read the same magazine found in possession of a rapist and not rape a woman. Studies like those conducted by Dietz, who worked with the criminally insane during the mid-eighties found rapists were more likely to read crime magazines like **True Detective** than erotica. Watson-Brown ignores the studies that confirm one consistent factor in men who rape, and that is their background of sexual repression within the family. Hijacking the Sarah Payne case for her own anti-porn stance Watson-Brown reminded everyone: *"Are we doing anything about it?"* Her friend Catherine Harper of Scottish Women Against Pornography used the **Sunday Herald** to expound their propaganda in a letter. *"We have a collective responsibility to object to and challenge pornography and its message of hate"*. That *"collective responsibility"* was manifest in yet another feature about 'galvanising action' against pædophiles, (and, by association, the consumption of 'pornography'). Watson-Brown wanted everybody *"opening their eyes to what actually exists between the covers of 'men's lifestyle' magazines in their local newsagent shop"*. She dismissed harmless men's wank-fodder as *"easily procured pornography"* full of *"abusive, exploitative images and text"* that *"glorifies child sexual abuse and the dehumanisation of women"*. She wanted the shelves cleared. After venting her frustration at *"a clown"* who had *"stood outside an Alldays store... distributing balloons to children"*, she charged him with *"encouraging"* children *"to see the store as a convenient, family-friendly place"*. Marching into the newsagent chain, she found, just above the comics, magazines with *"textual references to anal, oral and forced sex..."* and gasped: *"How should a parent explain to a child just learning to read what these words mean?"* Off Linda Watson-Brown trotted to complain to the manager before picking on some poor inadequate caught playing with himself while leafing through magazines in front of a shopkeeper. Watson-Brown insisted this showed *"what 'soft porn' is and does"*. Spouting her nonsense in another piece in **The Scotsman** she tried to establish how *"we live in a world which likes its women dead... Women are killed because they are women"*. Ignoring the fact that in relationships it is *men* who are most at risk of being murdered by their *female* partner, she spouted: *"Male sexual violence comes from patriarchy"* pointing the finger of blame on *"entire systems of social values which perpetuate hateful ideas and patriarchal slaughter"*. Her direction was entirely predictable: *"Consider the availability of exploitative magazines easily accessed* *through outlets such as local convenience stores, and question the glamorisation of violence and degradation in those publications".*

When news broke that the British Board of Film Classification was relaxing its rules, meaning films featuring sex and nudity would more easily gain an age '15' rating, the **Daily Mail** huffed: *"Censors allow more smut in movies rated for teenagers".* It meant that films like the *"notorious"* film 'Deep Throat' – according to **The Mail** - could now be seen uncut for the first time since its release almost 30 before. While BBFC director Robin Duval made a stand against Britain's obsessive nannying, **The Scotsman**'s Linda Watson-Brown went into paroxysms of finger-wagging: *"No matter how devotedly the pornographers adopt the language of the anti-censorship, free speech movement, what they produce is very often little more than documented evidence of criminal acts".* Eager to twist this into yet another excuse for some anti-porn hectoring, she barked: *"What can appear to be consensual may not be. What may appear to be liberal may not be. What may appear to be a blow for personal freedom may not be".*

Linda Watson-Brown went on to attack 'straight' lad's magazine, **Loaded**. *"The new pornbrokers..."* she gasped. *"Open a copy of any of the sad little lad's mags in your local filth-friendly newsagent and you will see just as much naked flesh and pathetic double-entendres as in honest pornographic fare higher up the shelves".*

Even a benign picture of a naked Germaine Greer had Watson-Brown sharply reprimanding Professor Greer for her *"NAKED STUPIDITY".* She set about filling in the blanks to her own questions. *"Is it not then a bit rich to deny these women the chance to cavort cheesily across the pages of this month's skin mags if that is what they opt for...? No it is not",* she sniffed. *"They may think they are posing for a tasteful photograph... but it comes with a price".* Watson-Brown suggested the **Daily Mail** *"and other family newspapers"* were trying to present such activities in *"a sanistised, acceptable manner"* while *"the lad mags who have made such a profitable industry of pornography for the masses resort to something slightly less than post-feminist analysis in their accompanying texts".* But is this really what the lads were looking for, to flick off to a bit of post-feminist analysis? Watson-Brown gave Greer a good slapping: *"Celebrities are no more than stripping slappers desperate for any attention, no matter what context".*

Linda Watson-Brown could hardly contain herself after having discovered PORNsweeper, a helpful device that filtered out all that nasty porn sent on the Internet while we are supposed to be working. It was supposed to recognise the harmless stuff by how the models struck their poses! It could even assess the amount of exposed skin on an image file! But it had some drawbacks. Because of the similarity in skin tone, you could have easily set off the alarm by downloading a few pictures of a pig! If it became popular, it could have sparked a revival in - if not dressed pigs - black and white Victorian prints of frilly knickerbockers and spanked bottoms that would've circumvented any need to display colour! Days later, Catherine Harper from Scottish Women Against Pornography once again wrote in to congratulate Ms Watson-Brown on her piece.

Linda Watson-Brown even turned her fire on those women who flaunted chastity! The apparently chaste, bobby-soxed and pigtailed pop star Britney Spears shouldered her argument. *"Some of the 101,500 teenage pregnancies which happen each year have been initiated by the likes of Ms Spears"*, she decided. Her disgust extended far beyond Britney's *"dull"* and talentless singing. She wrote how Britney, was *"peddling... paedophile fantasies... unattainable sex... Dressing up as a school girl, sucking a lollipop, putting her hair in pigtails, and clothing herself in the uniform of a million pornographic images... This is not cute and it is not harmless. It is dangerous..."* But how much sex does Britney Spears sell to kids? Or how much do they pick up naturally for themselves when they are good and ready in a natural process called 'growing up'? Britney's most enthusiastic young fans could be found on any night of the week in gay nightclubs. She didn't seem to have had much influence on them, stubbornly preferring to lift more shirt than skirt!

No stone was left unturned. When - as the **Scottish Daily Mail** described them - *"a growing library of more seedy images"* joined flying hearts and birthday cakes as images that could be sent by mobile phone, a 20-year-old from Renfrewshire became the first person to be charged for sending an offensive text message on his mobile. Accompanying the report was a picture of a mobile phone with the caption: *"potential nuisance"*.

Not just pictures were requiring extra vigilance, but words too. James Grylls of the **Scottish Daily Mail** wrote, *"Standards*

*at BBC Scotland are slipping. I am certain I heard the word 'bum...'
on Saturday. Even worse... I was shocked to hear* (Pierre Van
Hooijdonk, a Celtic striker), *swear at least five times... I won't
repeat it in a family newspaper but the word he used begins with an
's' and rhymes with 'twit'".* No shit!

Despite insisting in one of its editorials under Martin
Clarke, that the **Daily Record** was not prudish, words were
regularly censored. Amongst those banned: 'Pissed'. (Tom
Brown called himself a *"p\*\*\*ed off geriatric Labour"* supporter)!
'Bollocks', (when Professor Hugh Pennington challenged cooks
who claimed eating dirt was harmless: *"That is b\*\*\*\*\*\*s)".*
'Crap'. (Chef, Gordon Ramsey replied: *"I have never heard such
c\*\*p in my life...)"* And 'tosser', (after Coronation Street's hunk
Scott Wright commented about looking *"a right t\*\*\*\*r".* Steven
was talking about the python costume he wore for his on-
screen strip).

Reporting on a TV programme called 'A Brief History of the
F-Word', the **Record** suggested the word 'fuck' had been traced
to a Scottish poem of 1503 where it was used to rhyme with
'chukkit'. *"An academic claims that Scots caused the world wide
spread of the word f\*\*\*".*

Even gestures were in line for moral censorship with a full-
colour centre-page spread on the *"shocking"* practice of sticking
up two fingers! *"Whether one digit or two, a host of celebrities have
let their fingers do the talking - and the meaning they are getting
across is usually too blue to print in a family newspaper".* The
**Record** consulted Dr Doherty-Sneddon, a psychology lecturer
who explained that the use of one finger *"was rooted in rather
obvious sexual imagery".* As tennis fans cheered her opponents,
29-year-old Natasha Zvereva stuck her fingers up at the crowd,
the **Record** called it a *"shocking gesture, never before seen at
Wimbledon".*

It was suggested that through the conjoined efforts of religionists and feminists, sales of the **Big Issue in Scotland** in
Edinburgh had been slashed by around 1,000 copies and the
editor of this otherwise liberal publication, Ken Laird, decided
to axe their gay chatline and contact ads promising 'Live adult
fun'. Nancy Ott, a lecturer in Mental Health at Caledonian
University wrote to the **Big Issue in Scotland** to say she
thought the ads *"demean both women and men".* Another writer

thought the ads contributed to domestic violence and begged the magazine not to encourage the presentation of *"other people as sex objects"*. The ever-vigilant anti-porn campaigner, Catherine Harper found, *"pornographic phone lines are part of the multi-million pound industry that also exploits homosexuals"*. This comment would have been fine if she was using it as the basis of an argument for having erotica prescribed by the local GP on the NHS, but she wasn't! Harper tried to insist that the idea *"any opposition to pornography"* would be used against gay sexuality was *"illogical"*. But it certainly wasn't Scottish Women Against Pornography who became victims of the 1876 Customs Consolidation Act that prohibited the importation of material deemed 'indecent' by Customs officials, police, postal workers, sheriffs or magistrates. Harper was part of small group that regularly complained about 'sex crime' in the media. They deluded themselves about the real underlying causes and covered up their crusade's real aims by distorting research. Sexual violence has been around long before anyone made 'porn' films or sold **Rustler**. Surely, only those who see sex as 'defiling' or sexually active women as 'fallen' are ever likely to see sex as a means to hurt women.

The **Big Issue in Scotland**'s editor, Ken Laird explained: "The **Big Issue in Scotland** gives positive coverage to gay issues and I deplore much of the homophobic nonsense churned out by the mainstream Scottish press... Our vendors were coming in off the streets and telling us people were giving them £1 but not taking the magazine because of the adverts... We are opposed to censorship but we must always consider the position of our homeless vendors..." But after the virulent religious-inspired Section 28 campaign had swept Scotland, editor Ken Laird admitted he had been wrong to ban these advertisements.

Many newspapers throughout Scotland discriminate against gays, lesbians, bisexuals and people of transgender by refusing them permission to advertise for a partner in their columns of personal ads. Many of these same papers are highly critical of gays who find more unconventional ways of meeting, like cruising in parks and do not hesitate to expose them when caught.

Media-led crusades of moral outrage in recent times have

included the **News of the World**'s Name and Shame campaign following the death of young Sarah Payne, the one by a handful of popular papers in support of Section 2a in Scotland and the **Daily Record**'s SmutWatch: A small-minded and vindictive forerunner of editor Martin Clarke's ambitions to define the nation's morality.

*"We're not prudes, but..."* began the **Daily Record**'s chief apologist in earnest. *"...To keep track of where our television is heading we've launched SmutWatch. Every move they make we - and you - will be watching them"*. But prudish was exactly what it was. *"Throw out the trash"*, the **Daily Record** demanded. It's *"time to call a halt to television's bosses' obsession with nudity"*. Appalled at the *"lashings of flesh and fornication"* and *"unashamed salaciousness"*, journalist Kathleen Morgan rustled her hooped petticoat to implore: *"we've had enough..."* it's *"one big turn off"*. Morgan turned on the presenter of TV show 'Eurotrash', Antoine De Caunes *"dishing up clips of Europe's most tasteless television..."* and cried: *"It's all his fault"*.

The **Daily Record**'s SmutWatch had to ride the storm over *"an inflatable 32HHH bust"*. They dragged out Rev Jim Cowie, vice-convener of the Church of Scotland's Board of Social Responsibility who *"hit out"* at model Ashley Bond after her appearance on ITV's 'Richard and Judy' show. *"The show came under fire again last year when they featured naturists with their naughty bits covered up with pots"*. Naughty bits? How old were these people?

*"Spare our children from this sex-obsessed trash"* the **Daily Record** screamed in the face of a Broadcasting Standards Commission study. Only 15 per cent of those aged between 16 and 34 thought there was too much sex on TV compared with 73 per cent of over 65s who did. But never mind: *"Anyone with a channel-zapper knows there is too much tawdry sex on TV..."* the **Record** insisted. *" There is a time and a place for sex. It isn't when children are watching"*. The SmutWatchers at the **Record** were reeling after having just seen on TV, one of 'Harry Enfield's Yule Log Chums', *"Kevin the Teenager performing a sex act on himself... The viewers were left in no doubt about what he was doing"*. The **Daily Record** tried to make out the BBC had been bogged down with complaints over Kevin the Teenager's Christmas wank, but in actual fact, they only had *"the usual calls, some com-*

*plimentary, some not so complimentary"*. The 'Men Behaving Badly' Christmas special was also ticked off as *"seasonal smut... Stretching the boundaries of bad taste..."* Unfortunately, the **Daily Record** had forgotten they had recommended the programme to its readers as their *"Comedy Choice"* for viewing in what they regularly fence off in their TV guide as the *"9pm watershed"*. They topped the discussion with a few words from an embarrassed mother from Stirling expressing relief her kids hadn't asked her any difficult questions. The 'Sexfinder General' was recruited for some words of advice, and finally, they finished off the piece with a plea for anyone to write in to them if *"smutty TV"* had outraged them. The tabloid's agony aunt, 'Old Mother Burnie' expressed her alarm at the effect of programmes like 'Jerry Springer' on the great unwashed. *"They... push up their tolerance levels..."* she gasped, like it was a bad thing. *"All of us require some checks in our lives, along with solid values"*. An informative documentary programme on naturism, 'Full Frontal in Flip-Flops' was also hauled in front of SmutWatch to be belted across its bare arse. *"An excuse to thrust more naked bodies at an unsuspecting public"*, they snarled. But you can't win with the **Daily Record** with your clothes on either, as Edinburgh children's TV presenter Gail Porter found to her cost. *"...Her hair piled high and her make-up plastered on... Wearing just a bra and pants on the front page of FHM..."* the **Daily Record** warned that Gail's behaviour *"angered parents"*. And the church too after it was alleged she called herself 'a daughter of Satan'.

The **Scottish Daily Mail** usually mirrored moral campaigns by the **Daily Record**. At the same time as the **Record** mounted SmutWatch, the **Scottish Daily Mail** also laid claim to a moral victory. *"Has soap bowed to viewers' demands for less sex and violence?"* they asked after learning Scottish Television's soap 'Take the High Road' was to *"once again concentrate on the charm of the setting and the gentle eccentricity of its characters"* in a *"return to traditional Glendarroch values"*. New producer Mark Grindle told the **Scottish Daily Mail**: *"We have had complaints that people wouldn't watch again after we featured prostitution and lesbianism"*. Graham Stevens, chairman of the National Viewers and Listeners Association was hauled out of his Middle England armchair to express a wish that Grindle's twee storylines should be extended to other soaps, *"so that we no longer have this daily diet of sex and salaciousness"*.

Meanwhile, with the help of the **Daily Record**, the launch of Playboy TV was made to look as if sex was about to rammed down the throats of an apparently resentful nation. *"There will be programmes like The Art of Sexual Massage and 101 Ways to Excite Your Lover... No doubt the prospect delights the sniggers of the dirty mac brigade... Peddlers of soft porn try to sell it as innocent fun that helps spice up your love life. The new Playboy TV channel is carefully fronted by women to try and give it an air of respectability. But the reality is that most soft porn is sleazy titillation, degrading to both sexes and downright dangerous to women"*. In fact, some 12,000 of Playboy TV's 20,000 subscribers were women.

A hit in so many countries, the huge popularity surrounding the 'Big Brother' phenomenon, following the exploits of a group locked away from the outside world had the **Daily Record** backing the minority. While *"Big Brother pushed back the TV barriers as a bedroom sex scene forced the programme's website into near meltdown... Public criticism began to challenge the euphoria and there were some calls for an end to TV voyeurism"*. 'Some' being the operative word. The religious **Record** called on Tory Brian Monteith to warn: *"It must remember it is Channel 4 and not Channel Filth"*. Far from being an embarrassment, the *"meltdown"* provoked Tom 'Brigadier' Brown to decide the fate of one of the contestants. *"Flirty Claire, who seemed such a nice girl, has become Dirty Claire and her reputation is ruined"*. All for hopping into bed for what the editorial described as a *"tacky romp"* with winner Craig! The **Record** praised the rest of the inhabitants for not succumbing to *"carnal desire"*. Brown hit out at 'Big Brother': *"Not only have they been getting their kit off, they are also being mentally undressed and left psychologically naked. No-one knows what the long-term effects are likely to be"*. The religious **Record**'s editorial demanded: *"Clean it up, guys"* after finding *"producers are becoming more sex-starved than the contestants"*.

Moral vigilantism was not only confined to the **Daily Record**. In an attention-grabbing headline to boost its sales of sleaze, Scottish editions of the **News of the World** exclaimed: *"Porn peddling perverts have ripped off a town's £500,000 jobs slogan - to boost sales of sleaze"*. Laura Livingstone imaginatively changed the town slogan Life Is For Livingston to Life Is For

Living for her erotic magazine **Scottish Rendez-Vu** that the **News of the World** called *"sordid"* because, amongst other things, it *"promotes… gay sex"*. The Sunday tabloid flatly noted: **Scottish Rendez-Vu** *"shows men and women in a variety of undressed states… News of the World investigators replied to ads offering gay and lesbian sex… and did not receive a single reply!"*

It was not hard to see what inspired the tabloids in the way they presented sex. *"Sin!"* frothed the **Sunday Mail** with religious fervour over the making of a new game show starring camp comedian Julian Clary. In a *"sordid exposé"*, they admonished *"TV's latest seedy attempt to win the ratings war with a sinful, sex-and-sand game show"* which they claimed went *"to the very edge of decency and suggestiveness"*. And worse was to come! *"One of the contestants in Prickly Heat is former Glasgow hooker Yvonne Hay… During the day she played rude games like slipping grapes into other contestants' cossies… and squeezing out the juice. Or, even more disgustingly, running a relay that meant stuffing lard into the others' bikini bottoms… It begs the question how TV's controls could be so lax as to allow vice girls to participate. Or indeed, why anyone should fail to see that a seedy show like this will attract professional sex girls"*. Of course, Julian's programme was another one described as the one that had finally pushed TV over the edge. Of another programme, 'The Tribe' on BBC 2, the tabloid found *"their publicity bumph dubbed it a 'dark and erotic film' - a convenient metaphor for soft porn"*. The **Sunday Mail** dragged frail Christian morality campaigner Mary Whitehouse out of retirement assuring readers that *"at 88, she is still as active as ever in her chosen rôle as a TV obscenity watchdog"*. She confessed: *"If I had to choose between tennis… and drama, I'd choose tennis"*.

Scottish editions of the **News of the World** were equally prudish about Jeanne Tripplehorn co-starring in the film 'Sliding Doors', *"wearing a black slip and stockings - sat on a chair astride naked actor John Lynch… Broadcast by Scottish Television just MINUTES before the start of kids' TV"*. They dragged out the 'Sexfinder General', who hoped *"appropriate action would be taken"*. And Rev Roddie MacLeod, part of the dour Free Church of Scotland's *"religious and morals committee…"* who raged: *"This is another example of TV bringing the evil of pornography into people's homes"*.

So many of the Church's members have clung to a censorial

approach to sex and a belief it should only be confined to marriage. In many of their eyes, sex comes across as something intrinsically evil of which we should all be on our guard. Sex is linked to a notion of sin. Mrs Ann Allen from the Kirk's Board of Social Responsibility said: *"The more exposure there is to explicit material, the more people are anaesthetised to the inappropriateness of it and the more we lose a sense of our sexuality being something private"*. On behalf of the Catholics, the 'Sexfinder General' once said the Church had a major challenge chipping away at an industry that exposed *"the tension between man's will to be good and desire to be evil"*.

The **Scottish Mail** and the **Daily Record** both made much of a rise in complaints to the Broadcasting Complaints Commission in the summer of 2000. *"Complaints rocket over sex and swearing on TV"*, squealed the **Scottish Mail**. And *"television watchdogs are receiving more complaints from viewers than ever, with concerns about sex top of the agenda"*, the **Record** cried under the unlikely headline: *"Sex is a turn off for viewers"*. With such a paltry rise from 3559 to 5138 complaints, it was no wonder most other newspapers hadn't taken up the story. What didn't appear to evoke much concern was how sex got more complaints than violence.

On almost any sexual issue the **Sunday Mail** considered distasteful, (and that was most under the editorship of Jim Cassidy), the spokesman for the Catholic Church in Scotland had to be wheeled in. The superb documentary on Scottish Television, 'Vice: The Sex Trade' sent the 'Sexfinder General' into paroxysms of nannyism. *"I would applaud STV for resisting screening this so early. But it really shouldn't be on TV"*. The tabloid suggested *"STV wanted to ditch it before network chiefs stepped in"*. In the end, it was screened at 11pm; two hours after the rest of Britain had seen it. The **Sunday Mail**'s sister, the **Daily Record** found that once again: *"TV has finally hit rock bottom"*. Columnist Jack Maclean gasped: *"Without doubt, this was the most sleazy documentary I've ever seen... the like of which I never expected to tarnish our screens... sex is not a spectator sport..."*.

*"By 'adult' they mean SEX"*, spat Polly Toynbee in disgust, hauled out by the prudish **Sunday Mail** to support an unshakeable belief there was too much of it on the box. Watching the BBC doing it *"wearing auntie-like camouflage"* particularly got

her goat. Armed with a pail of cold water, she sniffed: *"The BBC needs to get a grip"*. For toeing the **Sunday Mail**'s line, Lord Melvyn Bragg - whose 'South Bank Show' had pushed a few boundaries in its time - was slapped on the back and praised for hosting a *"highly-acclaimed"* programme. And John Millar, poor dear - apparently tied to an armchair in front of a TV built without an 'off' switch - was forced to watch the *"utterly-awful"*, 'Vice: The Sex Trade', *"the most appalling documentary it has been my misfortune to see on British television"*. The **Sunday Mail** rallied the troops. *"Do you think TV's rubbish? Is your family bored with the stale ideas TV bosses keep churning out? Is there far too much sex and sleaze on the box?"* A cash incentive was up for grabs. *"We will pay for every letter that we publish"*.

The **Daily Record**'s ridiculous SmutWatch campaign rolled out the headline *"SEX IN THE SITTING ROOM"*. This was a tabloid more comfortable with 'doing it' doggy-style under crocheted bedspreads in the master bedroom. The **Record**'s agony aunt, 'Old Mother Burnie' whose professional approach to problem solving had reached a level where she referred to a transsexual as *"he, she or it"* and chastised soaps where *"gay sex is glamourised"*, underpinned this philosophy. While Channel 4's 'Sex in the City' doubled the number of viewers to Channel 4, it disgusted her. *"…This is filth, punctuated by the F word… Sex in the City is only the latest wave in this sea of sleaze… Where once cameras stopped dead at decency and the bedroom doors, now they glide right in and linger lustily through every grunt, groan and simulated orgasm"*. She was indignant that *"purchasers of porn… should be made to go out looking for it in their sleazy sex shops - and definitely not allowed to hijack mainstream television and deprive us of our entertainment for their perverted pleasures"*.

On the subject of *"this new craze adopted by… dim young things…"* of *"deliberately showing ones' knickers"* 'Old Mother Burnie' sniffed that it was *"not nice at all… It should provide perfect, unobtrusive support during the daylight hours and stay out of sight until peeled off at bedtime"*. This was an attitude not altogether surprising for a woman educated in a girls-only establishment from which all men – and sex education – were excluded. Burnie also warned readers: *"It is kinky to want three-in-bed"*. Seizing another opportunity to attack TV erotica and its *"false morals… Because, chums, as a direct result of programmes which are mad, bad and dangerous to watch..."* (And of these she included *"Fat Ladies, Naked Chefs, bra-less gardeners..."* and *"Queer As Folk...")"* She added, *"Fewer and fewer of us are actually bothering to turn on at all".* Then, turning on foppish designer Laurence Llewelyn-Bowen she insisted we *"get enough courage to decorate our bedrooms in magnolia if we want instead of purple because a bunch of daft, effete hyphenated decorators of indeterminate sex tells us that the only colour for this year's walls is purple".* Of 'Tinsel Town', a major drama on Glasgow nightlife for BBC Scotland, she wrote: *"Stir in the obligatory drugs and violence, punctuate it with four-letter words, loveless sex and McBob's your uncle for Auntie Beeb... May God forgive them although I am not so sure I can... But someone has to take a stand against this wholesome slander of our second city. Someone has to say Tinsel Town is not on... I recognise that the TV has a quota system and writers these days have to stick in the requisite number of four-letter words and copulations. And twice as many if it's based in Scotland... Why can't someone, somewhere write about Glasgow and its citizens as they are? Why can't they write about us as normal?"* she begged.

While the **Mail** found a 'liberal' commentator, Jonathan Freedland to write about *"how porn has turned us all into voyeurs",* their editorial suggested that programmes involving sex on television was the *"new tyranny".* 'Old Mother Burnie' moaned: *"...We viewing voyeurs swallow whole the endless diet of junk which would once have had us reaching for either a cold shower or the remote control... Sex has become a sort of DIY - except TV does it for us, something we watch other people do, forgetting it should never be a spectator sport. Sex is pleasurable but, above everything, intensely private... Even the trailers are bluer than a blue movie. They used to put porn high on the top shelves as something shameful and surreptitious. But now your friendly local pimps - the BBC, ITV and the rest - pump the filth right into our home, day after dreary day, until we've all become so accustomed to it we almost don't seem to notice any more. So, we sit there with our glazed-over jaded eyes as the nightly procession of sex - Sex And Shopping on 5 and Sex In The City on 4, straight sex, gay sex, under-age sex, geriatric sex, group sex, oral sex - parade through our living rooms".* Burnie watched what Monica Lewinsky did to Bill Clinton in the ITV drama, 'Metropolis' and gasped: *"...One of the characters showed us exactly how it's done. In full colour".*

Then came along another programme that would provoke the **Daily Record**'s displeasure. *"Is this the way for TV to come out of the closet?"* they begged. Trying on a Reithian mind in an MTV world, a suitably Victorian journalist was asked to do a piece on Channel 4's 'Queer As Folk' for SmutWatch. Before anyone had a chance to see the innovative drama set in Manchester's gay village, Kathleen Morgan had decided it *"will have viewers reaching for the off switch..."* In actual fact - nudging four million viewers an episode - Channel 4 substantially *increased* its share of viewers. It was the highest-rated drama series in Channel 4's history, half of whom were women. The video collection was the best-selling the station had released, out performing 'Ali G', 'Friends', 'Frasier' and the 'Brookside' specials. *"The most graphic homosexual sex scenes ever seen on British television..."* promptly sent Miss Morgan into hysterics. *"15-year-old boy... Writhing naked... 29-year-old man... Picking the boy up in a gay cruising area..."* (Well... Outside a gay bar anyway). *"Follows Nathan into a shower cubicle for a second helping of under-age sex..."* (Stretching it a bit, I thought. When Stuart stepped in the shower with Nathan all he grabbed was a kiss)! Miss Morgan insisted Nathan *"laughs when he discovers Nathan is underage..."* Again... At best a wry grin! The **Scottish Daily Mail** left it to the English to comment with Lynda Lee-Potter gasping at: *"Relentless homosexual sex... Ceaseless copulation..."* and *"a live sex show..."* With the fall of the Roman Empire echoing round her ears, she shrieked: *"Any nation which allows this..."* is *"hell-bent on destruction"*. Tom 'Brigadier' Brown in the **Record** *"couldn't stick"* the programme and used it as an opportunity to lash out at *"sad minorities..."* adding, *"I haven't met anyone who managed to make it to the first commercial break - but, then, maybe I move in the wrong (or right) circles"*. He stuck with 'Queer As Folk' long enough to notice there was *"not a mention in what I saw of HIV or Aids"*. (Like syphilis and chlamydia were going be shoved into the first few minutes of sexy TV hit 'Sex In The City'). Brown labelled gays *"the lowest form of sensation-seeking audience"* and accused Channel 4, the *"porn purveyors"* of having *"finally crossed the line"*. Neither was he too keen on the world's most popular TV show, 'Big Brother'. *"Just when you think tacky TV can't sink any lower someone - usually on Channel Four - is sure to prove you wrong... This is*

*the detritus of TV… How typical are this lot of their generation? If
they are thrown together as a bunch of strangers, do all 20 and 30-
somethings automatically get down to the basics of booze, smut and
empty-headed sexual banter? If so, let's blow the world up now".* A
black block screened readers from seeing the limp penis and
bare bottom of a guy, shut up in a house with a bunch of other
youngsters, naked and smeared in gunge, rammed up against
a wall by a naked girl. The **Record** dragged in 'Sexfinder
General' Monsignor Tom Connolly who advised: *"I am worried
about young people who may see this. If they see couples together on
TV, they will think it is all right".*

Believe the press, and you would believe the town of
Dunbar had not seen anything like it since the war! *"Telly viewers in a Scots town were left speechless when their sets could only pick
up GERMAN channels",* screamed Frank O'Donnell in the
**Scottish Sun** over hot weather interference. *"Worried parents
switched off their sets – fearing German porn channels would come on
their screens".* The **Scottish Daily Mail** added: *"Fortunately only
family shows were broadcast".* Otherwise, goodness knows what
might have popped up in the middle of 'Grandstand'!

After the Broadcasting Standards Commission, headed by
Lord Holme of Cheltenham criticised Channel 5 for introducing erotica to mainstream television, Channel 5 bosses tried to
hit back, calling them out of date and patronising. *"ITS DEFI-
NITELY NOT FAMILY VIEWING",* the **Daily Record** snorted
while the **Scottish Daily Mail** joined the SmutWatchers in condemning Channel 5's *"acres of writhing flesh".* Entrusted with
the duty of monitoring the nation's morals and policing standards, the married chairman of the Commission Lord Holmes
stood down after he was exposed by the **News of the World** for
making calls to sex chatlines and having two mistresses. The
**Scottish Daily Mail** gasped: *"Miss Kelly is said to have nicknamed
him 'Mr Toad' and the couple are reported to have indulged in sex
games including spanking".*

Nothing could have prepared Channel 5 for the froth that
marked its honest attempt at marking 50 years of naturism in
Britain with a game-show presented by a naked ex-children's
presenter, Keith Chegwin otherwise described as *"shamelessly
parading his portly frame".* The disgusted **Daily Mail** called it
*"the moment that British TV plumbed new depths of degradation".*

Its prudish reporter, Edward Heathcoat Amory *"sat stunned through an hour of Channel 5's Naked Jungle…"* Despite Amory claiming *"it left me slightly disgusted with myself for watching it…"* he carried on watching it anyway. The **Scottish Mail**'s report made amusing reading, and the pictures? *"As a family newspaper, the Mail has blacked out the parts which, sadly, can now be seen on mainstream TV"*.

Channel 5 notched up record viewers for the programme. The prudish **Daily Record** was jumping in the air. With words like: *"sleazy"* and *"tacky"*, they did a full-page job with pixelled pictures of presenter 'Cheggers' and his contestants, sniffing: *"Chegwin, once a children's favourite, showed no shame to go nude in a bid to boost his career"*. The **Record** dragged on the Kirk's Board of Social Responsibility's Mrs Ann Allen to air her thoughts on the matter. *"It condemns itself by the fact that it can be so childish as to use nudity as an attraction. I just hope viewers have the sense to switch off…"* 'Old Mother Burnie' featured a picture of 'Cheggers' with a number 5 blocking out his dick before administering him with a severe reprimand: *"Apologies. I have always maintained that size doesn't really matter. But Cheggers' vital bit is tiny isn't it? Hardly formed at all. It's not quite as small as the others who took part in Naked Jungle and those at Channel 5 who put it out - although the smallest of all was anyone who actually watched the programme. I refer to their brains. Or in Keith Chegwin's case, both"*.

Leo McKinstry, a columnist who turns prudery into an art form, appeared in the **Daily Mail** to declare: *"During the past four weeks, for the purposes of this article, I have been watching the station and I have been amazed at the deluge of filth a public broadcaster is willing to screen in the name of entertainment"*. McKinstry found a *"relentless pursuit of sleaze and smut"* on Channel 5. Displaying naturism in inverted commas, he wrote: *"Now 'naturism' has always attracted the interest of pornographers and voyeurs because of the opportunities it provides to display acres of naked flesh… What is so scandalous is not just that this kind of titillation should be presented as social analysis but, even worse, that it should be beamed into homes at a time when children are watching television"*.

In another feature chastising Channel 5, Stephen Glover attacked Channel 5 boss David Elstein in the **Daily Mail**. *"He who has read Gibbon and Macaulay, Proust and Shelley, what does he* *hand on to the less fortunate people who stand below him? Only filth".* The programme controller of Channel 5, Dawn Airey appeared on BBC's 'Question Time'. When she mentioned that a series about the porn industry was showing on Channel 5 at exactly that moment: 150,000 viewers promptly switched over!

Shortly before the sexually-repressed editor of the **Daily Record**, Martin Clarke left the tabloid there was another roar of canon fire over *"the controversial station - nicknamed Channel Filth..."* The headline: *"CHANNEL 5: WE WANT TO SHOW HARDCORE PORN"* rang out across Scotland. Moral spokespeople from the usual sources were given a platform to voice their disapproval: The Church of Scotland's Board of Social Responsibility, the Catholic Church and the odd renegade MP. Labour MSP, Ken Macintosh *"warned... 'Countries who produce shows that titillate are not stimulating viewers intellectually'".* The SNP's MSP, Mike Russell *"accused"* Channel 5 of *"seeking to shock"*. Father Danny McLaughlin for the Catholics said: *"Just because other countries do something doesn't mean we should"*, and Hugh Brown for the Board of Social Responsibility thought: *"They should be forced to tone down"*. The **Daily Record** never did explain what it meant by *"hardcore"*. Channel 5's chief executive, David Elstein had merely suggested showing erotica by encrypted pay-per-view as it is shown in Europe. *"The men responsible for station's smut"* were hauled across the coals. **Record** reporter Alistair Munro suggested Elstein *"could easily be considered for one of the station's murkier shows"* since he had a *"wife and mistress"*! And Adam Perry was labelled the station's *"king of tack"* for *"bringing us a naked Keith Chegwin"*, which, readers were reminded, was *"branded tacky"*.

Under its new editor, Peter Cox, the **Sunday Mail**'s columnist Melanie Reid was free to talk some sense. *"Had Naked Jungle's slot on Channel Five been filled by some third-rate cop movie, with a graphic rape scene and about 10 vicious murders filmed in slow motion, there wouldn't have been a murmur of protest. Had it been filled by some vile piece of megastar violence, such as Arnie Schwarzenegger gunning them down by the dozen in Terminator, viewing figures would have been even higher. But why some honest nudity - a harmless bit of late-night silliness - is seen as deeply corrupting and damaging simply beats me. Frankly, Naked Jungle isn't going to harm a fly. ...What* (Keith Chegwin's) *daft game show has*

*done is expose Scotland's massive hypocrisy about sex and shown us*
*to be an emotionally repressed bunch of small-time puritans. What on*
*earth is the problem with nudity? Why should we be hung up about*
*other people's bodies? It seems to me we're a country deeply hung up*
*about ourselves. We still think flesh is 'dirty' and get in a moral panic*
*when it is shown... And so we have young people who can happily*
*watch dreadful violence on screen, but feel unable to ask their*
*boyfriends to wear a condom".*

The Independent Television Commission threw out just 13
complaints attacking the programme on the grounds of taste
and decency, but only months later, Channel 5 boss, David
Elstein was sacked.

The **Scottish Daily Sport** launched their campaign for the
freedom of choice and begged: *"What's wrong with having sex on*
*telly?"* But locked between stories that described women as
*"stunnas"* and portrayed gay sexuality as something that is
either shocking or - in the case of women - for the benefit of
straight men, somewhat undermined the force of their argument. *"...Why should a gay minister tell you what to watch?"* they
begged. The **Daily Mail** celebrated the *"unprecedented rebuke*
*from the Culture Secretary"* on the front page. Chris Smith MP
had only made a few remarks about broadcaster's obligations
to *"take good account of the views of the public"* and not as the **Mail**
put it, *"spoke up for the millions of viewers appalled by the spread of*
*smut and sex across its schedules"*. The storm continued to rage
with the word *"SEX"* set in 24-point across the page of the
**Scottish Daily Mail** and described as *"the three-letter word that*
*sums up so much of Channel 5's output"*. The **Mail**'s editorial
warned: *"Last week the **Daily Mail** launched a campaign against*
*the vulgarity and smut that has made Channel 5 a disgrace to British*
*broadcasting"*. The editorial also managed to chip in how *"the*
*Scottish parliament has made a fetish of pressing ahead of*
*Westminster over such unnecessary measures as repeal of Section 28*
*and banning fox-hunting"*. And with an unyielding belief in 'the
majority of public opinion' on their side, homosexuality, along
with a sort of 'political-correctness-gone-mad' idealism, this
was just the sort of liberalisation against which moral conservatives were prepared to pitch battle.

When the **Daily Express** (and consequently the **Scottish
Daily Express**) went up for sale, a string of moral conservatives

circled the kill. Amongst them was the Daily Mail and General Trust, publishers of the **Scottish Daily Mail** and **Mail on Sunday**. The **Daily Telegraph**, Mohammed Al Fayed, the Harrods boss who thought the repeal of Section 28 sent the message it was OK for perverts to prey on kids. Also bidding were the Hinduja brothers who financed the Faith Zone in the Dome and the Barclay twins, owners of **The Scotsman** and **Scotland on Sunday** who live on a fortress island. Ephraim Hardcastle in the **Scottish Daily Mail**, added *"soft porn expert"* Richard Desmond of Northern & Shell to the list, gasping: *"Do you suppose we might hear from Saddam Hussein before bidding closes?"*

# Chapter Three
## *Dunblane, the 'Perv List' and Kids' Condoms*

*"She was 31 and I was 17,*
*I knew nothing 'bout love; she knew everything,*
*And I sat down beside her on the front-porch swing*
*Wondering what the coming night would bring*

*When she looked at me I heard her softly say: -*
*'I know you're young*
*And don't know what to do or say,*
*But stay with me intil the sun has gone away*
*And I will chase the boy in you away'."*
**Bobby Goldsboro**

When a survey revealed one in three kids having sex before the age of 15, the **Daily Record** accused them of *"losing their childhood innocence"*. Their agony aunt, 'Old Mother (Joan) Burnie' bemoaned the *"end of innocence... Today's kids go straight from nappies and the nursery to sex and grown-up games with no stops in between to enjoy being innocent, if not ignorant of our adult world"*. But have not children always imitated grown-ups? Mummies and Daddies, Doctors and Nurses, Cowboys and Indians or clacking down the road in mum's high-heels. How could children play if they weren't able to imitate adults? Displaying Victorian naïvety, Burnie scorned *"the 37 per cent of under 15s who are sexually experienced a year before what we laughingly call 'the age of consent'."* That was then 16 for everyone except gay men, and only then, if you agreed with what she laughingly called *"sexually experienced"*. She insisted: *"...Even in my day we wanted to be old before our time. It's natural, part of growing up, but the difference was that society didn't actually encourage us... But I'll tell you what we DID have. We had parents and other adults around us who knew their responsibilities towards us..."* Including adults who airbrushed out 'private parts' in magazines, thought Rock

Hudson was a 'real' man and administered electro-shock therapy to homosexuals. By now, she was up to her neck in nostalgia, rattling out her homily to 'childhood innocence'. It has been a dominant theme in contemporary mythology, like Barrie's, 'Peter Pan' or Kipling's, 'Mowgli', all solid investments in the utopian state of 'childhood innocence'. The Grimm Brothers had bought into this long before the **Daily Record** bought 'Old Mother Burnie'. Gone were their tales of sadism and eroticism, leaving only the violence and cruelty, explained away as a just retribution for the wicked. 'Sleeping Beauty', who gave birth to the Prince's twins in earlier versions, could now only be softly kissed. Disney bought the rights. In Barrie's famous play of 1904, Tinkerbell drinks poison and Peter Pan cried out to the audience: "Do you believe in fairies? Say quickly that you believe! If you believe, clap your hands!" Barrie, anxious no one would clap, paid someone to do it. But there was no need. The adults applauded their loyalty to the world of pretend and their children followed. This was not just about children believing in fairies, but the adult's unfaltering belief in childhood, personified by Peter Pan, the boy who never grew up. Sometimes we forget 'childhood innocence' is only fiction and reel in horror when hit by the reality, be they the little boys who murdered the toddler, James Bulger, children denouncing their families in China, or kids raping other children. 'Old Mother Burnie' would have done better acknowledging the irony of her words. Demanding the protection of the 'childhood innocents' as the **Daily Record** permitted youngsters to hang around the streets, late at night, selling the paper in pubs or to men driving around the streets. Anyone want their chimney cleaning?

When the Catholic Church's Committee on Relationships and Moral Education, ordered by the Bishops of Scotland, released new guidelines on sex education, they stopped short of referring to contraception. The document was supposed to update the Catholic Church's attitudes to sex education for the 21st century following the publication in 1995 of the Vatican document 'The Truth And Meaning Of Human Sexuality', prepared by the Pontifical Council for the Family, of which Cardinal Thomas Winning was a member. Father Joe Chambers, the chairperson of the committee whinged how society had made it *"necessary to discuss homosexuality with children..."* Parents were advised that they always had the option of removing their children from sex education classes and a section of the document entitled: *"Protecting The Age of Innocence"* was aimed at helping parents start their children's sex education at home, whilst secondary school pupils were advised on how to choose a partner as a basis for forming a relationship for marriage.

In a column in **The Scotsman**, Christopher Whyte, a gay catholic, described his experience of sex education when he recounted the response to a pupil's question of what it meant to be a homosexual. Whyte claimed the teacher had replied: *"A homosexual... is a person with a warped personality"*. Whyte recalled: *"This actually happened when I was 13. That was all ten relatively privileged years of education had to tell me. The only other mention at school was when the history teacher made some odd remarks about William of Orange's sexual proclivities... The awful truth is that gay and lesbian children often have to protect themselves from their own families... Schools are about education, which means stimulating greater insight and understanding than would otherwise be generally available. Where sexuality is concerned, it is no longer acceptable for them merely to reproduce the lowest common denominator of widespread prejudice"*.

When the Catholic Church in Scotland offered the parents of a 12-year-old English girl financial assistance to have her baby, the **Scottish Daily Mail** called on Dr Trevor Stammers to advise: *"Fear works better than condoms"*. He had born witness to the *"fear and self disgust which flashes across an apparently innocent face when I have to break the news to a schoolboy or schoolgirl that he or she has some sexual infection..."* His words were echoed by Catholic columnist Katie Grant in **Scotland on Sunday** who bemoaned *"the passing of good old-fashioned hypocrisy"*, adding, *"in order to try to stop teenagers having sex, it is not respect but fear that has to be instilled..."*

The Scottish media rarely disputes the concept of 'innocent' children. When three girls - one as young as 12 - let an 80-year-old man fondle their breasts for a packet of chips, it was the 80-year-old man Scottish editions of **The Sun** called a *"perv"*.

There was little in the way of 'sexual innocence' when, in a separate incident, police were called to investigate a 'honey-trap' gang in Glasgow that used kids to blackmail gays. It was alleged the gang would use rent boys to entrap men and then turn up at their door with a boy, demanding money.

In the classroom, a sobbing 10-year-old girl in Scotland explained how her classmates had raped her. Five boys, aged just nine and 10, allegedly dragged her into the school toilets, stripped and fondled her. Then three of the boys took it in turns to rape her... She cried: *"I was fighting in the toilet. I was going to scream but they put a coat over my mouth"*.

Larry Clark's film 'Kids' attempted to sweep away the taboo surrounding childhood sexuality and portray it with a degree of honesty. The **Daily Record** was shaken to the core. *"Kiddie porn"* they squealed. *"She is 12 years old... he is 15"*. In their opinion, director Larry Clark was apparently *"struggling to weather the storm of protest"* and called on Rev Bill Wallace to pronounce: *"...I think its time for society to say enough is enough"*. When Warner Cinemas, South of the Border refused to show the film, he expressed the hope that Scotland would follow suit. 'Kids' also upset the **Daily Record**'s sister, the **Sunday Mail** who winced: *"Anything that is offensive, illegal, immoral or involves bodily functions is squeezed into this film"*. Its showing on Channel 4 a few years later passed without comment and everyone lived to see another day. A still from the film was used by the **Daily Record** to illustrate a study conducted by Edinburgh's Family Planning Service which revealed a third of girls and 27% of boys under 16 were having sex. *"Sex mad schoolkids"*, the front-page headline screeched. The 'Sexfinder General' was *"stunned"*, but was brought round long enough to *"blast"* that a *"culture of sex"* was being forced on kids. *"They've lost the thrill of youth"* he blathered. Its editorial fumbled for an explanation, or something to blame, and came up with this cracker: *"It's regarded as trendy to tune in to... programmes shown by Channel 4"*. What the **Daily Record** didn't see fit to mention was that in the Netherlands, where the age of consent is 12 and there is a sex affirmative attitude to sex and sex education, kids actually start exploring sex *later* than their British counterparts and the teenage abortion rate is some *seven times* lower than Scotland's. The whole issue had the **Daily Record**'s 'hotline' buzzing. *"When you turn on the TV these days, whether it's Neighbours, Home And Away or whatever, the youngsters are getting* *into bed together"*, wrote one reader. Ann Cairns wrote: *"There's far too much sex on TV"*. A frustrated Christine McLeod wrote: *"It's a scandal that people are having sex before they're 16. I didn't..."* whilst a Mrs Rammage added: *"I've got two children aged two and five and I'll soon be worrying about them... The media these days seem to be telling kids it's all right to have sex"*. Goodness knows what newspaper she was reading; only I never saw it.

The **New York Times** revealed a disturbing trend in American schools where kids avoid showers after sports. Whilst that is not so unusual in itself, what *was* disturbing was evidence of parents picking children up and driving them home in order for them to shower in private. One school had even considered removing the showers altogether. It is not difficult to understand what was happening. The press are bullish about the term 'pervert'. It is rarely used in its proper context. A pædophile is an adult who has a sexual interest in pre-pubescent children, not lads over 14! This confuses school kids who are told that gays (or 'perverts') are everywhere, even in school.

The **Sunday Mail** headline: *"NAKED FURY. Outrage as police strip drug-search schoolboys"*, was centred not on the issues of drugs seizures or the civil liberties surrounding police making individual searches for drugs on five teenagers at a school in Clydebank but the fact *"police ordered five schoolboys to strip NAKED in front of their headmaster"*. In another story in the same tabloid, five pupils at the Queen Victoria School, a military boarding school in Dunblane, were expelled and a sixth suspended after they *"admitted"* having sex in a dormitory. The five expelled were three boys and two girls. Girls were accepted in this taxpayer-funded school for military personnel only in 1996. Headmaster Brian Raine said: *"It is worth noting that this type of behaviour has not been reported since"*. In another incident at the school, two female pupils were sent home from a Duke of Edinburgh Award trip to Fort William after disrupting fellow campers and stealing condoms. Poor MSP Lyndsay McIntosh, Tory deputy home affairs spokesperson expressed shock in the **Mail** at the pupils' behaviour. *"They should be concentrating on exams instead of doing things like this, heaven forbid. These children are supposed to be the cream of the country"*.

Consistently referring throughout their report to an *"assault"* and an *"attack"*, moral panic appeared to have overtaken £12,500-a-year Rannoch boarding school after the **Sunday Mail** interviewed the mum of a 15-year-old lad who had been alerted after her son was caught with his pants down with his 15 and 17-year old pals. The boy's sister demanded police, social workers and a doctor were called. The lad begged the police to drop the matter and not prosecute. The headteacher dismissed it as *"an incident that had got a bit out of hand"*, and the police sensibly decided not to take the matter any further after they had a word with the three lads. Still, the tabloid delivered a strong moral line: *"It was only after the Sunday Mail questioned headteacher Dr John Halliday about the attack, that he expelled the boys responsible"*.

Alan Rennie was newly installed as editor of the **Sunday Mail** when the paper attacked Marcus Woods, a graphic artist employed by Strathclyde University with his 'Glasgow Gangbang' swingers website. *"Sordid encounters"* sniffed Victoria Wood in her exclusive for the **Sunday Mail**. The tabloid downloaded his pictures of previous parties with *"graphic sex scenes"* and a woman *"performing a sexual act"*. Marco was *"confronted outside the University"* and promptly suspended after the **Mail** *"alerted bosses"*.

The Pecksniffian morality of the **Daily Record** challenged St David's Catholic High School in Dalkeith when teacher Adrian Meehan attempted to address important sexual issues to kids in their own language. It was a *"shock lesson"* when he *"ordered kids: Fill your jotters with *@!^*! words..."* Enter an *"outraged mum"* who was shown cuddling poor 12-year-old Donna who had to be removed from the school. The teacher had apparently *"asked the class for words to describe sex and people's private parts. The kids shouted out a list of mostly obscene terms"*. The **Daily Record** added that teacher; Adrian Meehan *"lives with his wife and a child..."* as if he also posed a threat to his own family.

Despite the obvious benefits of providing primary school children with better sex education, the media makes the subject of sex increasingly difficult for adults to impart to children. Bosses at the Theatre Workshop in Stockbridge, Edinburgh were forced to admit that the safer sex literature in their foyer aimed at young gays should have been kept out of sight and reach of children attending a panto. School head Julie Cunningham was supposed to have been *"horrified"*, poor dear, yet the information contained in the leaflets was both benign and matter of fact. Nonetheless, the **Daily Record** had to declare: *"KIDS PANTO ENDS IN GAY SEX FIASCO…"* after a rather prim Ms Cunningham remarked that one of the parent's sons *"had one of the leaflets and had been talking about the contents. The material is offensive in the extreme, even for adults"*, she complained.

The **Daily Record** reported anyone reacting badly to sex with relish. *"An angry mum yesterday called for a computer mag to be X-rated because of its smutty contents"*. The **Record** featured a front cover of **Playstation Plus** - aimed at a readership of between 15 and 23 - which pictured a woman showing her cleavage. It was described in the tabloid as a *"huge picture of a near-naked computer game heroine"*. The mum, who *"strictly vets"* her son's games and only buys him *"footballing or car racing games"* gasped: *"When I saw it, I was absolutely disgusted. I was horrified that my son had it. The January issue has a lot of things with double meanings and a lot of swearing. There are photos of a woman posing in underwear. There are no warnings on it whatsoever"*. The **Daily Record** reported how the mum *"wants it put on the top shelf along with seedy adult magazines and well out of the reach of children"*. Stirling MP Anne McGuire was called in. She was *"appalled"* and threatened to write to all the area's main retailers to have it put on the top shelf. 10-year-old Jamie was apparently unfazed.

In an effort to clamp down on the high rates of teenage pregnancies in Scotland, a telly ad was prepared by the Health Education Board for Scotland showing tortoises having sex and shown after the 9 pm watershed. The **Daily Record**'s headline begged: *"DO KIDS NEED HARD SHELL ABOUT SEX?"* And called on 'family values' campaigner Victoria Gillick from Wisbech in England, to say: *"I think it is a very nasty ploy. It will equate a human phenomenon such as irresponsibility and immorality with animals, which is grossly unfair"*. The **Scottish Sun** spoke to some kids and ran the headline: *"IT TORT US A LOT"*.

The Church is frequently at the root of efforts denying children appropriate sex education. The Catholic newspaper, **The Universe** bawled: *"Don't Shop at Boots"* on its front cover after the Glasgow branch of the pharmaceutical company offered free contraceptives to young people. Its editorial saw it as *"pro-*

*moting promiscuity…"* and editor Joe Kelly dismissed Boots's efforts as *"a money-making exercise"* in **The Herald**. Some religionists still insist that Scotland has never had proper sex education, defining 'proper' as one that works hand in hand with its strict moral agenda. They seriously believe a return to Victorian values would stem the natural desire for sexual experimentation and cut Scotland's shameful record of teenage pregnancies. The **Scottish Daily Mail** addressed the concerns of moral conservatives by visiting *"Britain's first drop-in family planning clinic"* run by Dr Tina Mackie at Boots. With a young stooge posing as a 15-year-old girl, they set out to discredit the valuable work the clinic was doing. *"I said I was 15, I spoke to a doctor, and they gave me a fistful of contraceptives"*, the girl told hungry reporters. The **Scottish Daily Mail** was outraged. *"The question of whether or not it was appropriate for Vicki to have a sexual relationship at the age of 15 or seek contraception without her parents' knowledge was never raised"*. The former convenor of the Church of Scotland's Board of Social Responsibility, Rev Bill Wallace was hauled in alongside the 'Sexfinder General' who moaned: *"It is dreadfully sad to see adults encouraging young people to be promiscuous"*. Valerie Riches of Family and Youth Concern, (otherwise portrayed as completely partisan), barked: *"The signal it will give children is 'Go out and have sex'."* They were all being very economical with the truth since Vicki *was* given appropriate counselling. The **Scottish Daily Mail** insisted: *"Yesterday Boots staff revealed they had received death threats and been subjected to a barrage of abuse from shoppers"*. The cashier I spoke to painted a different picture: *"Err… aye! I think I remember something…!"* she told me.

Another *"controversial sex clinic"* handed out *"free keyrings and orange juice along with contraception to attract under-age youngsters"* that caught the attention of the **Scottish Daily Mail**. Cornelia Oddie of Family and Youth Concern accused the Brook Clinic of *"abetting unlawful acts"* and the 'Sexfinder General' reminded everyone: *"It's against the law…"* There were no comments from anyone better qualified to discuss sexual matters.

*"CONDOMS FOR KIDS, 6"*, the **Daily Record** spluttered in another exclusive. In the collapse of society as we know it, *"little Christopher MacLaren"* walked into his house with a contra-

ceptive hanging out of its packet and his pal had one over his hand. 27-year-old mum, Fiona, said: *"I was furious I'd been put in a position where I had to explain sex to a six-year-old... He started asking me what it was for. One question led to another and I ended up having to explain the facts of life"*. Poor Fiona!

When the Royal College of Nursing suggested school nurses should be able to hand out contraceptives, it *"prompted outrage"* in the **Scottish Daily Mail**. The tabloid drew on the forked tongues of some of its old regulars. 'Sexfinder General' Monsignor Tom Connolly said: *"The simple fact is that this is wrong. It tells children that it is fine to indulge in these practices when it is not. As long as teenage girls think it is fine it will continue. The boys are out for what they can get but it leaves the girls soiled and disreputable"*. And *"what do you do with a pregnant 11-year-old girl?"* begged Colette Douglas Home, the wife of the **The Herald** editor in the **Scottish Daily Mail** after the Royal College of Nursing suggested some young girls might benefit from a morning-after pill. *"It is a difficult question. But I know what I would not do. I wouldn't hand her a morning-after pill and send her back to class"*, she insisted. *"If we believe they deserve a childhood, we need to go back to first principles. We need to clean up their magazines. We need to teach them the true complexity of human relationships. We need to teach them to value themselves"*. Bar the censorship of teen magazines, that is, of course, exactly what counsellors *do* hope to achieve. She also added: *"When the law established the age of consent at 16 it didn't set out to penalise youngsters. It set out to protect them"*. But what protection *does* an age of consent of 16 have to offer the majority of young people who are experimenting with their bodies at a much younger age?

*"A sex guide for schoolboys is set to cause a storm of protest"*, declared a Scottish edition of **The Sun** of a booklet issued to kids in the Grampians. And what was so shocking? *"The eight-page booklet shows how to put on a condom"*. Jack Irvine, who went on to organise the Keep the Clause campaign in Scotland, was the newspaper's editor in Scotland. The series of TV ads on Scottish Television, promoting the tabloid, declared: *"No Sun: no fun!"*

Under a picture of Health Minister Susan Deacon, Gerald Warner squealed in the **Scottish Daily Mail**: *"She is at it again... Promoting yet another permissive initiative - as usual, at taxpayers'* *expense - that will encourage sexual activity amongst under-age girls... How can this Minister be allowed to spend £3million encouraging girls to break the law on under-age sex?"* Deacon was apparently *"possessed of a crusading zeal to promote sexual activity among young people"* and had *"outraged parents and supporters of family values"* by setting up four Brook Advisory Centres offering: *"Abortion referrals and sex advice to females aged 12 to 25"*. Warner demanded readers *"note the age range"* for *"it is illegal for girls under 16 to have sexual intercourse"*. But does the law stop girls under 16 having sex? Round 'em up! Lock 'em up and make sure they're *"punished with the prescribed penalties"* was Warner's message. Warner's arguments were confused. First he records how many parents *"heaved a sigh of relief"* when they were *"excused the embarrassing 'bird and bees' routine"* after schools took on board sex education. Then he called it *"an ill-advised abdication of responsibility"*. But what was so responsible about telling children about 'the birds and the bees'? Moving on, he choked: *"Children have been nationalised"*. Instead of recognising how the Health Minister, led by the success of Scandinavian sex education programmes, was empowering young people, he accused Susan Deacon of adopting the policies of *"Red China"*. In the face of a failed sex education programme in Scotland, countless European studies on the healthy effects of proper sex education and the success of starting sex education at primary level, he closed his eyes, plugged his ears and distorted the facts: *"The pregnancy rate has risen in tandem with ever more ubiquitous sex education"*.

But if there was one defining moment in Scottish history that did more to mobilise our culture into tiptoeing delicately round the minefield of young people's sexuality, widen the gulf between adult and childhood sexuality and blow up a rationale and informed perspective otherwise provided by psychologists, historians and anthropologists on the sexual taboo surrounding pædophilia; it was a tragedy that befell the Scottish town of Dunblane. The media was ready, willing and able to fill the vacuum.

On March 13, 1996, Thomas Hamilton burst into the gymnasium at Dunblane Primary School, near Stirling and gunned down 16 children, their teacher and injured many others. The straight press tore at the corpse of 'spree killer,' Thomas

Hamilton: *"Pervert... monster... bachelor... fat, balding loner... rubbing his hands and walking with a stoop".* The Conservative Prime Minister, John Major summed up the incident: *"I have my own children. I looked at it firstly as a parent, as I think most people will..."*

The **Daily Record** went into orbit. The numbers of pages devoted to the massacre stretched across the front page for days: *"Pages 2, 3, 4, 5, 6, 7, 8, 9, 10, 11, 13, 15, 16, 17, 18, 19, 21 and 23".* No stone was left unturned as it gasped: Hamilton took boys swimming *"...wearing only swimming trunks".* Its editorial squealed: *"ALL schools - even in the sleepiest, safest-seeming villages - must have panic alarms and early-warning systems, including links with the police and data on local characters who may pose a threat".*

Why did Thomas Hamilton murder 16 children and their teacher? The **Daily Mail** hauled in a GP, who observed in him a marked resemblance to *"radical journalist"* and broadcaster, Beatrix Campbell who was supposed to have said that the anger of *"militant homosexuals was its own justification: I'm angry, therefore I'm right. Furthermore, if I'm angry, I have the right to do whatever I please".* The **Daily Mail** even summoned a graphologist to reveal: *"He was almost certainly a sexual misfit"* with *"homosexual leanings"* because *"...the lower loops of his handwriting lean heavily to the left".*

An otherwise innocuous picture of Hamilton steadying a boy vaulting in a gym was printed on the front page of **The Independent** and described in the **Daily Express** as the *"demon in disguise"* grabbing *"hold of a bare-chested child".*

Hamilton loved photography, and photographing youth was his passion. Without shame or embarrassment, he loved to show off his pictures and even sought to have them printed in the **Stirling Observer**. Their reporter told the **Daily Mail**: *"We spoke to the police and, on their advice, we never ran any pieces on the group's activities".* A Stirling camera shop also alerted police after Hamilton attempted to get his pictures developed there. Newspapers reported he was subject to over 240 separate interviews by four separate police units. No prosecutions resulted. In one case, a parent told the **Daily Mail**: *"The policeman's parting words to me were: 'One of these days he'll overstep the mark and that's when we'll catch him'".* The **Daily Record** set up a

hotline begging anyone to come forward who had been in contact with the killer. No one came forward with any substantial
evidence that could prove Hamilton had taken sexual advantage of the young boys in his charge.

**Daily Mail** columnist, Simon Heffer thought otherwise.
*"Thirty years ago a man like Hamilton would have been run out of
every town in which he attempted to practice his bizarre habits. The
police would have taken the closest possible interest in him, whether
he was breaking the law or not. They would have felt it their public
duty to do so"*. Simon Heffer played on rumours that Hamilton
was a homosexual pædophile. *"Our empire was bundled away...
We willingly surrendered the belief we had in ourselves as a world
power... The culture of self-reliance, family values and proprieties
that had prevailed in Britain until the war... swept away... Opinion-
formers worked to ensure that the social stigma - in some cases downright, illegality - attached to divorce, desertion of wives by husbands,
homosexuality, abortion and illegitimacy were cast away. With them
went notions of social normality and respectability... A culture has
grown up in which homosexual men, however isolated and repressed,
are told not just that it is acceptable for them to find gratification, but
that it is their right. The rest of society, terrorised by a political correctness... has been loath to impede this bandwagon"*.

Dismissed by the press as *"hate filled letters"* and the ranting
of a lunatic, Hamilton wrote: *"At Dunblane Primary School where
teachers have contaminated all of the older boys with this poison even
former cleaners and dinner ladies have been told by teachers at school
that I am a pervert... There have been reports at many schools of boys
being rounded up by staff and even warnings given to entire schools
by headteachers during assembly... I have no criminal record nor have
I ever been accused of sexual child abuse by any child and I am not a
pervert"*.

Boys not only called the man who gave them money for
sweets and fish suppers, a 'pervert'; they regularly stoned him
in the street. He also received vicious beatings from angry
fathers. One mum, Doreen Hagger proudly told **The Sun** how
she and her friend Janette Reilly *" collected pails of eggs, shampoo,
oil and flour and threw it over him..."* On another occasion,
Thomas Hamilton broke down in tears and hit back at the hateful campaign by distributing 7,000 leaflets to parents. Young
Jamie Thomson told the **Daily Express**: *"If we saw him he used to*

*be a target, he was the sort of man who would have his windows bro-*
*ken. Often kids used to throw stones at him"*. Neighbours told the
press how they peered through his windows and watched him
sitting alone looking at an array of pictures of little boys on his
wall. His neighbour, Grace told **The Herald**: *"He was a sinister,*
*sleazy sort of man who never talked about his personal life. I'm sure*
*he wasn't married or had children... He was kind of effeminate..."*
This clearly satisfied the **Daily Mail**'s Simon Heffer: *"To their*
*great credit as a community, the people of Dunblane read Hamilton*
*correctly. Locally, society performed its functions properly. He was*
*ostracised from contact with the children he so desired. Parents made*
*judgements about him, and acted upon them"*. But that didn't stop
the massacre of a classroom of children. Hamilton was proded
and poked until he launched a sick and vengeful attack. The
mere suggestion that Hamilton had been provoked drew a
storm from the media as in the case of Gary Rankin-Moore who
was labelled by the **Daily Record** a *"gun nut... sick English coun-*
*cillor... and a "loony Lib-Dem"*.

Thomas Hamilton pleaded with society: *"I am not a pervert"*.
Whether a statement of fact or a declaration in his defence, that
is what Thomas Hamilton wanted everyone to believe.
Hamilton wanted the respect of his community and fought
hard to shake off the notion he was a 'pervert'. The modern definition, one understood by Hamilton, is entirely media constructed. Where once it was defined as diverting from a perceived truth or propriety; deviating from a right course, now,
the media have redefined it to imply a homosexual. In playgrounds everywhere today in Britain, for a boy to be called a
'pervert' is as good as being called gay. Was this what Hamilton
sought to shake off? Was he indeed, in denial of his own sexuality? Had the media, in effect, contributed to the psychological
pandemonium that sparked one of the world's worst massacres? Thomas Hamilton was sexually naïve, born into a family that read the same tabloids and learned much of what they
knew and understood about sexual issues from them. His
grandmother - who led Thomas to believe his own mother was
his sister - brought him up. The community in which he lived
read the same tabloids that helped them define Thomas
Hamilton's supposed sexual persona. Rumour, innuendo and
distortion continued even after his death. Newspaper reports

that he had been caught cruising Calton Hill cemetery, a gay cruising area in Edinburgh, were fabricated, yet appeared in the press as truth. As a result, today, most people are left with the impression Thomas Hamilton was a homosexual pædophile.

The legacy of the Dunblane tragedy rumbled through the Scottish media. The first primary school built after the Dunblane tragedy was built with six-foot high perimeter fences, electronic doors, surveillance cameras and video controlled entry system. Soon after the massacre, a postman from Glenrothes in Fife who stole a *"hard-core video"* from a sorting room where he worked had his home raided by police. The **Daily Record** had an exclusive when police also found *"an arsenal of guns and rifles"*. They were all licensed, but this only prompted an insider to hint: *"This is all a bit weird, especially following the Dunblane tragedy"*. The **Paisley Daily Express** reported a 24-year-old man jailed for three months *"after being found on school grounds"*.

By Christmas, the children of Dunblane climbed to the number one slot of the nation's pop charts singing, 'Knocking on Heaven's Door' and new guidelines were issued by Jenners department store in Edinburgh preventing kids from sitting on Santa's knee unless their parents gave permission. Female staff was told they must be in attendance at all times while children were in the grotto.

In Livingston, West Lothian, an exhibition of Picasso etchings had to be axed after complaints over the explicit nature of some of the works. According to the **Daily Record**: *"People protested that children might see them"*.

Scottish editions of the **Daily Star** found a *"PERV POOL!"* and warned parents: *"Killers and rapists will be let out to visit a swimming pool near two schools and a play park... Hours after a mums-and-toddlers' group has had a dip"*. Despite the doors being bolted and the men being accompanied by five wardens and nurses, the tabloid stormed: *"Mums fight pool pervys"* and *"...frightened mother Caroline Tweedlie raged: 'After Dunblane, what can these people be thinking about'?"*

A young man, caught looking at two 14-year-old boys in the changing rooms of a swimming pool was jailed for two months and a 77-year-old man, described as a *"beast"* was jailed for more than four years after he was caught taking photographs of children at the seaside.

Teachers were advised not to rub sunscreen into pupils and mum, Margaret Ross slashed her two children with a Stanley knife, scarring them for life, believing them "better off dead than living in a world full of child-sex abusers".

Three years after the incident at Dunblane, the case of Julian Danskin was splashed over the pages of the Scottish media. In the **Daily Star of Scotland** he was a *"MARKED MAN... Shamed... Beast... Jeered by the angry crowd... Child sex pervert... Balding, bespectacled bachelor..."* and *"evil..."* The **Scottish Sun** joined in. *"You shamed our boys, you shamed our club"*, they bawled at the *"gay video lawyer..."* after thieves blackmailed *"balding bachelor Danskin – who lives with his mum"* over a gay video he watched being made in his office. He was promptly *"booted out as a Boys' Brigade leader"* and told to quit as chairman of East Fife soccer club. It was open day for the tabloids. The **Scottish Sun** quoted a *"dad"* who *"immediately"* stopped his son going to the Boys' Brigade saying, *"I just don't trust Mr Danskin at all now. He can no longer be trusted with children"*. (His 'child' was 15). The **Daily Record** pictured one mum - one of many who had *"queued up to condemn Julian Danskin"* – hugging her son, and berating the Law Society which had apparently *"refused to take action"*. A young man, just back from Benidorm did his best to quench the **Daily Record**'s lust for news of Danskin's 'perverted' interest in children. *"He told how the bachelor wakened boys on camps by tickling their toes"*. The lad claimed: *"Every morning he would walk into a room and shout – 'Get up'."* And worse: *"The youngster also said Danskin demanded a breath test on boys as a way of checking if they had been drinking. 'If you were over the limit he grounded you'."* And to top it all *"...his favourite phrase when he was annoyed was to call you a 'friggin' prat'."* Others felt sufficiently *"uneasy"* about him; they either left or were withdrawn by their parents from the Boys' Brigade. What had started out as a court case involving a man who had been blackmailed by two thugs who stole a video from his office, was now about a man facing prosecution and a trial by media into offences against children. High Court judge, John Wheatley said: *"Even on the most charitable view, there is something very unsatisfactory and unwholesome about Mr Danskin which lies at the heart of this case"*. And, to the two men convicted of blackmailing him: *"It is possible you have very little regard and respect for a solicitor who involves himself in the making of this type of video tape and purports to hide behind the pretence of professional confidentiality"*. In actual fact, Julian Danskin wanted to *protect* the identity of the two guys in the erotic video. One of the lads, 19-year-old Steven Paterson who had taken part in the video film took his own life after police interviewed him. His brother was reported saying: *"My brother died through this case. He was in the video and he was ashamed that it might come out in the press"*. The **Daily Record** resorted to a joke from a local barman: *"The wisecrack has Danskin discussing which video to rent for a quiet night in. His mother says, 'Why don't we get Aladdin?' and Danskin replies, 'For goodness sake mother, I'm in enough trouble already'."* A spokesman for Fife police suggested to the **Daily Record** *"disgraced Danskin also faces a police investigation over his part in the making of the sleazy video"*. Julian Danskin was convicted of 'shameless indecency' towards a 25-year-old when he was between 14 and 18 and two offences against a boy aged between eight and 14. Danskin denied all charges. The defence argued both were heroin addicts and proven liars. The **Sunday Mail**, whose reporters sparked the investigation, gloated: *"POLICE PRAISE MAIL FOR NAILING B.B. SEX BEAST... Fife Police thanked the* **Sunday Mail** *for the 'responsible' way we dealt with the information"*. The **Daily Star of Scotland** concentrated on the drama: *"One woman screamed: 'You're a beast, Danskin...' As the pervert was whisked away to face a three week wait before sentencing, an angry crowd jeered and a woman screamed: 'I know what you look like Danskin. It will be me who will be appearing in the dock next for murder'"*. Julian Danskin was jailed for 18 months. The **Daily Record** called it *"a kind of justice"* and asked: *"Have YOU seen Julian Danskin? If so, call the* **Daily Record** *immediately on 0141 242 3252"*.

In January 2000, the **Sunday Mail** reported how *"sex-case lawyer returns to haunt town"*. The *"pervert"* was *"back to work in new Jag"*. They claimed: *"Incredibly, he's gone back to work at the town centre law firm he owns"*. He was *"spotted though the window of his plush offices"* and even seen to be *"chatting and laughing on the telephone"*. Readers were reminded: *"Tormented Jimmy Paterson was just 10 when Danskin began his sickening campaign. His teenage brother Steven killed himself with a massive heroin over-*

*dose after being caught in Danskin's evil clutches. Choking back tears,
Jimmy of Leven, said he was horrified...".*

If the concept of a child's supposed 'innocence' was challenged, the children themselves became a target of the same
venomous reportage in the media as adults, instantly turned
into wholly sexual beings from which the public had to be protected. The **Paisley Daily Express** reported a *"24-HOUR
WATCH ON FLASHER..."* over the sad case of 17-year-old
Thomas Morrison, a *"pervert"* who had served four months in
detention after performing indecent acts in front of women. He
had put *"seven women in a state of fear and alarm"* when he *"began
to stare"* at one woman and took to *"'peeking' out at her"*. He
*"carried out an indecent act on himself"* in front of another. *"He
pulled open his jeans"* in front of a couple of young women who
*"laughed"* and went on to flash at a few more.

One of the youngest boys to be put on the sex offenders' register in Scotland was 11-years-old. The mother of a girl with
cystic fibrosis found the boy naked with his cousin and called
the police. The incident was blamed on the boy having an attention deficit disorder and he was promptly administered medication. Judge David Hodgson told the boy: *"Every option will be
open - that includes you being sent away"*. According to the **Daily
Record**, *"Edinburgh Council caused a storm..."* by allowing him
to attend school. *"Angry parents said he had been at the school
until... the day before his court appearance"*.

Elsewhere, the **Scottish Sun** declared: *"A 14-year-old boy...
has been put on the pervs register"* by a court in Paisley, he was
ordered to attend a special school until he was sentenced. The
lad was discovered playing 'doctors and nurses' with his eight-
year-old cousin. His defence counsel blamed the incidents on
sex education lessons, which they thought stimulated his interest in sexual matters.

*"Sex beasts at 12 and 13"* cried the **Scottish Sun**; *"boys... put
on sex pervs list"*, the **Daily Record** added and *"schoolboys
shamed"* chorused the **Scottish Mail** over two brothers convicted of indecent assault of an 11-year-old girl. The girl gave evidence from behind a screen and said the boys asked her out to
play football before performing oral sex and forcing her to do
the same on them. Another boy said he saw them pulling down
their pants and jumping on her. They were described as the

youngest ever to go on the sex offenders' register by a Scottish court. The **Scottish Mail** suggested: *"Their home is in a block of renovated tenement flats which overlooks a nearby primary school. Last night local parents said they feared for the safety of other children who live in the area".*

Huge protests in both Germany and Switzerland, backed by the Swiss tabloid, **Blick** followed the case of an 11-year-old Swiss-American boy who faced charges in the States of aggravated incest and sexual assault on his five-year-old sister. A neighbour reported seeing him engaging in 'predatory sexual behaviour'. His family claimed he was only helping his little sister to pee. He was woken up in his home in Evergreen, Colorado, was forced to wear shackles and thrown in a juvenile prison cell before being put into foster care. The boy insisted he had done nothing wrong while US prosecutors tried to say he had been exposed to erotic videos shown at the parent's home.

Academics were not immune from being targeted by the media. University psychology doctor Chris Brand was branded *"sick"* after he referred to research that - as the **Daily Record** chose to put - found *"paedophile sex is HARMLESS"*. The taboloid was indignant. *"Criminal nonsense... Anybody who still thinks Brand is a fit person to be educating young people is a bigger lunatic than he is".* He was labelled a *"dangerous loony, who deserves to be slung out on his neck...* Brand wanted to promote the line followed by some other European countries where the age of consent is 12 and kids are empowered to distinguish between abusive and consensual sex. The **Record** reported that Brand had *"tried to defend his views"* to the **Daily Record**, but only a string of outrage from Childline, the Royal Scottish Society for the Prevention of Cruelty to Children, Barnardos and the Edinburgh University Students' Association followed. The **Scottish News of the World** returned to Brand during its Naming and Shaming of pædophiles campaign, asking: *"Is this the sickest man in Britain...?* The headline read: *"Paedophile sex 'good for kids' says Scots author".* Brand was supposed to have said: *"Kids in some countries learn a lot from sex with clever grown-ups".* Brand had referred to a sexual practice in Papua New Guinea where a standard greeting for a boy who meets an elder is to open his trousers. Brand blamed the media for confusing pædophilia with serious violence against children, a point of view even backed by conservative **Daily Mail** columnist Lynda Lee Potter who challenged the opinion that all pædophiles were the same, separating the 'park flasher' from the child rapist. The sacking of lecturer Chris Brand from Edinburgh University didn't go unnoticed. *"The loathsome psychologist believes that sex with a child over 12 is fine as long as both pervert and young partner have an above-average IQ"*. The **Daily Record** boasted that it *"took great pride in exposing Brand"*. The editorial warned: *"We give him fair warning. Whatever stone you crawl back under... we'll be watching"*. Outspoken and controversial academic Chris Brand had made the mistake of providing commentary, debate and moral judgement in an area exclusively occupied by the media.

Protecting the concept of 'childhood innocence' and the fall-out after the Dunblane tragedy left gay men having access to children through fostering, adoption or other means, such as leading a troop of Scouts, open to populist attack by the media.

Scotland's leading Catholic, Cardinal Winning told the **Sunday Mail**: *"Homosexual Scout leaders could be attracted to youngsters of the same sex"*. (Much like priests, I should think)! He reckoned homosexuality was a *"disorder in a person's make-up"* and thought there was a *"further risk"* of gays abusing young children.

Of course, many gays not only lead or teach children but have them too. This is particularly so in Scotland where the pressure for young gays to marry is so great and many 'come out' as gay at a time when they are already parents.

Shock-jock, Scottie McClue hit out at lesbians bringing up children on Scot FM. *"Ridiculous!"* he exclaimed. And of a woman who claimed her lesbian friends had considered using a sperm bank: *"What a piece of nonsense! What a pair of pathetic farts!"* Perhaps his attention should have been drawn to foster parents Judy Weeks and Pat Roman who tartly told the **Daily Telegraph**: *"There is nothing magic about heterosexuals that make them good parents. We would not have had to foster 52 children if that was the case"*.

The prospect of gays adopting children positively rocked the homophobic **Daily Record**. *"I don't know what the fuss is about"*, said a neighbour. *"They make super parents"*, said friends and family. *"Jon comes in here with Jacob and thinks nothing of *spending £100 a time"*, said a delighted manageress of a Gourock children's clothes shop. *"We are not going to become involved"*, said a top social worker. And *"there is no reason for our involvement"*, added the Greenock Police. The **Daily Record** turned to Rev Bill Wallace of the Kirk's Board of Social Responsibility in their determination to condemn Jon Ioannou and Ted Mitchell from Gourock for having a son: *"The whole thing is totally wrong... There should be one male, one female and one home"* and followed it with similar judgements from the Catholic Church. In its editorial, the thunder rumbled on: *"How will* (the child) *cope with the playground taunts of others who see their classmate as different?"* In other words: Assimilate with the bullies, or you're on your own! And as for that delicate flower of male heterosexuality: *"...How will the child come to terms with his own sexuality?"* 'Old Mother Burnie' was ushered in to administer a dose of her corrective treatment. *"Gays... bleating about their... absolute RIGHT to a baby... Frankly, I don't care what or who they sleep with as long as it doesn't frighten the horses"*, she opined. *"This isn't blind homophobia..."* she begged, *"although it has to be acknowledged that gay relationships are even less stable than those of straights"*. (In its defilement of gay relationships, the **Daily Record** had already made a significant contribution). But Ted and Jon had been so successful raising Jacob, four years later they pledged to do the same again. *"Timeshare gay parents 'storing up troubles' for children"*, the **Scottish Daily Mail** fumed, claiming support from *"experts"*. The only 'expert' they quoted was an unnamed *"eminent Scottish psychologist"*. He told the **Scottish Daily Mail**: *"I don't know of any long-term studies into the effect of gay parenting on children..."* before launching into a tirade of personal prejudice. Dr Fiona Tasker, a psychologist at Birkbeck College in London *had* made a comparative study, and after 14 years, returned to her study samples to find the children of lesbian parents emotionally better off!

Whilst the issue of gays adopting received support from Dame Elizabeth Butler-Sloss, one of the country's top judges, **The Herald** countered the argument with political loser Dr Adrian Rogers of Family Focus whose links with far-right religionists in the States, permitted him to declare: *"Research in the USA has shown that where a gay couple brings up a child there is a greater incidence of abuse and homosexuality"*. This 'research' clearly did not cover the State of Indiana where Earl 'Butch' Kimmerling, a noted evangelical with a record for slamming gay rights and protesting at his foster daughter joining her three brothers who had been adopted by a gay couple, was sentenced to 40 years after he forced the girl to engage in oral sex.

The **Scottish Daily Mail** continued their blistering attack on Jacob's parents announcing, *"...both couples have moved to Hillhead in Glasgow"* and printed a picture of Ruth and Adrienne's home. They also printed a picture of Jon and five-year-old Jacob, somewhat undermining the paper's concern for the bullying they claimed the child might receive if he was identified. To completely drive the nail home, they quoted Valerie Riches of the potty group Family and Youth Concern, who squealed: *"How dare they...?"* Hugh Brown of the Kirk's Board of Social Responsibility said it was all *"extremely peculiar"* and the 'Sexfinder General,' Monsignor Tom Connolly, said a child *"should not be treated as if you are going into a supermarket to get one"*.

Tom 'Brigadier' Brown participated in a television debate on Grampian Television, observing: *"One homosexual chap announced he was 'broody' and desperately wanted a child. The lesbians on the programme saw nothing wrong with a loveless coming-together with a stranger (or gay male friend) for the purpose of producing a baby as an accessory to their otherwise man-hating relationships... It ain't natural. And what ain't natural ain't right - and can be damaging for the child"*.

Although mimicking heterosexual partnership rites doesn't necessarily appeal to all gays, otherwise brought up in Gourock, Jon Ioannou and social worker, Ted Mitchell adopted the only social markers they knew to confirm and endorse a genuine commitment to each other by getting 'married'. A point the **Scottish Daily Mail** clearly missed in its eagerness to trash the arrangement once their second child Olivia was born. In **The Herald**, the 'Sexfinder General,' Monsignor Tom Connolly ranted: *"A child is meant to be the fruit of the expression of love between two people in a stable loving relationship... The ideal situation is for a husband and wife to raise a child in a committed relationship"*, which, if that was the only qualifying factor would have made Fred and Rosemary West the perfect parents. **The Herald** wheeled in Hugh Brown, a spokesman for the Kirk's

Board of Social Responsibility to wave a fist in the face of the couples' obvious success. *"I don't see how a child can... get a conventional upbringing by being brought up by two lesbians. Family life is critical as far as the Kirk is concerned and by family life we mean living with a mother and father"*. Gary Keown in the **Sunday Mail** squealed: *"No one seems to criticise such behaviour"*.

When comedian Michael Barrymore dropped a hint he would like to adopt when the circumstances were right, he explained: *"The child would be loved"* and *"would be given all the opportunities it would not normally have had... I'd like to adopt a child from one of the countries where they are genuine orphans and will suffer if no-one takes them home"*. The **Daily Record** found this an *"extraordinary revelation..."* and a *"shock admission"*. For 'Old Mother Burnie', this was certainly not 'awlright', warning him and his *"toyboy"* lover – otherwise only described as his 'pal' - that they *"shouldn't be allowed to adopt so much as a stuffed budgie"*.

Dr Gill Dunne, a senior research fellow at the Gender Institute of the London School of Economics was dismissed as a *"controversial... feminist academic"* by **Scotland on Sunday** for claiming gay men made better dads. Mrs Ann Allen of the Church of Scotland's Board of Social Responsibility supported Stephen Fraser's report by referring to *"the thousands of years behind the traditional, biblical model of a family structure, which we believe is the best and most effective sway to bring children up"*. Despite agreeing gay dads could indeed be good dads, she insisted: *"...We cannot condone anything that presents homosexuality as a social norm"*. The Church intended to use all its influence to put its view across. It would be operating from a position of some strength, boasting the healthiest bank balance it had ever had in its entire history. According to its Board of Stewardship and Finance, the total income from congregations was reported in 2000 to have gone up by more than two per cent to £82 million. **Scotland on Sunday**'s editorial sniffed that *"inevitably the research will be used to advance the cause of male gay couples who want to adopt children. There are, though, anxieties here that go beyond basic human rights for gay people, and they concern the welfare of children"*. The editorial added that a child *"reared in the environs of a committed and stable relationship between a man and a woman"* was *"one of the most cherished"* values of our society.

And, *"when the fine balance between their joint input to the emotional an intellectual development of children is distorted the consequences can be devastating"*. Like, I suppose when one of the parents can no longer conceal their homosexuality.

The **Daily Record** was ready to call on the Church at a moment's notice for advice on any moral issue, particularly if it concerned gay people and children. All too often, it was the Church calling the media, ready with story, pictures and supporting quotes if necessary. Under the heading: *"Concern"*, the **Daily Record** ushered in the 'Sexfinder General,' and Mrs Anne Allen for some more finger wagging on the subject. This time: *"A woman who lost her lesbian lover in a road smash is to bring up her partner's daughter with the blessing of the youngster's grandparents"*, their headline gasped. Mrs Allen was quick to remind everyone: *"The church view is that couples of the same sex are not regarded in the same light as married couples and in law do not have the same rights"*. But who were they to moralise? In one case, fire and brimstone preacher, Keith Offor who wrote the Pulpit and the Pew column in his local paper in Stranraer, left his wife and ran off with a parishoner. He told his congregation *"they would end up in Hell if they committed adultery"*. According to one parishioner: *"Once he stood in the pulpit and said if a man walked down the road and even looked at another women it was adultery"*.

When the **Daily Record** discovered *"LESBIAN LOVERS TO HAVE DONOR BABIES"*, they couched their exclusive in heterosexisms: *"Lesbians Jeanette Smith and Margaret Fleming say they will act as mother AND father to their babies"*. It reminded me of that scene from the film 'Great Moments In Aviation' when a surprised Vanessa Redgrave told Dorothy Tutin: *"32 years you kept this secret...? Now you tell me that for 32 years you felt the same way for me as a man feels for a woman?"* Dorothy delivered the crashing reply: *"No actually, I love you as a woman loves a woman"*. The meaning behind that would have been quite lost to much of the pond-life working for the **Daily Record**, otherwise too busy indulging its readers in more of the finer details: *"Jeanette, 31, even injected Margaret with the donated sperm herself"*. More shocks were to follow: *"The lesbians... revealed they have already helped bring up one child"*. (The *"child"* was 16 when she moved in with them)! *"Opinion"* was never very far away in the shape of the 'Sexfinder General' who dismissed it all as *"unnatural"*.

That wasn't all the 'Sexfinder General' found unnatural. The Catholic Church had made it quite clear what their opinion was of homosexuality was and had no intention of giving ground in the face of changing attitudes on the subject.

In the early nineties, a MORI poll found a startling 36% of Scots baying for homosexuality to be made a criminal offence. And whereas 74% of the UK supported an equal age of consent in a Harris poll, only a meagre 9% of Scots could stomach it. But was this, as some believed, a sexual temerity symptomatic of a Scottish malaise or a lack of self-confidence that stemmed from Scotland's status as a subject nation? Or had Scotland just been conditioned by years of Church and media propaganda? Either way, such statistics demonstrated homosexuality was ripe for exploitation by Conservative politicians and the populist press. Not until the crashing defeat by the Tories in the election of 2001 and the publication of the Scottish Social Attitudes Survey of 2000 did a different picture emerge. The Church and media were shown lagging behind Scottish social values when the report revealed only 8% thought pre-marital sex was wrong compared to 21% back in 1983! Also, the report revealed no significant differences in attitude to soft drugs and abortion between Scotland and south of the border. In 1983, six out of every 10 Scots believed homosexuality 'was always wrong' but now it was showing up as less than four in 10. As with all surveys of this nature, strong generational differences were often concealed in newspaper reports.

Young gays are sharply defined by their sexuality in a way that young heterosexuals are not. The civil rights of gays surrounding the debate over an equal age of consent could be measured by the attitudes to sexuality in society as a whole. In Scotland, that was not good. The **Daily Record**'s attitude to all young people's sexual habits was displayed on its front page when it wrote them off as the *"generation of the damned"*. A report from the Scottish Youth Issues Unit had the tabloid in a frenzy when it announced: *"Most teenagers have experimented with sex, drugs and alcohol"*. This was described as a *"bleak"* picture that offered *"little evidence of hope for the future among Scotland's younger generation"*.

That was nothing compared to the outrage reserved for a lonely 'straight' teenager using the screen name Wee Bear to post messages on the Internet to seek friendship and a possible relationship. The **Sunday Mail** was not amused. *"Sick student Steven McCory goes looking for under-age sex on the Internet... The baby-faced 19-year-old sends messages begging 'innocent girls, 14-16, for casual sex'"*. They contacted *"furious Strathclyde University bosses"* and *"told them what he had been doing"*. He hid his face behind a rucksack as the reporters *"confronted"* him at the bus stop. To add to his shame, the **Sunday Mail** mentioned he was *"still a virgin because he suffers from an embarrassing sexual condition"*. Then they printed his photo, indicated his address and blasted him with their vitriol: He was *"Sick... twisted... devious"* and a *"cheat"* before adding that the *"sleaze student"* had boasted and was even a liar. The Wee Bear had entered into correspondence with a **Sunday Mail** reporter, posing as 15-year-old girl.

The Labour administration under Tony Blair was determined to equalise the age of consent across the whole country for gay men from 18 to 16. Unlike the repeal of Section 28, the age of consent originated in the House of Commons so would be immune from blocking measures by the House of Lords. The **Daily Record**'s *"voice of authority"*, Tom 'Brigadier' Brown named and gave *"full marks"* to Scotland's four renegade MPs: *"So our politically correct (but hopelessly wrong) MPs have voted to lower the age of homosexual consent to 16. Only four Scottish MPs voted against lowering the age of consent..."*.

With young people having sex earlier than 16 some thought it made sense to assist those educating youngsters with a new age of consent for everybody at 14. The suggestion brought about the wrath of the Church. Mrs Ann Allen said: *"We would be 100% opposed to lowering the age of consent to 14. It would give entirely the wrong message to adolescents and would put enormous pressure on young people who are not at the point of wanting to be sexually active"*. For Catholics, the 'Sexfinder General' added: *"Our position on this matter is quite clear. We believe any sexual relationship outwith marriage is wrong at any time irrespective of age"*. Judging by general practice, of course, the majority of its member begs to differ!

Jim Sillars, a former SNP MP, was so right-wing that the **Scottish Sun** gave him his own column in the tabloid where he could write about, amongst other things, MPs' vote to give - as he saw it - *"mature men the right, for their homosexual pleasure, to seduce young boys aged 16"*. Of course, lowering the age of consent was intended to do no such thing, only to reduce the distress, criminalisation and suicides in young gay men, as it did in the Netherlands when they reduced *their* age of consent. Neither was it, as Sillars believed, introduced to *"extend the realm of the gay brigade…"* But he used his influential platform to inform a nation of rather less educated readers the politics of prejudice: *"These young boys that the homosexual lobby have in their sights…can be used for homosexual acts. Let me tell you a blunt truth. Homosexual relations don't produce homosexual children who grow into prospective sexual partners for others like them. So there is no stock of homosexual young males. The answer is to legalise it and get the age as low as possible to ensure a continuous supply of sexual partners. …Sex objects, to be used"*. The header marched to the sound of his jackboots: *"THIS VILE CHARTER IS WRONG, WRONG, WRONG"*. Sillars was shocked *"there is no backlash"* and attacked gays trying to live their lives in a culture otherwise committed to the ruthless promotion of heterosexism. *"Cruising gay pick-up areas, assignations in public toilets, one night stands for sodomy and obscenity, with all that they threaten in terms of sexual diseases, are prevalent. It is into that unsavoury world that the gay lobby want to drag more young people… We are asked to accept that heterosexual relations, and the family unit they create, are of no higher moral value than sodomy. And our society knuckles under"*. Of course, if sodomy really was the issue, it is not gay men, but straight men that are its chief practitioners, a fact that conveniently escaped Sillars notice.

Spokespeople for an array of religionists and moral conservatives lined up to have their say on the equalisation of the age of consent. The Reverend John Macleod squealed: *"The Bible… speaks of sodomy as a vile, unnatural and heaven-provoking sin"*. Tory MP Nicholas Winterton declared: *"If the Lord Almighty had meant men to commit sodomy with other men their bodies would have been built differently"*. (What? Like putting a hole there)? And Sir Patrick Cormack, deputy Tory shadow leader of the House advised *"gay men were 'not only different', but should not be recognised 'as equal or equivalent' to heterosexuals"*.

**Scotland on Sunday** had already set space aside for Gerald Warner to denounce Blair *"the self proclaimed champion of family*

*values, proving his credentials by legalising sodomy of 16-year-olds".*
He regarded the vote in the Commons as *"a slap in the face to
every parent in Britain".* Warner begged for the *"decent majority"*
to rise up and say that *"liberal legislation has gone too far"* and
warned: *"There will have to be a campaign to repeal it under the next
government".* Warner bordered on being racist too. The homophobic speechwriter for former Tory Scottish Secretary, Michael
Forsyth also writes in the **Scottish Daily Mail** where he dismissed figures by the Commission for Racial Equality showing
racism in Scotland more rampant than in England, a *"myth..."*
Nothing more than *"creative juggling",* he wrote. He reckoned
the *"sponsors of the race relations industry"* were *"at it again"* and
accused both them, and the Government and its *"battalions of
politically correct agents provocateurs",* of having a *"vested interest"* in the *"race relations industry".* He scorned the media for
focusing on racial harassment at all and poo-pooed a year-long
enquiry by the Scottish Parliament as *"more waste of taxpayers
money".* He considered the police were best qualified to tackle
the problem. With his rants appearing in a cluster of newspapers and his continuous harping on about the 'gay lobby',
many wondered how many times it would take to flush before
Gerald Warner would disappear. **Scotland on Sunday** allowed
him to bewail how *"Labour bends over backwards for cottagers";*
spread more distortion and lies how, by equalising the age of
consent, gays wanted *"to recruit emotionally insecure boys..."* and
chide gays for *"claiming that sexual orientation is not a matter of
choice".* A fact he insisted was *"aimed at preventing medical and
psychiatric support reclaiming any of its victims for normality".* His
tormented soul was torched by the *"Paedophiles' Charter... as
MPs laid down the new, permissive ground rules for The Cottager's
Saturday Night. Labour is so bent (figuratively speaking) on foisting
this repellent law on the public that it is prepared to use the
Parliament Act to reverse any further rejection by the Lords. That is
how fanatically committed the government is to declaring open season
on adolescent boys".* Warner painted a picture of *"patients on trol-
leys clutching feverishly at the white coat of the Angel of Islington..."*
(Tony Blair) and declared this a reason to halt *"the legalisation of
sodomy of young boys".* He was sent rustling through documents
to find what he claimed was the earliest record of sodomy in
Scotland, in 1570 and declared it a time when more cases of bes-

tiality were documented, adding: *"That hardly suggests a large proportion of the population genetically predisposed to that vice".* Which says what...? That sodomy bothered no one until it became so much of a nuisance that a law had to be passed to curb it in the 1530s? Even then, sodomy was not then considered necessarily a homosexual offence.

The **Daily Record** unleashed its own bulldog, 'Brigadier' Brown to air his views under the header: *"PINK POWER... THE PARTY NO-ONE VOTED FOR".* Forgetting how, in a previous column he had requested that *"private lives shouldn't be public"*, he turned on gay MP Stephen Twigg, asking: *"How many voters of... Enfield Southgate, where Twigg ousted Michael Portillo - KNEW they were voting in a homosexual MP?"*

In the **Scottish Mirror**, a regular column had been set-aside for ex-**Sun** editor Jack Irvine. His commentary on Labour's *"Pink Mafia"* and their efforts to equalise the age of consent were particularly strident. *"You know the tired old argument - if you're old enough to get married, you're old enough for a slobbering old queer to have his evil way with you... Let's remember what male homosexuals like to do with each other. They like to indulge in anal sex... Anal sex is illegal... Anal sex is liable to give a chap AIDS... And remember, the next time an old fruit gets caught with his hands in a 14-year-old's pants, he will probably get off when he lisps: 'but I thought the boy looked 16'".* Brian Souter, the multi-millionaire entrepreneur and owner of the Stagecoach empire, avidly read these comments before choosing Irvine to lead his homophobic campaign that would set Scotland alight with homophobic billboard posters supporting Section 2a, the only anti-gay law a democracy has introduced in modern times.

The age of consent debate sparked a furore in the **Scottish Daily Mail**. They hauled in a former convener of the Church of Scotland's Board of Social Responsibility, Reverend Bill Wallace. He managed to squeeze in at least four apologies to tame his homophobic rant. *"I despise the victimisation of individuals because of their sexual orientation... **But**... People should not be excluded because they happen to be part of a minority group **but**... No one can possibly condone homophobia or racism... **but**... I abhor homophobia **but**..."* One of the big 'buts' was being *"deeply disturbed when one very small minority group dictates the moral code and legislation of our country".* An extraordinary accusation considering how religionists in the House of Lords had effectively disenfranchised gays by blocking any equal rights legislation proposed by elected representatives in the House of Commons. Reverend Wallace added: *"The allegation that at one stage one quarter of the present Cabinet were gay coupled with this present rush to lower the age of consent makes you wonder who runs the country…"* (Rush…? France adopted their equal age of consent in 1791)! Reverend Wallace chastised gays for dictating *"the legislative programme of our country… A sharp warning to all fairminded people that all is not well with our society…"* and advised how *"we should fear for the future"*. He saw himself as being ruthlessly *"attacked and marginalised by small militant minorities"*, grouping gays with *"animal rights activists willing to plant bombs to further their cause…"* To him, gays were *"among the most determined and ruthless campaigners we have seen in recent times"*. He mentioned those *"right and just struggles"* like *"votes for women"* which, if he had read history properly, he would have known to be particularly violent. *"Or the abolition of slavery…"* which was opposed by the Church. The minister insisted: *"The impression given time and time again in the media is that to be gay is as normal and healthy a lifestyle as being straight"*. He didn't want the removal of legislation that protected people *"passing through a transitional stage"*. Thinking, *"it might well lead to adopting a lifestyle which they may deeply regret in later life"*. Presumably, like so many gay men who marry. He addressed immature men who were uncertain of their orientation *"well beyond their teens"*. Considering such doubts over sexual orientation have been identified in men well past retirement age, perhaps he was suggesting the age of consent for gay men should have been set at 73!

The Scottish Executive overwhelmingly supported an equal age of consent of 16. Although it was a devolved issue, they gave the go-ahead for Westminster to enact the change in Scotland. The House of Lords consistently blocked attempts by the elected House of Commons to make the age of consent equal at 16, (17 in Northern Ireland). The House of Lords rejected moves to equalise the age of consent for gay men three times. Baroness Young focused on the "age of buggery" suggesting the matter "far more important than the Dome". (The London Dome, a structure built for the new millennium, was also grabbing the headlines at this time). At 94, the late Lord Longford who was at various times a **Daily Mail** leader writer and Catholic layman, insisted homosexuals shouldn't be condemned. Such compassion was neatly demonstrated when he went on to describe the practice both "sad" and a "handicap", claiming it turned teenagers into rent boys! But in November 2000, the Government invoked the Parliament Acts to bypass the Lords' opposition and the Sexual Offences (Amendment) Act 2000 was passed. Gerald Warner spluttered: *"The Great Charlatan, when seeking election, pledged to defend family values. He has done so by using the Parliament Act - unconstitutionally - to force through legislation permitting buggery of 16-year-old boys and girls. This sodomites' charter was forced onto the statute book on the eve of World Aids Day - the politically correct Masque of the Red Death which impudently celebrates the triumph of perversion, while futilely seeking means of alleviating its unforgiving consequences. The Scottish parliament is to make its own contribution to the conquest of Aids by legalising group sex among men... Wendy Alexander and Susan Deacon - have done more in one year to undermine the family and debauch young people's morals than a century of suits on green benches. Repeal of Section 28 and the ironically titled 'Healthy Respect' campaign among youngsters are milestones in moral decline"*.

Failing to provide young gays with adequate sex education was just one of the failings of an unequal age of consent. It was therefore unlikely to have been described as anything other than a *"radical new report"* commissioned by Lothian Health to look at the health education needs of gay men, to suggest sex education should include safer sex for *all* young men and women. *"GAY SEX LESSONS CALL FOR SCHOOLS"*, squealed the **Daily Record**, wasting no time at all in digging up the 'Sexfinder General' to splutter: *"These sort of reports only encourage young people to experiment at an inappropriate age"*. The World Health Organisation had already studied the effect of sex education – counselling, education and access to contraceptives – on schoolchildren and study after study showed no evidence of children experimenting with sex earlier, in fact, many of the studies showed schoolchildren starting sex later or even decreasing sexual activity. Considering the likelihood of **Daily Record** readers having gay sex without identifying themselves as gay, *they* were the ones in most need of sex education. The 'Sexfinder General' insisted: *"It is far healthier for teenagers to work out this normal part of growing up themselves without having this propaganda".*

Any aspect of sex education aimed at gays was subject to the scrutiny of particular sections of the Scottish media. The **Daily Record** was furious that Gay Men's Health tackled the high level of recreational drug taking amongst young gays in a non-judgemental manner, producing postcards explaining 'safe' ways of taking Ecstasy and Speed. A suitably bold headline pointed out how the organisation got *"£135,000 a year of public money".* The **Daily Record** boasted how a gay man had handed the leaflet to them. Tory councillor, Daphne Sleigh thought it *"about time Lothian Health reviewed their position"* and the tabloid reminded readers how *"Gay Men's Health were criticised when their magazine, Spurt! promoted gay sex in public and offered advice on how to pick up straight men".*

Sex had already proved powerful and explosive enough to almost topple the leader of the world's most powerful nation. So, while Bill Clinton's future hung on semen found on a dress not cleaned for four years, men in frocks lined with ermine held the British government to ransom over buggery. The unelected House of Lords accused the Government of *"sending the wrong message"* and as the Bentleys drove in from the country estates for the vote in the upper chamber, it was clear they were not likely to change behaviour, only legislate for the continued criminalisation of it. The House of Lords voted to block the House of Commons from equalising the age of consent. Or at least until the Government evoked the seldom-used Parliament Act to force it through or had their hand forced by Europe. The moral conservatives were jubilant. Flushed with success, they were already plotting their next moral battle: Section 28. This legislation originated in House of Lords, so only the Lords could legislate to repeal it in England and Wales. In Scotland, as a devolved issue, it would be up to the Scottish Parliament at Holyrood.

Throughout the debate over equalising the age of consent, the moral conservatives succeeded to some extent in drawing attention away from the young gay men and teenagers who were directly affected by this iniquitous law and exploited a link between 'vulnerable and innocent children' and 'responsible adults'. It was not the first or last time that children would be used to conceal adults' insecurity over sexual issues.

# Chapter Four
## *Moral Panic and PervertWatch!*

*"Billy's poppa found out all about the style of Billy's life
And it didn't take long before he came round and he had a knife.
He cut up Johnny, stole all his money.
He called him all the names he could find
Said he'd wait for Billy at the factory tomorrow
And show them what they'd do to Billy's kind.
Under One Roof, sharing one love
Now all the world knew about them."*
**The Rubettes**

A report conducted by the Conservative Government's Economic & Social Research Council demanded radical improvements to sex education following comparisons made between Britain and the Netherlands. The sex-negating Scottish press belittled the report, hid it, focused on something else, or dropped it altogether for a story better fitting its own moral stance. The latter came in the shape of Wester Hailes GP, Penny Watson who wasted no time in putting the study's findings into action. She made some birthday cards containing - as the **Daily Record** put it - *"explicit advice on how to put on condoms, birth control and sexual diseases..."* and posted them *"to 14-year-olds"*. (They were, in actual fact, sent to their parents!) Scottish editions of **The Express** whipped up: *"Church leaders' anger of GP's condom cards"*, a story which contained only a small half-tone block containing details of the Government's report. The Church's Wallace and Connolly were wheeled in for the occasion. In the **Daily Record**, the Catholic's 'Sexfinder General' thought *"people of that age are not mature enough..."* and Reverend Bill Wallace of the Kirk's Board of Social Responsibility said he preferred kids were taught *"the value and importance of making responsible moral decisions"*. *"Absurd..."* scorned Tom Connolly the 'Sexfinder General' in **The Herald**. *"Appalling"*, he added in the **Scottish Daily Mail** who appeared aghast to find Dr Penny Watson *"unrepentant"*. In **The Herald**, the Reverend Wallace said: *"I think it is very short-sighted of her and quite wrong for her to impose her amoral views on these young people"*.

Readers of Scottish editions of **The Sun** were left with radio shock jock, Scottie McClue who reminisced over an *"innocent age"*. He blamed the *"worst teenage pregnancy record in Europe"* on *"daft liberals"*. Sex education for kids was *"crazy"*, he added. *"Make their life easier and tell them NOTHING about sex"*.

By the end of 2000, Health Minister, Susan Deacon was locking horns with the Pro-Life Alliance who were challenging her initiative, Healthy Respect. Amongst much else, she outlined her intention to send birthday cards out to 14-year-olds containing sex advice. Under the campaign banner of Parent Truth, 20,000 leaflets were distributed in her constituency of Edinburgh East and Musselburgh highlighting 'the filth that is going into schools'.

The **Daily Record**, dropped any mention of the report altogether to wallow in its *"Charter for our Children"* campaign. The **Daily Record** took to handling the complex and sensitive issue of pædophilia with a number of sensational reports. *"Some of our readers' experiences were so shocking that even our own trained counsellor needed counselling herself"*, its leader gasped. *"Almost every day, every week, the Daily Record reports harrowing cases of corruption of the young. And we're sick of it. Every one is a major crime, a life - often several lives - ruined. Let us bring this secret shame out into the open. Let us confront the monsters. Let us cure those who can be cured and cage those who can't"*.

The **Daily Record**'s PervertWatch campaign was launched prior to the introduction of the Conservative Home Secretary's sex offenders' register. The tabloid's demands for a national register of pædophiles was accompanied by a rogue's gallery of *"perverts and paedophiles"* which included gay men found guilty of breaching the law governing an unequal age of consent. These were certainly not pædophiles by any stretch of the imagination. While the gallery featured gym teacher, Kevin Drumgoole who was jailed for having sex with 14 to 17-year-olds, another gym teacher, George Brough, who had walked free following *"spiritual conversion"* to the Catholic Church after non-consensual sex with two 15-year-old girls, was not. The gallery also included *"pervert priest"*, Desmond Lynagh who was described as a *"WALKING TIMEBOMB!"* and a *"paedophile"* that had sex with *"kids"*. Newspapers reported Lynagh having sex with kids over 15 years old. The **Daily Record**'s leader boasted: *"We knew the civil libertarians would wring their hands. We knew we would be accused of setting ourselves above and against the law".* Their letters page revealed to whom the campaign was reaching: They should be *"put down..."*, demanded one, *"castrate them..."*, said another, and *"lock them up for life..."*, added yet one more.

Children were used to bolster the concept of the 'family', justify prudery and support a moral agenda dictated by the Church. If sex was to be denigrated, it took place near 'children playing'. If sex was to be portrayed as harmful, children had to be protected. The media's notion of 'childhood innocence' was exploited so earnestly that virtually no rational discussion of children's sexuality could be tolerated without involving the police, social services and moral campaigners. A subject once entrusted to professionals was now hijacked by the press pandering to the public's 'demands' for the simplistic values of good and evil: Victim and abuser.

In the nation's psyche, the 'professionals' were not to be trusted. In November 1990, social workers and police descended on the isle of South Ronaldsay in the Orkneys and took nine children from their families in a dawn raid. Three of the children described organised sexual abuse to police and interviewers from the Royal Society of the Protection of Cruelty to Children. Stories of 'satanic abuse' were fuelled by references to dancing in a circle, cloaked figures and strange lights. The media ensured that the 'ritual abuse' on 'Devil's Island' was embedded in the nation's memory before the finger of blame was planted on over-zealous officials and social workers.

Stories of sex with minors were often constructed with words more suitable for a story about five-year-olds. *"This is the pervert who terrorised a generation of young Celtic footballers"*, squealed the **Daily Record**. *"Trusted team boss... lured innocent lads... molested the babes who idolised him... a major figure in the Parkhead talent nursery"*. Scott Sinclair was 14 when - if the report was to be believed - apparently thought fondling the balls of a Celtic Boys' Club boss in the front of his car while his mates were all sitting watching in the back as fair exchange for promotion. The **Daily Record** considerately printed the number of the Samaritans underneath their own, urging any other Celtic boys who might have been abused, to get in touch. As everyone knew, Scotland's best-selling tabloid always paid well for a good story: the **Daily Record** hadn't long to wait.

The de-humanising front page said it all: *"SEX BEAST NAILED BY DAILY RECORD... CAGED: 18 years for care worker who preyed on boys... Evil Iain MacDonald, 39, put a boy of 14 through hell for almost a year… James - not his real name - told how MacDonald's sickening abuse had torn his life apart"*. The **Daily Record** said 'James' was *"terrified of being branded gay"*. He told them: *"The sentence will give me the chance to get my life together"*. 'James', whose real name was Charles Kumar, didn't waste any time.

When I interviewed 32-year-old Steven Fallon at his home in Glenrothes, Fife in 1995 on his record-breaking attempt to raise money for charity, climbing all of Scotland's 277 Munros in just 40 days, I didn't expect his story to appear outside of a gay magazine. Despite stories of similar record-breaking attempts appearing in the Scottish press, this wasn't the sort of story that interested them. Steven's 39-year-old lover, Iain MacDonald was instead about to deliver a 'gay' story the press liked better. My first impression of Iain was a thoughtful, caring young man sitting proudly beside his boyfriend Steven on the sofa. That was not how the **Daily Record** saw him. *"SEX BEAST NAILED BY THE DAILY RECORD. CAGED: 18 years for care worker who preyed on boys... Evil Iain MacDonald, 39, put a boy of 14 through hell for almost a year... James - not his real name - told how MacDonald's sickening abuse had torn his life apart"*.

"Before I met Steven", Iain told me, "I had a lover in the army who was killed in an accident. Afterwards I was drinking about a bottle of vodka day. I was 20".

As a commissioned officer from a public school, Iain completed his term and rose to the rank of lieutenant. After leaving the army, his grandmother died, leaving him homeless and unemployed. His newfound boyfriend, Steven, was at college in Stirling, but would regularly cycle over 100 miles to where Iain stayed with an elderly gay man in Edinburgh. Iain was scathing. "He charged for everything. I was skint by the end of the week, so he let me have a bit of bread and jam for 5p. Steven didn't believe me until I showed him the wee list. I could have a boiled egg for the same price as a bit of bread and jam. This was on top of the rent. It wasn't until weeks or months later I actually found out he'd been telling folk I was his affair. Some affair...!" he laughed. "Charging me 5p an egg!"

When Steven's mother discovered a love-letter from Iain, his family threw him out. There was just one place Steven could go. Iain said his new landlord was delighted. "The guy's hands were everywhere", Iain told me. "I managed to get another flat within a week, so we both moved into that. It was a box room in a flat with two other students". 13 years on and there was no disguising the affection Steven and Iain still had for each other.

All the same, there was a period when Iain would spice up his sex life outside their relationship. 'Cottaging' is not a remedy most 'straights' readily understand, but in a rural an area like Glenrothes, the public conveniences was all there was of what passed as local gay life. Most 'cottages' in the country often attract lads who are looking for gay sex at an age when their contemporaries are predominantly experimenting with the opposite sex. This is not so surprising when viewed in its proper context. Half the UK population have their first sexual experience (not necessarily intercourse) before the age of 16. Given the fears surrounding under-age sex and the closeted men who also use public conveniences to make contact with other men, the isolation of young gay men is often compounded. However, it was not in a 'cottage', but after a school concert, 14-year-old Charles Kumar claimed he first had sex with Iain. The experience was supposed to have so traumatised him he was unable to tell anyone what had happened - that was before he plucked enough courage to call Scotland's most homophobic newspaper. *"MacDonald came up and offered me a lift"*, Charles told the **Daily Record**. *"I said I didn't know about getting into a stranger's car, but he said he was a teacher at my school. On the way, he stopped the car and seemed to get really violent. I was getting really scared, so I said it would be all right if I walked home from there. I went to get out but he pulled the door shut, grabbed my wrist and told me he wanted sex. I said no, but he said I wouldn't be going anywhere if I didn't. I started to cry and he started hitting me. He said I'd better do it or he would kill me. I was still really scared and he was* *still hitting me so I went along with it. After he'd done it, he just sat there. I was still crying"*. Charles arrived home at three in the morning and told his stepfather he'd been at a party. The **Daily Record** claimed Charles was *"terrified of being branded gay"*. He told them, Iain's sentence *"would give me time to get my life together"*. Soon after, however, he launched himself on the Edinburgh gay scene. While Iain languished in jail, Charles's photo appeared in the pages of **Gay Scotland**, joining in a ceilidh organised by the Lothian Gay Switchboard. He pursued his ambition to become an actor and appeared on the front page of **ScotsGay** magazine in a musical presented by the Stonewall Youth Project. He was even interviewed by **The Scotsman** newspaper at the time of parliament's age of consent debate on his difficulties in 'coming out'. He told them: *"It will be nice not to feel worried that I could be arrested for doing something I don't feel is wrong"*. Charles Kumar won the heat of the Mr Gay UK contest and even appeared in **Boyz** magazine working in a gay sauna in Edinburgh before he was dismissed.

Iain denies ever picking Charles Kumar up after a concert. "I met Charles in a toilet", he said frankly. "He flashed his cock. We introduced ourselves, went to some nearby woods and had a wank. He asked me if he could give me a blowjob. I, of course, said, yes! He was not nervous. He knew what he was doing all the time. After we finished, I drove him home. We agreed to meet later, but he never turned up".

"I met Charles again a few days later 'trolling' the same toilet", Iain recalled. "We went out again to the woods. He wanted me to fuck him. I had a condom. I tried... But was too nervous. We had more sex. I blew him; he blew me. I drove him home. He said: 'What are you doing at the weekend?' I met him again on Saturday, we went back to my place, and we fucked. He fucked me, and I did the same to him. He was not nervous about fucking. I remember saying I wouldn't do anything he did not want me to do. He replied: 'If I didn't want to do it: I wouldn't be here'. I remember that". Whilst Charles claimed he was physically forced, Iain emphatically denied it: "At no time did I physically harm him, or force him. He even borrowed some of my porn films". Charles described them to the **Daily Record** as *"child pornography videos"*. Iain was indignant: "There were no pædophile films!"

"I brought him to my house once more before he started coming on his own. Even the neighbours saw him. He was not nervous, or scared. Our little fling went on for eight or nine months. I must say, I think he had a crush. I would meet him outside his school, but always a few streets away. I liked him, but I loved Steven. And I still do... God, how I miss Steven!" Iain sighed.

"Towards the end he started to ask for money. £5, then £10. At the end it was £15. He said, 'You know, I could blackmail you,' then sort of laughed... but just left it at that. The last I saw of him was when he asked me to take him to the theatre to see the Pearlfishers at Kirkcaldy. He was going with friends and asked me to pick him up afterwards. Somehow, I missed him. He phoned my home and spoke to Steven. Steven picked him up, drove him home and had a furious row with me about it afterwards. I didn't see Charles for a while until I saw him 'trolling' again. He got a bit aggressive, so I left him to it".

"One year later he's given his story to the **Daily Record** and I'm arrested for *raping* him!"

Most gay cruising areas or public conveniences - 'cottages,' in the gay vernacular - throughout the country have been frequented by youths of about 14-years-old seeking gay sex. If they find someone prepared to know them as a person and not just have sex, they would have been lucky. Most likely they will be shunned. Avoided by the hordes of married and closeted men; men epidemiologists prefer to call Mesmacs: men who have sex with men. These are often the type who seek drive-in, fast food sex as quickly and discreetly as they can, without picking up any gay labels at the checkout. Such denial has a debilitating effect on many youngsters. If they are not already in denial themselves - perhaps by excusing their proclivities by labelling themselves 'just rentboys' - their inability to find a replicate of their conditioned heterosexual ideal can be immensely frustrating: A loving boyfriend prepared to fulfil both their sexual *and* emotional needs. Whilst the public, media and government focus on the older 'pervert' we are failing young gays, struggling to come to terms with their sexuality in a world that would rather they didn't. Not all young gays intentionally indulge in promiscuous sex, but receive it as one after another married or closeted man, with their emotions hooked safely behind the bedroom door of the family home, pulls over in the lay-by for furtive, hurried, clandestine and very occasionally unsafe gay sex with the dish of the day. Research at the University of Frankfurt has shown that whilst two-thirds of gay men, (a third of lesbians), have their first experience of sex between the ages of 14 and 16, 30% of young gays under 18 will have sex with boys the same age. Only 34% of youngsters end up with a man over 18. Young gays don't necessarily fare any better in the hands of their straight peers. It has been estimated that upon learning of their siblings' burgeoning sexuality one in seven parents send them to psychiatrists.

With a picture of Iain looking slightly manic, throwing his head back and laughing, the **Daily Record** carried their 'exclusive' on the front page: *"We passed his evidence to the police and the beast was arrested… Stunned Iain MacDonald's legs almost gave way when he heard the sentence…"*.

"Charles told the **Daily Record** I was having sex with residents at my work", explained Iain. "This had came about because I had taken Charles to a 21st birthday party for a handicapped guy called Jason. He is also gay, although he denies it now. My workmates all knew Jason had a crush on me. I was never violent towards him. He is catheterised, so is unable to sustain an erection. He is also incontinent. Don't believe what the **Daily Record** said about Jason being *"barely able to talk"*. Jason is very vocal. If I had slapped him in the Home, he would have told. It could not have been covered up. Jason's condition makes his testament unreliable. He would say anything. I was always going to plead to having had consensual sex with Charles, but not with any residents in the Home. I faced six charges: three against Charles, and three with residents in the Home. All were violent". (Under British law, the charge of 'indecent assault' arises because young people under the age of 16 are deemed incapable of giving their consent). "My lawyer (Branislav Sudjic) kept saying to me, this must not go to trial, because as soon as a jury see wheelchairs, I am done!"

"My lawyer scared me into a deal with the Crown. They would drop four charges if I plead to two. I said 'no' at first, because there was violence in them. My lawyer said to me that if I went into court I could be found guilty on all six charges because there is in Scotland the Moorov Law of Corroboration. I had no choice. Damned if I do. Damned if I don't".

Scotland's Moorov Law of Corroboration appeared in the thirties when the High Court ruled it necessary to have two witnesses to another, similar crime, committed at around the same time. The law has recently been extended to make it easier to get convictions, so that now, only one witness is needed to convict someone of two crimes. In Iain MacDonald's case, that witness was Charles Kumar.

"I thought, if we could get the violence out, I would think about it", Iain explained. "My lawyer said if I plead the two charges, it would be the same as one charge, because I was going to plead to having had sex with Charles anyway. This way, I was supposed to avoid a trial and maybe a big sentence! In fact, he said the sentence would be the same, at least five years, or ten at the most. He made me write on a piece of paper that I was guilty of two charges. I thought this was for the Crown and was expecting six or seven years. He was on his feet for just three minutes. He kept telling the judge I was expecting a lengthy sentence. Three times he said this! It was a bad deal. I went and pleaded 'guilty' to something I did not do". Iain claimed his defence lawyer had appeared to write him off, telling the court there was little he could find to say in Iain's defence.

Now illegal in Scotland, a temporary judge, Alexander Wilkinson QC, adjudicated in Iain's trial telling him he had 'shamelessly exploited his victims' and sentenced Iain to a staggering 18 years which he began serving in Shotts Prison in Lanarkshire. He was sentenced to six years for having sex with Charles and 12 years for having sex with Jason, both to run consecutively. Iain's MacDonald's sentence of six years for sex with Kumar was substantially more than that given in recent Scottish cases involving pre-pubescent children. Sandra Alves, a 28-year-old mum got six months for asking two boys, 11 and 13-years-old, for sex. She was found on top of the 11-year-old. 27-year-old David Skelding got a three years supervision order and asked to seek psychiatric help after being found guilty of lewd and libidinous behaviour with a seven-year-old girl. 30-year-old Gregory Smith, convicted of indecent behaviour toward a 13-year-old girl in her tent on a camping trip, was freed on appeal. A married teacher who seduced a 14-year-old boy in her care at a special school in Dundee was reported only as having to face being barred from teaching.

Iain's lover, Steven was adamant after the sentence of Iain's innocence: "I should know Iain better than I should know anybody. And I know he wouldn't hurt anyone".

When approached, the Scottish press appeared reticent over Iain's story. *"Not with the present editor-in-chief..."* said one paper. *"Our straight readers wouldn't understand"*, said another. *"A good story... but too sensitive at the moment"* was a reply from another. The growing climate of moral panic in Scotland went some way towards explaining this sensitivity.

In the spring of 1997, the **Daily Record**'s notorious PervertWatch campaign under its editor, Terry Quinn came in for some heavy criticism from the Scottish Council for Civil Liberties. Because tabloids like the **Daily Record** blurred the boundaries between *"gay"* and *"pervert"* in so many people's minds, headlines like: *"Protect me from mob begs pervert"* made uncomfortable reading for some gay men or single men living alone or with elderly parents. But was it the rule of law or the baying of the lynch-mob the **Daily Record** supported when it revealed: *"Child molester will get support from council"*? While vigilantes hounded Alan Christie out of the Raploch area of Stirling, the **Daily Record** was on hand to share with their readers' news of his next location. *"He has since been staying in secret all over Scotland, including, as the Record exclusively revealed, at a Church of Scotland hostel in Edinburgh - next to a children's nursery"*.

The **Scottish Daily Mail** nonetheless declared themselves: *"POWERLESS TO PROTECT OUR OWN CHILDREN"* after finding themselves obstructed by efforts to conceal the identity of a man who had been jailed for a year for indecency with a four-year-old girl. *"But we can reveal the paedophile to be Alan Christie..."* squealed the apparently helpless **Scottish Daily Mail**. *"Christie moved to a bed and breakfast in Callander. But he was told to leave there and is now understood to be staying in a bed and breakfast not far from his former home in the Raploch area in Stirling... The entire shameful affair underlines the urgent need for a national register of paedophiles... And if that infringes the human rights of paedophiles, then we'll see them in the European Court... if* *they are lucky"*. The lynch-mob against 50-year-old Alan Christie was led by 'Big Mags' Haney, pounding on the door of his bed and breakfast, screaming: 'Beast out!' She was eventually caught selling up to 600 £10 heroin deals each week to desperate junkies under the nose of her eight-year-old twin grandchildren. Her daughter went on to serve three-and-a-half years for dealing heroin from the same Stirling council block as her mother.

Soon after, two men, innocent of any charges of sex with children, were forced to flee their home by a baying mob of vigilantes hunting for a sex offender. The terrified pair escaped as the gang of almost 100 teenagers and young women smashed up their property on a council estate in Aberdeen.

When 17-year-old Bryan Hillan was convicted of sexual misconduct, he moved from Clydebank to stay with his mother in Possil. The **Daily Record** reported how Clydebank residents called Possil residents who stormed his parent's home - as the **Record** advised - in *"Balmoral Road, Possil"*. The family fled and council workers had to board up the house. Others were not so lucky. Some had their homes torched, or in Andrew Green's case, was driven out of his council flat by a mob of kids, some as young as nine screaming 'beast' as they hammered on the door. Green had a conviction for sex crimes against a young girl. Days later, a gang of adults broke into his flat and threw his furniture out into the street from the third-floor balcony.

Other newspapers jumped on the bandwagon as more and more people were encouraged to take the law into their own hands. The **Sunday Post** reported a group who had formed themselves into Campaign Against Paedophiles. They held up a picture of 42-year-old William Hoggan who was soon to be released from Barlinnie Prison following a three-month sentence for gross indecency with a 14-year-old boy. The **Post** advised, he *"...owns a home in the village of Slamannan"* and quoted village resident, Ann Aageson who told them: *"We have nothing against the family of this man but if he's taken back then they will have a life of hell. His wife will lose the friends she has here if she stands by him.."*. In fact, his marriage had already broken up and William Hoggan was planning to stay with his father. Aberdeen's **Press and Journal** added to the furore by reporting that William had planned to set up home *"just yards from a* *school packed with young children"*.

Both the **Daily Record** and Scottish editions of **The Sun** were each fined £5,000 for publishing stories about sex offender John Cronin that amounted to a contempt of court. Terry Quinn, editor or the **Daily Record** and Scottish editor of **The Sun**, Bob Bird were each fined £250.

This was not the last time a tabloid would have to put its hand in its pocket over a damage claim, although in the case of Father Noel Barry, the **Scottish Sun** had my sympathy. They were prosecuted for just suggesting someone had had sex! Cardinal Winning's press secretary told the court that while he and Miss Clinton enjoyed *"a very healthy and wholesome"* friendship, the **Scottish Sun** had implied he had breached his vow of celibacy. And because Barry believed Miss Clinton's honour was also at stake, they both decided to take **The Sun** to the cleaners for a staggering £200,000 each! Barry won £45,000 and Miss Clinton £120,000. I think it unlikely Miss Clinton would be willing to split her winnings after it was disclosed in court that Father Barry had spent the night in a hotel with a nun! He admitted a hotel room tryst with virgin ex-nun Caroline Brown but insisted they never had sex! In a front-page story headed: *"RETURN OF THE SEX SHAME PRIEST"*, the **Scottish News of the World** claimed Barry's attempt at going back to being a parish priest had been blocked by Cardinal Winning.

When the Conservative Home Secretary, Michael Howard promised to set up a sex offenders' register, gays were amongst those Aberdeen's **Press and Journal** dismissed as a *"few people"* who would *"quibble with the new, tougher regime of penalties for sex offenders..."* Its editorial sniffed: *"Protectors of civil liberties may shuffle their feet a little and express disquiet.."*. But they had every reason to. At first, even gay men and bisexuals over the age of 20 who were prosecuted for consensual sex were destined for the pædophile list. Although that matter was later addressed, a 20-year-old man who had consenting gay sex with a man aged 17 was still destined to be categorised as a pædophile and forced to sign the sex offenders register whilst a 19-year-old heterosexual man who had unlawful sexual intercourse with a girl aged 13 would not. Scottish gay campaigners had to persuade Michael Forsyth that 'offences,' involving everyone from rent boys, to consenting Scottish gay and bisexual men over 20, should not land them a place amongst rapists and child abusers on a national register. Forsyth left it to the last possible moment before changing his mind.

Michael Howard's register was hailed as a victory for the **Daily Record**: *"CRACKDOWN ON PERVERTS THANKS TO DAILY RECORD"*, they crowed over news of: *"Perv alert power for the police"*. The paper's editorial sagely advised: *"The violation of children is the vilest of crimes and is bound to provoke anger… No-one needs to apologise for these feelings"*. The Tory Home Secretary extended the sentence of Robert Thompson and Jon Venables to fifteen years following their murder of Liverpool toddler Jamie Bulger. The European Court of Human Rights, who had to remind him that only judges in a court were entitled to sentence, was later forced to overturn his decision.

On the anniversary of the Dunblane massacre, the **Daily Record** reflected on *"how good came out of pure evil"* and slapped itself on the back for introducing PervertWatch prior to the introduction of Michael Howard's sex offenders' register. After 59-year-old James Murphy, suspected of sex crimes, was beaten by a masked gang in Port Glasgow, the **Record** wrote: *"People are no longer prepared to sit silently by if they suspect someone of being a weirdo or a pervert"*.

After this, a new Crime and Disorder Act was introduced in 1998 across Scotland in a further crackdown. Unlimited fines and tougher sentences were introduced to control sex offenders giving police power to apply to sheriffs for civil orders against convicted offenders. The orders effectively banned convicted offenders from going to parts of a community - such as play areas and schools - that officers thought might put members of the public at risk. By the beginning of 2001, following recommendations by the Voluntary Issues Review Group, £1million was set aside for voluntary organisations in Scotland to be given free access to check on the criminal records of all job applicants.

The first person to be jailed for flouting the sex offender's register occurred two years later in 2000. It was - in the words of the **Daily Record** - a *"peeping Tom"*. A 24-year-old mother was brushing her hair in her bedroom when she saw Scots-born Donald Ross's face leering through the window of her home near Stockport. He ran off, chased by an off-duty policeman who had spotted him. The paper reported how the mother could no longer sleep alone and was on the waiting list to be rehoused.

The definition of 'pervert' continued to widen as **The Herald** demonstrated when it reported: *"Girls praised for trapping pervert with camera"*. Apparently they were *"preyed on"* by 46-year-old William Robertson of Invergordon, Easter Ross as they walked home from a party at five-thirty in the morning. He allegedly took out an erotic magazine and flicked through it in front of them. Instead of fleeing from the flasher, one of the girls took a photograph and Robertson was jailed for three months.

Sometimes, the word 'pervert' was used by the media without any proper indication of exactly what was meant by it. The **Lanark & Carluke Advertiser** found a mother who gave up her children to live with a *"pervert"*. The paper didn't hesitate releasing the address after reporting how the 23-year-old mum had gone to live with 27-year-old farm labourer Peter Kemp *"at Wellhead Cottages, Cleghorn"* after he was ordered to carry out 150 hours of community service for three charges of lewd and libidinous behaviour and one assault. The paper went on to report how the young mother's parents had been hounded out of their home and had boiling coffee thrown over them.

Another *"SICK peeping Tom"* was also labelled a 'pervert' when he climbed onto a bench and leered at a woman as she slipped out of her swimming costume in a cubicle. *"...Horrified Paula Adam spotted the perv perched above her and hit the roof"*, reported the **Scottish News of the World**. His *"disgusting"* behaviour was reported to police and he was charged at Perth District Court with conducting himself in a disorderly manner. A neighbour was aghast, saying: *"I thought that he was a normal family man with a wife and a couple of young kids to look after"*. The tabloid begged: *"IS there a pervert in YOUR town? Help us expose them by calling us on 0141 420 5301. We'll ring straight back"*.

Once the term 'pervert' had gained - not just an element of notoriety - but also the stamp of legitimacy, it was applied with increasing confidence. *"Branded a pervert"*, the newspaper billboards screamed of an exclusive for Glasgow's **Evening Times** when Councillor Heather Ritchie stood *"accused of branding a Party member a paedophile"*. Brian McKenna claimed Mrs Ritchie orchestrated a poisonous campaign accusing him of being a gay sex offender. The **Evening Times** quoted a *"respected"* member of the community council: *"She said: 'You know he's a homosexual,' and I went 'Uh-huh?' And she said: 'Well, we are trying to get someone in the social work to look into it, but we suspect he's a paedophile...'."*

'Old Mother Burnie' waved her broom at her favourite bête noire: The *"perverts"* who had found their way up her telephone wires. *"The Internet is an excellent way of communicating with all sorts of people from around the world - it's just a huge pity that it also gives the perverts a chance to invade your home via a computer and e-mail"*.

What was lacking in criticism or intellectual debate in the media's campaign against 'perverts': bullying more than made up for it.

*"We're glad to nail pervert"*, boasted the **Daily Record** after they tracked down and confronted Alan Rozenski. Four years ago, driving instructor Rozenski was fined £350 for indecently assaulting two of his pupils. He told the **Record**: *"I am a legitimate qualified instructor and what's in the past is in the past. I am not a danger to anybody. I am a law-abiding citizen"*. He moved to a new area and changed his name. Rozenski begged the paper to leave him alone, saying it could lead to his ruin. They *went ahead anyway and printed his picture on the front page boasting: "We make no apologies... And will continue to expose... perverts like him... The podgy pervert calls himself Alan Wilson and unsuspecting learners have been for lessons with him, unaware of his murky past"*.

When former champion boxer 52-year-old Ken Buchanan battered 17-stone Murdo Macleod to a pulp after waking up to find *"the naked beast"* groping him, Scottish editions of **The Sun** toasted the champion on their front page. Buchanan had struggled with a drink problem, angina and had a string of failed relationships. He had already been convicted of assaulting the 22-year-old daughter of his former girlfriend at their house in Coatbridge when he had gone back to claim some of the prizes and medals he won during his boxing career. After having been fined and bound over for a year, Buchanan was admonished, on grounds of good behaviour. But according to Robert Tait in **The Scotsman**, Buchanan had *"far worse ghosts to exorcise"* following an incident that occurred after Buchanan claimed he fell unconscious when he took sleeping pills and woke to find his pal naked in bed with him. "*Sobbing Ken - who has lost his girlfriend and job since the attack - admitted no punishment could make up for the torment he has endured…*" Boxing hero Ken Buchanan pummelled his gay sex attacker to a blood-soaked pulp. *'This was my best ever fight, I beat him to a pulp'*", Buchanan boasted. **The Sun** took a ringside seat to cheer him on, gasping: "*And as the red mist descended he once again became a brutal fighting machine - raining down one crushing blow after another*". Buchanan added: "*It was as if I was back fighting again. I was never better. It was like I had him on a string. I couldn't hit him hard enough. At one point I missed a punch and felt sick that I had wasted a swing. He ran into his room, but I went after him and kicked his door in. He was lying on the bed naked saying: 'Don't, don't, please don't'. I was just pounding his face in and wouldn't let up.* **I screamed at him, 'Thank Christ it was a boxer and not some kid you picked on…'** *I might have been up for murder… …I would have killed that guy*". Murdo Macleod went hysterical after the attack and had to spend several days in hospital. He vociferously denied being gay and said: "*I'm an innocent man. I have done nothing. I was married and have two kids. I've also got a girlfriend now*". Macleod was later convicted of indecent assault. Buchanan, on the other hand told the press: "*the gay sex attack ruined my life*" before declaring his intention to counsel "*sex abuse kids*" and "*others who have suffered at the hands of perverts…*" He told **The Sun**: "*I feel so sorry for people, especially all the young children who have been sexually abused by some dirty man like the one who did this to me*".

Famous for his reactionary opinions on sexual politics and on the subject of burglary, the **Sunday Mail**'s Gary Keown advised: "*Far better to hit first and ask questions later. Give the guttersnipe a good kicking because that's more likely to knock some decency into him… It's dog eat dog. That's why you're entitled to do what it takes to deal with scum*".

After serving time for a sex attack on Judy X, John Cronin attempted to start a new life. The **Scottish News of the World** quoted a former neighbour who told them: "*…For the first few years of his life, his mum dressed him up as a girl. She wanted a girl so she dressed John in bows and frilly blouses. No wonder he's such a mess now*". He wanted to return home but the **Scottish News of**

**the World** reported, *"local vigilantes have threatened to lynch him…"* Reporters from its sister paper, the **Scottish Sun** found the *"monster in hiding"* at a farm cottage and printed a picture of the: *"Isolated… remote East Lothian cottage where Cronin is holed up".* No longer so isolated, the **Daily Record** reported: *"Cronin came to the door of the cottage last night, but turned around and ran back inside and refused to talk"* adding indignantly: *"The move to the village of East Linton, in East Lothian was supposed to be secret".* A villager who didn't want to give his name told the **Record**: *"'I passed him on the bridge… I asked him what he was doing and he said it was none of my business. I told him it was my business, because I have a wife and three kids and wanted to know where he was staying'.* Cronin replied: *'I have never touched any kids'."* The **Scottish News of the World** found a villager who reckoned he had heard Cronin whisper to him: *"The beast is back"* and another villager was photographed in his *"gallery of hate"*, a garage with the walls plastered in tabloid cuttings on Cronin. The **Scottish News of the World** called on all their readers to *"HELP US KEEP TABS ON THE BEAST. Women and children are living in fear because sick Cronin is to walk free. Help us to keep them safe by telling us what you know of his whereabouts…"* The **Scottish News of the World** added: *"We warned you of the exact day when evil pervert John Cronin would be let out of jail. Thanks to us, local mums and dads were ready and chased the sex monster to England".*

Residents in close-knit Scottish villages could be a fiery source of vigilantism, less accepting of the cities and their liberal ways. Gardenstown has five places of worship for a population of just 1,200 with planning permission for a sixth church and four meeting houses after a section of the congregation formed links with the Reverend Ian Paisley's fire and brimstone brigade, the Free Presbyterian Church of Ulster. Ian Paisley attracted around a couple of hundred people when he preached at Gordonstown in 1998. Reverend Noel Hughes insisted in Aberdeen's **Press and Journal**, *"People know where Dr Paisley stands".* When it became known that a Church of Scotland minister, Helen Percy had allegedly struck up a relationship with a married man in the Perthshire village of Kilry, parishioners declared her a witch based on tales that she preached in her nightdress.

The **Scottish News of the World** was fast establishing itself as the champion of the vigilantes. In another headline they declared: *"Vigilante villagers drive out a pervert"*. George McPhee had just served two years and had gone home to find *"a vigilante crowd of parents gathered outside his home - yards from a school playground - in a bid to force him to move away"*. The story finished with an extraordinary report of a mum fighting *"to have her own son listed on a sex offenders' register after it emerged he fantasised about raping a teenage girl..."* She was reported saying: *"I wish he'd never been born"*. When George McPhee moved to Cornton, residents held an emergency meeting and the **Stirling Observer** reported their claims that their community was being used as a dumping ground for perverts. A mother of two said: *"We knew there was a former resident who had returned to stay in the area after serving a prison sentence. We didn't have enough time to try and prevent him coming back but we now hear that there may be another one already here and the possibility of a further two moving in. We simply can't allow that"*.

The **Scottish News of the World** sneered when a pastor backed *"the pervs in his pews..."* Sandie Jamieson caused uproar when he welcomed three convicted *"perverts"* into the Lighthouse Christian Centre in Dumfries. The pastor faced chastisement from the **Scottish News of the World** because he defended his decision *"to let three vile sex offenders join his congregation"*. The pastor recognised in all humans the potential for murder, sex crime or mental breakdown. It was Nazi law that famously made the distinction between murderers, 'perverts', the mentally challenged and 'normal' people. They encouraged, first the segregation of 'subnormals,' then their elimination for the good of mankind.

Two girls of six and 10 were pictured in their school uniforms, standing by their PC with a built-in video camera alongside their *"horrified mum"* in the **Scottish News of the World** after she revealed they were being targeted by *"cyberspace sickos"* when they found *"INTERNET MONSTER FLASHES AT KIDS"*. The mother told the tabloid how she hadn't realised a PC *"was a perfect medium for perverts to get their kicks"*. The tabloid was hungry for more: *" Do you know a story about a sex perv?"* the **Scottish News of the World** begged. *"Is a fiend stalking your town? Call us on 0141 420 5301. We'll ring you back"*.

The hysteria over pædophilia that had developed in

Scotland in the wake of the Dunblane tragedy knew no boundaries. *"Don't worry about the paedophile next door, we'll build you a 6ft fence"*, quipped the **Scottish Daily Mail** who were afforded the opportunity to detail how *"housing managers and social workers agreed to erect a high wooden fence down one side of Mr Currie's garden..."* In *"Etive Place, Cornton, Stirling"*, the **Daily Record** added helpfully, *"to block the view from his window into the neighbouring garden"*. Mr Currie, whose wife, it was claimed, was a 'born-again' Christian, was imprisoned for molesting three girls and had returned to his three-bedroomed terraced house in Stirling. Mr Currie, who was 79-years-old, suffered from a heart complaint, senile dementia, suffered a chronic skin complaint, was almost deaf and walked with a stick. The **Scottish Express** quoted neighbour Pauline Smith with two girls of three and four who asked: *"...In summer loads of children congregate in the nearby quadrant. What happens if he is out and about near them?"* Another neighbours' application to have a fence erected round his garden was refused. Living two doors away with three boys, he stamped: *"If I do not get my fence by summer I'll have to stop the kids going out"*.

David Rivers was 70-years-old. He was already on probation after offences relating to indecency involving young girls when he approached a 15-year-old boy in a park in the borders town of Hawick and suggested they had sex. The boy said no and told his parents. After police were involved Sheriff Kevin Drummond recommended Rivers should be placed in a secure institution, but since none were available was warned he would be imprisoned if he did it again. Led by SNP councillor David Paterson, a campaign was soon underway to have Rivers moved from his sheltered housing which was deemed too close to a primary school.

In another incident involving an elderly man, the **Daily Record** headlined: *"MAN OF 74 CHARGED WITH SEX ATTACK ON WOMAN, 100"*. William Bowman appeared before Ayr Sheriff Court charged with attempted rape. Whilst nursing staff in the old people's home where the incident occurred were reported being *"devastated"*, the woman was reported to have been *"remarkably resilient"*. In another incident, wheelchair-bound and partially paralysed war hero, 77-year-old John Boyle, found himself ousted from Fernan Street day centre in Shettleston, Glasgow after he was accused of thrusting his hand between the legs of a wheelchair-bound friend. The widower tried to explain he had no movement in his left hand and only partial movement in his right.

Visiting Somerfield supermarket with his wife Rose and sister Margaret just before Christmas, pensioner James Reid found he needed to use the toilet. Because the gent's toilet was out of order, the assistant advised him to use the disabled toilet and gave him a key. He used the ladies by mistake. When he heard someone in the next cubicle he 'did the gentlemanly thing' and waited until she had left. Unfortunately, he emerged from the cubicle too soon and was spotted by a lady who started screaming 'pervert' at the top of her voice. Much to his embarrassment, Mr Reid, who walks with a stick and has a heart condition, was escorted out by security.

Once disempowered by sexual shame and ignorance, people were now encouraged to speak out about their past by the media. Even more "perverts" were "exposed". Captain David Neill, the married former captain of the paddle steamer, the Waverley, conveniently parked outside the offices of the **Daily Record**, was forced to publicly face his previous indiscretions. The **Scottish Daily Express** called it: *"innocence lost"* when they reported the *"kindly captain"* was really the *"Waverley pervert who robbed boys"* - they were reported as being aged between 12 and 15 - *"of their innocence and their dreams… He pretended he was helping innocent children gain experience of the sea, but was only interested in furthering his depraved lusts"*. A large picture of the former 'doon the watter' Waverely paddle steamer skipper appeared in the paper following his release from Glasgow's Barlinnie prison. The **Daily Record** followed him to *"his parents' home in Balloch estate, Cumbernauld… a detached bungalow"* which was noted as being near a school, *"a five-minute walk from Eastfield Primary School"*. The **Daily Record** was thanked by a senior police officer for drawing this to their attention. Police are supposed to be informed of a sex offender's whereabouts, but they implied they had not kept track of David Neill, suggesting: *"Problems might have arisen because of a local public holiday"*.

The pursuance of sex offenders is often guided by our own prejudices. The first assumption is that an offender is a man, and secondly, that he is an adult, something John Merrilees, 33, from Glenrothes in Fife found out to his cost when he was accused of raping and abducting a six-year-old girl. The crime resulted in massive roadblocks in the area. The Scottish Executive Minister Henry McLeish had to step in to reassure the community in the face of vigilantism and hundreds of parents locking up their children before a 15-year-old youth later confessed to the rape and the hysteria died down.

Moral panic is incited when the media masks sexual crime behind references to 'perverts' or 'beasts' engaging in 'sick acts'. There is often very little in a report to make any intelligent deduction of the seriousness of the crime to draw any other conclusion other than that there is a 'beast' about to be let loose in the community. It is also, to some extent, the dumbing down of violence in our society that ensures moral panic pays little part in attacking men who are released from prison into the community after serving a sentence of atrocious crimes of violence, yet is provoked into action by crimes of a sexual nature. The **Sunday Post** was waiting at the prison gates for *"convicted child molester Andrew Doharty (51) from Sandyhills, Glasgow"*. When it comes to housing, Doharty is at the mercy of local authorities. With little choice but to move in with his brother *"…in Shettleston, the area where he carried out a horrific catalogue of sexual abuse"*, his future also rested with the **Sunday Post**. Mrs X told the **Sunday Post**: *"My daughter has been too afraid to go to school all week and my little boy hasn't been to school for four years"*. The **Post** reported how *"Mr and Mrs X have themselves been in and out of hospital with psychological problems and the family is on medication. Their 14-year-old son suffers from agoraphobia and post-traumatic stress disorder. He needs special tutors at home. The two girls, now 11 and 18, have also struggled to cope"*. The **Post** also pointed out that Doharty's brother's house was *"just 10 minutes from the family's home and near the school their youngest daughter attends"*. Doharty was on parole after serving two and a half years of a four-year sentence. Nowhere in the report did it attempt with any degree of honesty, to explain what Doharty actually did, let alone what he felt about his crime after a lengthy prison sentence.

Press reports played on the public's fear of pædophiles stalking the country in search of prey. *"Inquiries after man*

*approaches boy in park"*, reported **The Scotsman** after *"a man jos-
tled a five-year-old boy in Kirkcaldy"*. They reported police *"playing down"* suggestions it might have led to abduction.

Often, the subsequent furore over sex offences can contribute to any damage that might already be inflicted on a victim. In the west of Scotland, an aunt set about questioning a 14-
year-old boy about 'abuse' after he casually remarked to her
how he thought men who murdered children ought be sent
away for a very long time. *"Sex beasts"*, Charles O'Neill, 35, and
William Lauchlan, 21, as the **Largs & Millport Weekly News**
referred to them were arrested. O'Neill was sent down for eight
years and Lauchlan, six. Soon after, the 14-year-old was admitted to hospital following an overdose.

Fears over vigilantism rose again after the **Scottish Sun**
printed a large, clear, colour picture of the man nicknamed
'Catweazle,' *"sex pest George Belmonte"* and his *"hideaway"* in a
*"Dumfries-shire graveyard"*, where he had tried to set up home.
The **Scottish Sun** hadn't revealed much more than the fact that
*"angry families hounded him out of his home"*, where police claim
Belmonte was effectively under house arrest. The reality was
more serious. A 70-strong crowd had gathered round his house
and smashed the windows. Posters had gone up all around
Kirkcudbright forcing a distressed older man, bearing a resemblance to 'Catweazle' Belmonte, to put a disclamatory notice in
the local press. Bandaged windows and scattered shards of
glass bore witness to what had happened to Belmonte in
Kirkcudbright. The **Scottish Sun** said he had *"fled to local woodland"*. Local councillors failed to allay people's fears as action
groups held petitions, meetings and poster campaigns to have
him driven out from their communities until Scottish Local
Government Minister Frank McAveety was forced to intervene,
holding talks with Dumfries and Galloway Council chiefs to
discuss the future of the 68-year-old man. 32-year-old Brian
McEntagart who kicked open Belmonte's Lockerbie flat under
the influence of drink and caused him an injury on the fore-
head, was jailed for three months.

The **Airdrie & Coatbridge Advertiser** publicly involved
itself in a *"rape victim's national campaign to keep sex beasts off the
streets"*. In an area were vigilantism could easily get out of
hand, their campaign followed the rape of a 15-year-old girl by

*"evil"* John Locke from Coatbridge. Throwing petrol on the flames was doing nothing to attack the root of such sex pathology and crime.

Soon, a supermarket chain was experimenting with electronic tagging for toddlers and the National Society for the Protection of Cruelty to Children advised parents to be careful when asking youngsters to kiss or hug their grandparents. Not that any of this would have prevented young James Bulger being abducted and led away to his death by two children.

Sexual criminals were pariahs in and out of prison. The tabloids castigated the Prisons Ombudsman Dr Jim McManus for suggesting at a conference in Dunblane that victims could benefit from mediation and reparation with a sex offender. He stated that sex offending, first and foremost, should be seen as a personal crime against a victim, rather than an abstract crime against society. He wanted the victim to become very much more the master of the process. The **Scottish Daily Mail** only reported an *"anger over prison expert's pleas for sex offenders"*. David McKenna, assistant director of Victim Support (Scotland) said Dr Jim McManus had *"missed the point"*. Roseanna Cunningham MP riled him for his *"eccentric approach"* and Pauline Thomson, of Scottish People Against Child Abuse dismissed him as *"crazy"*, blaming vigilantism on a lack of effective deterrents. The **Daily Record** described it as *"a controversial bid… to give (sex offenders) therapy…"* and hauled 'Big Mags' Haney up to say: *"The last person an abuse victim wants to meet in the street is their abuser"*.

When Gordon Spain, an art teacher at Irvine Royal Academy, ran off *"with tall brunette"*, 16-year-old pupil Laura Priestley, the **Scottish Sun** gave Laura plenty of space to justify her two-month old affair to readers. Quite a different picture was painted of the *"sinister Sir"* who, according to the **Scottish Mirror**, *"molested boys"*. Far from being sinister, Deputy Head Nigel Craik used to greet the boys on their skiing holiday in the USA calling: 'Hello boys, do you still love me?' Lanark Sheriff Court portrayed an altogether darker side to the 46-year-old's character when they heard how he massaged aftersun cream into a 14-year-old's face when he entered what was unusually described as *"a 15-year-old boys' room"* and *"rubbed his back and legs while telling him to 'relax'"*. An 'indecent assault' on a 13-

year-old was not elaborated on in the **Mirror**, but its sister, the **Daily Record** mentioned *"two occasions (Nigel Craik) sat on a 13-year-old's bed with his forearm on the boy's private parts until he was brushed away. On one occasion, he also tickled his body"*. The **Daily Record** added *"he tickled boys to get them out of bed"*. Unlike the **Sun**'s story, there were no references to the colour of any of the boys' hair. Craik was placed on the sex offenders' register and only escaped a jail term because the Sheriff was assured his career would be over. The judge told the court how he recognised in the geography teacher's behaviour a *"sinister element"*.

The attack on 'perverts' and the tight moral code already established by the churches and maintained by the media on gay sexuality caused genuine suffering to gay people and their families. Behind the **Dumfries and Galloway Standard**'s headline: *"Leave us alone!"* was a sorry tale. Rosemary Hush and Andrea Turnbull claimed their lives had been made a misery by constant abuse since they set up home together. It reached a peak when the word 'GAY' was daubed on the front door of their Lincluden home in giant blue letters and mother-of-four Rosemary, who had split with her husband to be with Andrea, begged people to just leave them alone to get on with their lives. She said: *"When I get visitors, people are shouting abuse... The kids are getting picked on - one of my sons doesn't like staying here... They tried to write lesbian the last time but I don't think they could spell it"*. She claimed her children were being spat at or hit by other youngsters. *"There's no need for it - I don't go out and flaunt anything... Unless you actually catch them the police can't really do anything either"*, she added sadly.

Michael, a gay 35-year-old care worker told the **Sunday Herald**: *"I had to move house because of the attitude of my neighbours. They daubed graffiti on the walls, accusing me of being a paedophile, and eventually they burned my house down. I gave the police names and addresses, but they said they couldn't do anything. Their attitude was appalling"*.

A gay couple and owners of a restaurant in Durness, Sutherland were forced to obtain a written statement from the police confirming they were not pædophiles to halt malicious rumours circulating their small Highland community.

Soon, in a paper written by Professor Brackenridge and Dr Jaques' in the **British Journal of Sports Medicine** doctors involved in sports medicine were being urged to watch out for the warning signs of pædophile abuse – such as a youngster's subdued and inhibited demeanour, signs of disordered eating, or an adult in charge appearing 'a little too dominating'.

The line adopted by many investigating police officers in cases of alleged child abuse is often the reverse of normal policing methods. They start with the suspect: then seek out the crime. In the case of investigating children's homes, hundreds of often damaged individuals with police records have to be interviewed, fuelled by the media and sometimes tempted by the prospect of compensation by the Criminal Injuries Compensation Authority. According to a report in **Community Care** magazine, following the interview of 200 former residents by Gwent police in Wales, 60 members of staff at one home faced accusations of abuse and the police intended to interview another 6,800. On Tyneside, Operation Rose resulted in the police interviews of 100 care workers, so many in fact that solicitors had to employ a team of five barristers. To encourage people to come forward, police involved with Operation Care in Merseyside begged former residents to contact them with 'any complaint' they might have in addition to those of physical and sexual abuse which resulted in as many as 80 former members of staff facing allegations against them. Richard Webster wrote in the **New Statesman** *"given the statistics already in the public domain, it is reasonable to assume that the number of care workers implicated by trawled allegations is now in excess of 3,000 and may well be approaching 5,000"*. In December 2000, after losing his job, seeing his children bullied and wife driven to the brink of despair, English premiership football manager David Jones was cleared of a string of sex abuse allegations at Liverpool Crown Court. His lawyer, Stephen Pollard claimed he had 20 or more witnesses ready to discredit the evidence of the alleged victims, two of whom were serving prison sentences. He also claimed to have been *"besieged"* by volunteers prepared to come to court to testify that the complainants were fabricating the allegation in the hope of winning compensation. They included former prisoners who had volunteered information to prison staff about the alleged victims' plans. In his summing up, Judge David Clarke criticised Merseyside Police for their 'trawling' methods.

Law and order sometimes took a back seat in the pursuit of sex criminals. The police were forced to launch an internal enquiry over a likely breach of data protection measures when an insider leaked the story of James Clark to the press. Police officers at Lothian and Borders scrapped the continual surveillance of convicted pædophile James Clark following his release from prison after a three-year sentence for attempting to kidnap a nine-year-old girl. Clark's picture appeared in the press. A host of politicians backed the **Sunday Mail**'s fury: "*Police boss spends more time spying on his own staff than trailing paedophiles*".

RDSI, a European research company, showed 1,000 men a photograph of an adult man, surrounded by small children playing soccer. While in Europe men concluded the picture depicted a family man, in Britain, they called him a pædophile. The researchers presented the findings as proof that the British remain petrified of anything touchy-feely, that our deep, puritanical instincts continue to see sex and evil in innocent situations.

The suspicion and mistrust that had developed around men with children had a father of three writing to the **Daily Mail** blaming "*political correctness*" and "*feminists*" for his fear of being branded a pædophile if he attended to "*a lost, little child, in tears*". A senior pædiatrician at a Glasgow hospital claimed the climate of hysteria was making it difficult to do the necessary studies – involving examination of large numbers of school-age girls - to explain the huge rise in girls treated for early puberty.

Columnist Susan Flockhart was mother of a 12-year-old when she wrung her hands in the  over Scotland's obsession with "*stranger danger*". She found "*people who won't let their toddlers play naked in their own living rooms for fear a passing paedophile should glimpse them through the window*". And recalled "*one educational film which showed a swing park full of happy children. Cut to an innocuous-looking chap on the park bench. 'He may look friendly,' said the plummy-voiced commentator. 'But...' And suddenly, the stranger turned into a red-eyed monster. Cut again, to a child in a darkened room, biting her nails and whimpering as a menacing shadow of a man enveloped her shivering form... 'This child took a lift from a stranger...'*" For Susan Flockhart, "*the nightmares which ensued were stoked by a mysterious, unexplained word.*

*Harmed"*. She begged we loosen up and implored that children should not be made strangers to sexual culture. Susan Flockhart pointed out that so-called 'childhood innocence', in other words, sexual ignorance, was exactly what true pædophiles thrived on and blasted the Church for getting into such a furore over a drawing in Glasgow's Fruitmarket Gallery, which showed the back of a naked child eating an apple and writing off teenage magazines **Mizz** and **Sugar** as *"immoral poison"*.

The former **Sunday Mail** columnist Gary Keown wouldn't have agreed with her, after ticking off social workers for being *"meddling do-gooders who can't tell the difference between right and wrong"*: he presented his 'solution' to the popularity of teenage magazines. *"First, we should start a bonfire with all those silly girls' magazines that tell kids how to get into trouble. Then throw the parents of these 13 and 14-year-old mothers into the flames, too"*.

The **News of the World** was still warming itself up for a much bigger anti-pædophile *"crusade"*. *"Is there a sex beast in your town?"* they begged. Or *"a perv?"* Words were carefully chosen to make a clear distinction between 'good' and 'evil'. *"INNOCENT children laugh and smile as they skip happily to school – unaware that they're passing just yards from the lair of two evil kiddie-sex fiends"*. The tabloid even measured it: *"Only 200 yards..."* Michael Garven, 29 was convicted of a sexual encounter with a four-year-old girl and was undergoing psychiatric treatment. Robin Millar, 55 had fondled a handicapped girl. They were moved to a chalet in Kilmartin, Argyll, owned and run by learning disabilities charity ENABLE and booked by mental health experts treating the two sex offenders. The **Scottish News of the World** told how *"the lair overlooks the playground"* and demanded to know why parents weren't told. Probably because, as one man told their reporter: *"Everyone will be horrified when word gets around about who these men are and why they are here. I can't see them staying around very long after that. They will have to move on somewhere else before some of the local men get to them"*. A local mum cried: *"...These perverts could be watching my child"*. The tabloid soon crowed over its hard-won victory. *"YOUR SCOTTISH NEWS OF THE WORLD GETS THINGS DONE... FAST"* And so they had! *"SORTED IT!"* They cried over the case of the *"two sick paedophiles"* that were forced to move to another address revealed by the tabloid: *"...A cottage near the town of Ardrishaig"*. Readers sent in their letters congratulating the **Scottish News of the World** for its efforts. *"Once again the News of the World has done the public proud..."*, they boasted.

*"It is every parent's right to protect their children..."*, wrote one reader.

*"Paedophiles like them should be sentenced to live on a deserted island for the rest of their natural lives. They should be left there with no food and no shelter – only the clothes they stand in..."*

*"They should have locked them up and thrown away the key..."*

*"If Garven and Miller are hounded everywhere they go, then they deserve it..."*

*"I felt physically sick when I read about those two awful paedophiles – I can't even bring myself to write their names..."*

*"Why are they still free to do as they like...?"*

Another sex offender, Francis Ward, 60, was described by the **Scottish News of the World** as *"twisted... scum"* and *"the beast"* who had *"had holed up..."* in a rusty camper van *"yards from a primary school"* in Aberdeen. *"Furious locals now want action..."* so Ward was forced to move his van inside a nearby police station compound.

Gary Keown wrote in the **Sunday Mail**: *"There has probably never been a better time to be a child molester..."* He had reached this conclusion after reading the stories of a girl who lived next door to an Ayrshire man who had interfered with her, and the sex offender who had been taken to a pub by a social worker. *"Angered and appalled by all that?"* he spat. *"You certainly should be... These vermin shouldn't even be allowed out on the streets. They are the kind of gutter dwellers that capital punishment was invented for".*

PervertWatch was of nothing compared to the anti-pædophile campaign organised by the **News of the World** in England after the body of missing child, Sarah Payne was found in a field. Amidst falling circulation figures, the **News of the World** under editor Rebekah Wade, published the names and locations of 50 convicted pædophiles. *"The murder of Sarah Payne has proved police monitoring of these beasts is not enough... We do so in memory of Sarah Payne... As a tribute to Sarah we have named our campaign the 'For Sarah' crusade..."* They reminded readers that there is one sex offender for every square mile in Britain. Fifteen Scottish names were added, including ex-Bay City Roller, pop star Derek Longmuir who *"narrowly avoided jail for having computer kiddy porn"*. A spokesman for the paper promised more names and insisted: *"The important thing is that the vast number of people believe what we are doing is right"*. They informed readers: *"Our website maps beasts"* and invited parents to *"protect their children"* by logging onto the interactive database *"to see if they have a paedophile living in their area"*. The editorial warned: *"That is not all. We are demanding that, in future, life must mean life for the worst child-sex perverts. No more parole. No more early release. No more soft options. No more freedom for the fiends. And we have the support of the people. A MORI opinion survey taken two days ago reveals massive backing for our demands"*. Their competitor, **The People** called for the reintroduction of the death penalty for child abusers.

One of the problems with such a campaign was that of the estimated 80 or so children murdered in Britain each year, only around seven of these were by people the child did not know.

Scores of letters poured into the **Scottish News of the World**. *"If it was left to me, I'd suggest tattooing these beast's noses with a luminous green substance. This way they'd be recognised even in the dark and would be hard to conceal"*. Further letters in support included R M from Glasgow wanting the whole Scottish Executive put on the list and a Pat Gordon via e-mail who turned on the *"politically correct do-gooders"* who were shouting in defence of *"these monsters"*. D Mitchell from Aberdeen wrote: *"You just have to look at Sarah Payne's angelic picture to know what's the right thing to do"*. C Munro from Irvine wrote: *"Scum like these should never be allowed back into society without being castrated. The crimes they commit are the vilest of the vile... Keep up your fight"*.

The tabloid's headlines promised: *"More names and photographs of child sex offenders living near you... PARENT POWER CAN CHANGE LAW"*. The tabloid campaigned for a 'Sarah's Law', named after 'Megan's Law' which had been established in the States in similar circumstances. The editorial surrounded itself in photographs of victims dating back to 1963. *"Never in the long history of this great campaigning newspaper have we had a bigger response, or stronger support, from the great British public...*

*We vow we will not rest until the government take action. And put Sarah's Law on the statute book"*. Very soon, the agenda widened. American-born photographer Tierney Gearon's exhibition of photos of naked children at the Saatchi gallery in London had been running for eight weeks before the **News of the World** condemned it as *"a revolting exhibition of perversion under the guise of art"*. The paper said police raids followed complaints from members of the public, but the police said they were following up complaints from journalists.

Linda Watson-Brown in **The Scotsman** hijacked the case to promote her anti-porn campaign in this paper. *"Bear in mind the paedophiliac pornography masquerading as straight news reporting in the Sarah Payne case"*. She found the reportage surrounding Sarah Payne was *"titillating"* and *"a paedophile's dream"*. She asked: *"...Am I the only one to feel nauseous each time I read of the pretty little girl in the white socks found naked in a field?"*

In complete contrast, the day after the **News of the World** published its *"name and shame"* feature against the recommendations of police and Home Secretary Jack Straw, 80 loyalist and republican terrorists were released from The Maze prison in Northern Ireland as part of the Good Friday Agreement. Amongst them was Michael Stone who murdered three mourners and injured 68 in a grenade and gun attack at an IRA funeral; Sean Kelly who bombed a fish shop in 1993 and killed ten; Torrens Knight who killed seven; and James McArdie who served two years of a 25-year sentence for the London Docklands bomb in 1996, which killed two people and injured 40.

The **News of the World** sparked a spate of attacks. George Belmonte, one of the named Scottish offenders, went on a hunger strike out of fear, claiming he was a victim of a witch-hunt and a prisoner in a room above a Dumfries pub. He had by now been forced out of various locations about a dozen times. A 300-strong stone-throwing mob mistook Iain Armstrong for Peter Smith, one of the offenders pictured in the **News of the World** who lived in the same area and also wore a neck-brace. By Sunday night, a brick was sent crashing through his window.

Whilst the war against repeal of Section 2a (Clause 28) raged in Scotland, Richard Wilshin, a registrar for the General Optical

Council battled with the **Sunday Mail**. Optician Gordon MacGregor, 36, had been found guilty of holding indecent pictures of children on his PC. He was fined £1,500 and placed on the sex offenders' register for five years. Wilshin was adamant MacGregor should not be struck off and said: *"The council was not satisfied from the evidence that what was alleged to have happened had happened... The pillorying this person received in the Press and the calls that he be struck off were also given in evidence at the hearing. The council considered he had been the subject of Press publicity to such an extent that he had his reputation very much affected... The situation is quite straightforward. We needed to be satisfied the photographs were what they were alleged to be. The disciplinary committee had evidence on oath from Mr MacGregor about what the photographs were, which the committee did not consider to be indecent"*. The **Sunday Mail**, however, were clearly satisfied they were even though they hadn't seen them. They sought the opinion of former Tory MP Phil Gallie who said: *"Given the conviction this man has, I think that makes him fair game for the media"*. MacGregor had practices in Glasgow, Tiree and Ayrshire. The **Sunday Mail**'s Russell Findlay reported: *"Locals in Newmilns, Ayrshire, hounded him out of the town and warned him never to return... He is understood to be now working as a locum optician travelling around nursing homes in Glasgow... MacGregor's neighbours in Leven Street, Pollokshields, Glasgow, posted leaflets after the court case, written in Punjabi and English, warning about his behaviour. One local said: 'Everyone has been warned about this man as there are a lot of young children in the area'."* His name appeared on the **News of the World**'s printed list of 'perverts', which was launched on their website and became the subject of further damning reports.

In Ayrshire, an innocent man's home was vandalised by a vigilante mob and daubed in offensive slogans. They smashed his windows and raised a petition of 300 signatures demanding he be barred from moving to the Ayrshire town of Cumnock. He was in fact a married man with two children due to move to the property the following day because it afforded easy access for his disabled son who used a wheelchair. The **Scottish News of the World** denied responsibility for this attack, claiming it took place a day before they published their list.

In Plymouth, police had to rescue an innocent man, his wife

and three children from a 60-strong mob who attacked his home, threw paint and carried placards chanting: "Pædophiles out!"

The worst rioting took place on the Paulsgrove estate in Portsmouth where five families were forced from their homes. Around 100 riot police were called to stop an almost 200-strong mob attacking Victor Burnett, a 53-year-old man on the **News of the World**'s list. A car was overturned and set on fire, a number of policemen injured and windows smashed. Burnett's house had to be boarded up.

Andy Chandler, his wife and their twin seven-year-old boys had to be evacuated by police from their home on the Paulsgrove estate after three-days of rioting when protesters were seen carrying petrol bombs to his house. Chandler's house was also boarded-up.

Michael Horgan, 55 and his family in Brockley, London had to be put under police protection after 500 houses in the area received letters stated incorrectly he was a twice-convicted child molester.

Police had to investigate a suspicious fire at the home of a man in Bingley, Yorkshire who was due to be sentenced for possessing indecent images of children.

A father and three children narrowly escaped an arson attack on their home in Norwich once owned by Roy Reynolds who had been jailed for life for sexual assaults on children.

A group of residents gathered outside the house of Thomas Maxwell who escaped jail for lewd, indecent and libidinous practices with a 12-year-old girl when Sheriff William Reid learned this devoted Jehovah's Witness would live in 'voluntary exile' on the Hebridean isle of Harris.

In another incident, the **Record** reported: *"PAEDO KILLS HIMSELF IN MOB ATTACK"*. James White, a 50-year-old father of five fled after a 70-strong mob stormed his house in Manchester. He died in hospital after taking an overdose.

A motorcycle dealer, arrested for alleged offences against two 15-year-old boys was found dead at his garage in Herne Bay, Kent with shotgun wounds to the head.

The **Coatbridge and Airdrie Advertiser**'s editor, John Murdoch was condemned for *"irresponsible journalism"* by North Lanarkshire Council over protests outside a homeless unit in Airdrie which had been named as the home of Graham Campbell, an 18-year-old convicted of using lewd and libidinous practices toward a five-year-old girl in Motherwell and placed on the sex offender's register. Despite Campbell not being at the Blue Triangle home, 200 people surrounding the unit had frightened the residents. SNP councillor Richard Lyle said: *"Many people have fears which are not being addressed and think it is time that they were addressed"*.

Three vigilantes were jailed for life after killing William O'Kane from Glasgow. He was found slumped across his bed with blood dripping onto his Celtic football shirt. Patrick Moran, 26, Daniel Greaney, 23 and Vincent Gill, 26, all from north London, murdered O'Kane with various weapons including an iron bar after they discovered he had molested a young boy. The judge said: "There is evidence that Willie had behaved certainly in a suspicious way towards that child. But Willie is dead. He is not here to put his side of the story".

Sex offenders, particularly those suspected of abusing children were shunned. The **Sunday Mail** reported how at a stage version of 'Lolita' at the Edinburgh Fringe, the stage director Ruth Cooper-Brown handed out warnings to pædophiles to stay away.

If sex was sometimes perceived as something 'dirty', the reporting of so-called 'perverts' only endorsed this belief. Under a picture of *"smelly Paul McCormack leaving Airdrie Sheriff Court"*, the **Record** reported *"uproar as court is cleared to get rid of pervert's stench"*. This *"smelly pervert called Lardy…"* was an unfortunate 22-year-old found guilty of *"carrying out a sex act on himself in public outside the home of a neighbour…"*

Mere suspicion of sexual abuse became a justification in itself for appalling violence as became clear in the case of Ms 'Frankie' Fawcet-Reid and the handyman who smashed up her mansion in Perthshire. The handyman, 31-year-old Gus McConnell said he found a photo of *"a little boy with an old man"* and added: *"I just lost the plot. I pulled the four-poster bed apart and went through the house, smashing everything up. Then I set a settee alight"*.

Although the **News of the World** promised to put on hold its listing of pædophiles after the second week, the paper threatened to revive the idea if the Government didn't comply with its demands and introduce 'Sarah's Law'. The paper's continued hysterical reportage led to a second night of rioting on the Paulsgrove estate in Hampshire as a 300-strong mob took to the streets and attacked the home of a frightened victim in his early forties who had to be smuggled away by police.

The three-year-old son of mother-of-four Katrina Kessel, one of the megaphone-wielding ringleaders of the protesting mothers on the Paulsgrove estate, was found wandering the streets naked while his mum was busy giving interviews. She still insisted she was a good mother. If she had not been, "social services would have taken my children away", Katrina insisted.

After reading the case of John Adair and Amanda Wharrie, both in their early twenties, some people began to wonder if this hysteria demonstrated a false sense of priorities. While scapegoating pædophiles, attention was being distracted from the vast majority of cases of child abuse by members of a child's own family. Investigators at Hamilton Sheriff Court told how they discovered a fully clothed three-year-old boy in bed, soaked in urine, and his 17-month-old sister in a filthy nappy, barricaded in a squalid room full of dog excrement.

In Paisley Sheriff Court, a mother denied assault and causing injuries to a three-year-old's hand with something like a cigarette lighter. She pleaded guilty of wilfully ill-treating and neglecting him.

In January 2001, a 24-year-old car mechanic, Robert Leitch wept in court after he was released from his year-long ordeal and four-day trial, accused of sexually assaulting his nine-month old baby. This occurred after he and his wife found blood on their baby's nappy and took her to Monkland's General Hospital in Airdrie where doctors examined the baby. Mhairi Richards, his defence, asked WPC Smith who charged him if this had been done because he was a man and she had too readily accepted the word of the mother that she had not harmed the child. The mother later admitted she might have scratched the baby when she changed her nappy and also that her three-year-old son had been playing with the baby earlier that day. It was later revealed that controversial consultant pædiatrician Marietta Higgs had examined the baby. Dr Higgs was central to the Cleveland affair in 1987 when, using an unproven medical theory – anal reflex dilatation – she and Dr Geoffrey Wyatt diagnosed 121 children with sexual abuse in Cleveland. Although five of those children were not returned to their parents, she was accused of being over-zealous by an enquiry and moved to Scotland after losing her licence to practice in Teesside.

Dr Yvette Cloete, a pædiatrician at Royal Gwent Hospital in Newport was forced to flee her home after it was daubed with the word 'paedo'. Police investigating claimed vigilantes had confused the word pædophile with pædiatrician.

Married, dad-of-two Lloyd Beat, 36, hung himself after he was accused of sexually assaulting a 15-year-old boy. He left a suicide note to Scottish Tory leader David McLetchie. Beat had stood against Sir David Steel in his Borders constituency.

The **Sunday Herald** headed a feature on a group challenging the hysteria raging in Scotland with the headline: "*'Sinister' paedophile group set to campaign in Scotland*". This was hardly a fair opening gambit, laying such emphasis on a quote used against them. Action Against False Allegations of Abuse (AAFAA) was a group clearly operating in hysterical times. Isobel George, who believed her husband Alex, a prison warder had been wrongly convicted, headed the group. In the feature, she explained in the feature how a sentence for a sex offender was one of life since it continued after the offender had left prison. On her husband's release, she told how they would have to move house because of its proximity to a primary school and once the public were alerted, could end up moving around the country like nomads. The organisation also campaigned against the Moorov Doctrine, the Scottish law that allowed a number of victims to convict a sex offender if the offences took place around the same time and for the testimonies to be accepted as corroborated.

Mr Robin Corbett, chairman of the House of Commons Home Affairs Select Committee asked the Home Office to consider prosecuting the **News of the World** for the incitement of public order offences. In its third week, there was no let up from the paper. The front page of the **News of the World** insisted: "*Since Sarah Payne was murdered more than 460 sex offences have been committed against children. Today there will be another 10. How many more must suffer before the law is changed?*" The pages inside spoke of *"tears, teddybears and a dozen white doves"*. The words *"for Sarah"* appeared under the newspaper's masthead and they promised to keep it there until 'Sarah's Law' was introduced. In a piece on the growing menace, little information was given other than to stir fear in the hearts of its readers of the presence of pædophiles in their midst. The editorial dismissed it as *"an unfortunate fact that, pushed to the extreme, otherwise reasonable citizens are forced into vigilante action"*.

Stuart Carnie's group Freedom For Children was featured on BBC's 'Newsnight Scotland' showing off his new, Aberdeen-based Internet site with searchable database designed to locate sex offenders living in any particular region. The site was designed to provide offenders' names, addresses, and details of their conviction and the level of danger they posed. The website came in for heavy criticism in the press and particularly from Grampian Police. At the same time, Deputy Home Secretary, Paul Boateng introduced what he described as 'Sarah's Law'. These amendments - introduced whilst the Criminal Justice and Court Services Bill was still being debated - put on a statutory footing elements of risk assessment and the management of sexual offenders. Stuart Carnie was later accused in 2001 of plotting to abduct a nine-year-old girl.

Reminding readers of its own PervertWatch campaign, the **Daily Record**'s 'Brigadier' Brown blasted *"pious commentators and the be-kind-to-criminals industry"* for *"sneering at ordinary people..."* He wrote: *"When the Daily Record 'named and shamed' Scotland's child sex offenders, we came in for the same kind of do-gooder backlash... I was astonished..."* and *"found myself in radio and TV studios defending the right of parents to know when there is a convicted pervert in their neighbourhood"*. He demanded local authorities *"provide innocents with protection"*.

Dissatisfied with the official sex offenders register, Scottish police forces had already been keeping an 'unofficial' one. The 'unofficial' register listed more than 6,000 sex offenders who were not required by law to be on the official register. Most of these, unable to challenge what information was kept on them, were convicted of offences before the Dunblane massacre and the introduction of the sex offenders register. 80-year-old George Fraser spent £70,000 and fifty years trying to clear his name after he had been accused in 1948 of abusing his young niece, Nina. She admitted lying and George Fraser was pardoned after his case became the first to be sent to the Scottish Criminal Cases Review Commission.

Whatever impression the media gave of incurable child molesters released from prison, the Home Office state only 2% of those convicted of child sex offences go on to commit another sex crime against a youngster. And, in the vast majority of cases, pædophiles that commit a sexual crime against a child are not strangers to them. In most of these cases, these people are often victims of abuse themselves; the very same people the media were demanding to be protected.

Vern Bullough, director of the Center for Sex Research in Northridge, California wrote for the magazine, **The Position** explaining the workings behind the efforts of some moral conservatives and uncovered some uncomfortable parallels in Scotland: *"The problem for those most hostile to change is finding a way to disseminate their message to the public without alienating them. They adopt several tactics including painting the past in unreal, idealistic terms. But their most effective weapon is to seize on hot-button issues that revolve around children".* Vern Bullough had himself been attacked for being a "self-confessed" pædophile and now admitted: *"I now find it professionally difficult to study the sexual activities of children under any condition—in particular, paedophilia. Anyone in the U.S. who disseminates or even possesses child porn is subject to prosecution. Any therapist who attempts to treat a paedophile - even someone who admits to fantasizing about engaging in sex with an under-aged person - is required by law to turn that client over to the authorities, or risk arrest himself or herself. Researches into paedophilia thus have few sources to rely on - either the accounts of convicted paedophiles or the memories of children actually or allegedly sexually abused. The former are not particularly reliable, and the latter have often been manipulated by a therapist".*

Interestingly enough, it was not the **News of the World**'s exercise in 'Name and Shame', but a spoof documentary called 'Brass Eye' on Channel Four in the summer of 2001 that evoked calls for a tightening of regulations and media censorship. *"…Drowned in a sea of bad taste and offensiveness",* wrote Allan Laing in **The Scotsman**. *"The sickest TV show ever",* headlined the **Daily Mail**. *"Oh, Chris Morris, what have you done?"* gasped

Linda Watson-Brown of the series' writer. Pages and pages of media outrage followed 600 complaints to the television watchdog, ITC and caused Home Office junior minister Beverley Hughes to go on BBC Radio 4's 'Today' programme to call 'unspeakably sick' - a show she'd not even seen! Richard Littlejohn, in **The Sun** raged: "...*Under-age gay sex; a man having a colostomy bag emptied over his head; rent boys; bestiality; lesbianism; necrophilia; bondage; grown men in nappies. It was only a matter of time before it got round to child molesting*". The irony of Morris's satirical take on pædophilia, itself evoking so much media hysteria was lost. But Chris Morris had proved his point. Channel Four refused to apologise and repeated the programme.

By the end of 1999, further proposals to tighten the law against pædophiles were put forward by Scottish education minister Sam Galbraith following recommendations by Lord Cullen in a report commissioned after the Dunblane tragedy. The Index of Adults Unsuitable to Work with Children meant anyone even *suspected* of being a pædophile or a risk to children by police, local authorities and social workers faced up to five years in jail or unlimited fines. *"This is to stop paedophiles and weirdos infiltrating volunteer groups and charities"*, wrote the **Scottish News of the World**. Whatever the intentions of the Index, it did nothing to separate, in the public eye, gropers, flashers, men who downloaded erotica, women or men who had sex with teenage boys, men who met other guys 'in public' or children guilty of inappropriate behaviour from violent sexual offenders.

Further proposals from by the McLean Committee suggested the use of satellite tracking systems to monitor the movements of violent criminals and sex offenders when they were released from prison together with a new sentence, the Lifelong Restrictions Order to be imposed on offenders considered a potential danger to the public. Sex offenders would be placed under tight and continuous surveillance, wearing electronic tags, sometimes for their whole lives, or paged regularly by police armed with voice-recognition equipment. Following widespread trials, offenders were expected to wear devices set to go off if a stalker went near a victim or an area forbidden to them, like a playground. Also under consideration were global satellite-tracking systems to follow criminals when they left the country. Scotland's justice minister, Jim Wallace said: 'We are committed to building a safer Scotland'. The **Daily Record** gave it a ringing endorsement. The editorial made clear: *"Electronic tagging, exclusion orders, drink and drug tests, random visits and giving details of their personal lives, as recommended by the McLean Committee, may seem harsh to some in the civil rights lobby… No one wants a vigilante law. But for the protection of children, parents have the right to know when a pervert is in their midst"*. High Court judge Lord MacLean suggested it might affect just a dozen people a year.

By 2000, the **Daily Record** was reporting how a £25million Internet surveillance centre built by M15 would boost Scotland's *"war against porn and paedophiles"*. They quoted Tory spokesman, Phil Gallie who advised: *"This will root out use of the Internet by paedophiles and for pornography"* and in the following year, at Skye's Portree Sheriff Court, uniformed police were forced to use CS gas in the courtroom as they clashed with members of the public. 35-year-old Nicholas Walker, an Englishman who lived alone in a Skye croft, pleaded guilty to taking indecent photographs of four young girls and a boy between the ages of four and 13 years when attempts were made to drag him from the dock. Walker claimed the pictures were 'naturist' but was arrested when he picked up the photographs at his local chemist. He later fled Skye after threats on his life. The Sheriff imposed the maximum penalty of three months on each charge.

By the summer of 2001, police in Lincolnshire launched an investigation after a list containing the names, addresses and contact details of over 200 sex offenders was found in a supermarket car park and handed in to the **Sunday Times**, a sister publication of the **News of the World**.

# Chapter Five

## *Homophobia, Double Standards, 'Old Mother Burnie' and Fairy Cakes*

*"The British police are the best in the world.*
*I don't believe one of these stories I've heard*
*About pretty policemen in leather and jeans*
*Showing their leg through a split in the seams.*
*Leering at people, and leading them on,*
*Then running them in, when they start to respond.*
*The press all ignore it, they don't want to see.*
*Except when the case is a Scottish QC.*
*Sing if you're glad to be gay..."*
**Tom Robinson**

Over the years, lesbians, gays, bisexuals and the transgendered have suffered mercilessly at the hands of the Scottish media. The **Daily Star** in Scotland's front-page story of a gay party held on board the famous paddle steamer, Waverley screamed: *"Puff Off!"* after printing: *"Queers want PINK Gay-verley"*. The homophobic rhetoric was unapologetic. *"Hello sailor gays asked ship bosses to bend over backwards ...and repaint the world-famous Waverley PINK. Hundreds of homos are going down the watter for a special AIDS awareness conference in RothesGAY on the Isle of Bute this weekend"*. The **Daily Star** in Scotland even included a photo of the black and white paddle steamer carefully doctored to look pink. On the day of the sailing, straight kids mooned at the gays the tabloid had already described as *"REAR ADMIRALS"*. Because of this adverse publicity, the gay group were banned from making any further bookings on the paddle steamer despite protests to David Duncanson of the PS Waverley's management committee from John Wilkes of Phace West. It was not the last time the paddle steamer made the front page of a tabloid. Months later, the **Sunday Mail** carried the headline: *"RIOT ON THE CLYDE"*. A police helicopter had to shadow the paddle steamer up the Clyde where 40 police officers - some with Alsatians - stood by. Four police vans and an ambulance waited after two groups had staged a pitched battle over an argument erupted into violence over football in one of the paddle steamer's bars while terrified day-trippers looked on. 10 men who had been drinking heavily all day were arrested. One passenger was quoted saying: "It was a stupid fight caused by bigotry. They were all shouting Rangers and Celtic chants".

In another example of blatant homophobia, Scottish editions of **The Sun** reported: *"Uproar as shy gays get clinic for lesbians only"*. This, as the **Scottish Daily Mail** explained, *"will cater exclusively for women who refuse medical services used by heterosexual women and are too embarrassed to 'come out' to their own GP".* To start the ball rolling, **The Sun** dug up the Rev Bill Wallace, then convenor of the Kirk's Board of Social Responsibility, to opine: *"To provide special facilities for a minority group who just want to be different seems to me a waste of public money"*. Adding, in the **Scottish Daily Mail**, that: *"It inevitably means there is less money for others"*, whilst the 'Sexfinder General' added: *"I would have thought they would have wanted to be treated as normal people…"*. Otherwise, no more fuss was made of a *"casualty for phobics"*; a new Patients' Advocacy and Support Service funded by the local authorities for anyone who is afraid of going to their doctor, dentist or optician than a few column inches in **The Glaswegian**. Jenny Campbell, a counsellor at the Lesbian Health Centre explained to me how studies in America had indicated lesbians could be at higher risk of developing breast cancer. "Being a lesbian doesn't constitute a high risk in itself, but factors in the lesbian community, such as smoking, a higher intake of alcohol and reluctance to take part in screening programmes can contribute".

Scottish editions of **The Sun** also blasted the way lottery cash was being spent. In its editorial, it reckoned people were *"sick of seeing their cash given to lesbians, gays, prostitutes, rent boys, junkies and asylum seekers"*.

Unlike heterosexuals, homosexuals are largely defined in society by sexuality. Because of this, gays are encouraged to be more liberal in attitudes to sex than heterosexuals. Gays will be confronted by more sexual images in gay lifestyle magazines and speak more openly about sexuality with friends. This is a generalisation, of course, since gay sexuality also embraces many who are bisexual, closeted or in a heterosexual marriage. But gays are less likely to meet a sexual partner on a works' night out and conversely, 'straights' are not likely to consider the local park an option for meeting a partner. Naturally, targeting sex education at gay men requires a different approach from that used for heterosexuals. It was therefore surprising to see in the **Daily Star**: *"A gay charity which gets public cash sparked outrage yesterday by publishing explicit details of sex acts in their magazine - Spurt"*. The spunky new magazine leaped ahead of the shy and retiring tabloid: *"Brand new and sporting rather a big willy, it's SPURT!"* But the closest they got to showing a willy was a full-blown coloured photograph of a bunch of bananas on the front cover! The Edinburgh-based gay magazine, published by Gay Men's Health and *"funded by taxpayers"* - as **The Herald** was quick to point out - soon shot its load and was forced to close. The **Herald** was prompted to drag out Conservative Councillor Daphne Sleigh to cover the grave and remark: *"Such explicit sexual messages should never have been entitled to funding from the public purse"*. **The Herald** pointed out that *"the third issue of the magazine contained only one article that tackled HIV and Aids issues"*. Perhaps **The Herald** was suggesting **Spurt!** should have looked to **The Lancet** for inspiration?

When the Arts and Humanities Research Board awarded a government grant of £12,252 to Dr Lucille Cairns for research on lesbian desire in post-1968 French realist literature, the **Scottish Daily Mail** found Tory Phil Gallie to brand it a *"total waste of public money"* while Fenland family values campaigner, Victoria Gillick described it as *"disgraceful... absolutely outrageous"*.

Asked why anyone should ban gays from their employ, the **Scottish Sun** found a company boss who said: *"The honest answer is most people don't accept that homosexuals should be allowed in"*. Most trained and qualified members of senior management would consider that an inappropriate statement to issue under any circumstances. So how come the **Scottish Sun** couldn't find one? Perhaps because their opinion on the subject is at a level that considers: *"The effete world of gay hairdressers... a rich seam for comedy material"*. They had come to this conclusion after reviewing a new film, starring Scots comic Craig

Ferguson who was described as *"red-blooded"* after he explained his new rôle, playing a camp hairdresser who was *"a little light on his loafers"*. Ferguson told the **Scottish Sun**: *"As a totally straight guy I did find it weird mincing around like a big p\*\*f"*. The tabloid coined the phrase: *"THE FULL MINCY..."* for what they described as: *"The hottest film for the Millennium"*.

The **Scottish Sun** also turned on *"barmy plans to establish a San Francisco-style gay quarter and a women-only housing complex in Scotland..."* They first lambasted *"gender-bender"* Barnaby Miln, the former aide to the Archbishop of Canterbury who expressed a rather stretched optimism suggesting that *"Edinburgh could become the gay capital of Europe"*. Then, the tabloid warned: *"Women want to build a male-free estate in Glasgow"*. In a piece headed *"Barny's barmy army"*, the **Sunday Mail**'s Melanie Reid, sniffed: *"Barnaby Miln... would like to put up bright flags around the gay part of Edinburgh..."* The **Daily Record** sighed: *"For 25 years, the father-of-two was a pillar of the establishment..."* It was really all too much! *"Thousands of homosexuals are flocking to Edinburgh..."* they shrieked. Sounding terribly middle-England, Edinburgh's local Tory councillor, Daphne Sleigh sniffed: *"It sounds so terribly un-Scottish"*.

Gays didn't get much reprieve from supposedly more liberal papers. When the **Scottish Daily Express** editorialised on the army's manpower crisis, they wrote that it was *"so severe... it has decided to turn female recruits into pretend men. Through sweaty exercises, drill sergeants will endeavour to broaden their shoulders and equip them with legs like the pistons of steam locomotives"*. It was suggested Generals *"might help these new Amazones to grow macho moustaches, which will make them more acceptable when they apply to join the SAS"*.

Margaret Garth of the Edinburgh School of Domestic Engineering wrote the 'Daily Express Home Management Book'. In its review, the **Scottish Daily Express** reminisced over *"innocent times"*, when they *"could publish a front-page advert reading 'Camp Coffee is simply made for men' without anyone sniggering... Days when gay meant happy and camp was for boy scouts"*.

Also in the **Scottish Daily Express**, columnist Peter McKay discovered *"Sir Dirk Bogarde, who has died at 78, was a closet homosexual... Unlike movie hunks who turn into needy queens when the camera's off, Sir Dirk was no cream puff. He was a young captain* *at the Normandy landings".*

The **Express** had its moments though. Former editor of **The Independent** Rosie Boycott was *"delighted"* in the **Scottish Daily Express** by the performance of *"Blonde Bombsite"*, drag performer Lily Savage at the Edinburgh Festival, *"fag in hand, staggering through Edinburgh's grandest hotel"* after being jumped on by security guards as she *"teetered toward the PM's bedroom"*. Her frock was ruined. Ms Savage was unyielding: *"Prime Minister or not, he's getting the bill. New Labour, new frock, that's what I say"*.

Another self-proclaimed liberal publication, the **Big Issue in Scotland**, printed a scurrilous letter that, had it had been aimed at any other minority group, would not have seen the light of day. *"Gays are freaks and perverts"*, wrote a Mr L Taylor from Stenhousemuir. He wanted gays *"isolated from the mainstream of our society"* because they *"can cause havoc in communities amongst our young and most vulnerable"*. He went on to declare the sanctity of young men's bodies in the face of homosexual *"perversion"*. A judiciary and police force that mete out punishment in accordance with Britain's discriminatory sexual legislation and ethics back him. As far as the 'young and most vulnerable' are concerned, courts often rule it not in the interests of the family to publicly name sexual offenders, so all too often their non-consensual, abusive, sexual misdemeanours remain hidden: brushed under the carpet. On the other hand, the names of sexual offenders outside of the family will have their names, addresses and pictures printed in newspapers. Homosexuals in particular make the perfect scapegoat for one of the tawdriest secrets of the heterosexual family: sexual abuse.

If public outrage sells newspapers, then transsexuals have wrapped it up for them. The **Scottish Daily Mail** found a transsexual sitting on a Children's Panel. Despite government agents seeing *"no reason for complaint"*, the *"tall and glamorous blonde who rolls up… to give advice and guidance to troubled youngsters across Aberdeenshire"* worried the tabloid. They declared *"her background has been greeted with concern by family groups…"* The tabloid remarked how she *"lives alone"* and turns up for work *"dressed in a dark skirt…"* This quickly became the *"Strange case of a transsexual who sits in judgement of youngsters"*. But why shouldn't she? Zara Strange had fought hard enough to get access to see her *own* children. Niall David, clerk of the Aberdeenshire Children's Panel advisory committee sharply told the **Scottish Daily Mail**: *"Aberdeenshire Children's Panel has a transsexual member. What is wrong with that?"* Reporter Lesley Roberts soon found an unnamed panel member to malign her. *"No amount of make-up or feminine clothes can hide obvious masculine features. There are difficulties in working in the uneasy atmosphere that has been created"*. Then the paper dragged Dr Adrian Rogers of Family Focus to proclaim her a *"recipe for chaos"*. A bit rich considering this rabidly homophobic and controversial character, after standing for election in Exeter for the Conservative Party, lost the seat to an 'out' homosexual!

You would think journalists should be sufficiently clued up on transsexuality to avoid the level of sloppy reporting exhibited by Ben Rankin in **The Herald** over the decision by a father-of-two fireman from West Sussex to undergo gender re-assignment. This supposedly serious report in the broadsheet advised how *"he was a woman trapped in a fireman's body"* and *"Mr (or should that be Ms?) Hyland"* was pleased to say how he had the full support of his colleagues and nobody in the service laughed or sniggered. Ms Hyland was also backed by a working equal opportunities policy operating within the fire service.

It was also Kevin Hutchin's status as a *"cash-strapped transsexual"* that dominated an otherwise minor story of a shoplifting offence in the **Daily Record**. The headlines revealed an undercurrent of prejudice. *"SKINT TRANSEXUAL NICKS SIX FAIRY CAKES"*. Kevin Hutchins had his name, address, age and a colour photo printed in the tabloid. Kevin's defence solicitor claimed that, when Kevin found himself a bit short before his giro came through, he would usually borrow money from his mother, but since she had been away on holiday, he had been forced to steal food. The **Daily Record** seized the opportunity to get a cheap laugh at Kevin's expense. *"Call me Debs says fairycake thief Kev"*. It didn't matter that the 69p packet of cakes Kevin stole from Iceland stores in Milngavie were not 'fairycakes' at all. Paul Crozier, defending Kevin Hutchins, told the court how his client had since been shunned by his mother and was ridiculed by locals after the newspaper reports. Kevin, who had started gender re-assignment, didn't turn up in court and neither did Prosecutor Lorna Revie ask for a warrant for his arrest. The **Daily Record** responded by printing another picture of Kevin with his full name and address under the title: *"Sex-change for court dodger"*.

Sandra Rae, a transsexual solicitor imprisoned for embezzlement, was described as *"a former burly rugby player"* by the tabloid. She appeared under the headline: *"Bent brief faces a stretch in women's prison"*. The **Daily Record** also reported: *"AC-DC PC gets marching orders from the police"* and declared: *"A gender bender policeman who wanted to become a WPC has been sacked"*. One of the most difficult challenges facing those undergoing sexual reassignment is getting used to living life in their chosen gender rôle. That meant, for 31-year-old Alex Horwood of Edinburgh, going to work dressed as a woman. The **Daily Record** reported the story with an astonishing lack of compassion. *"He used to turn up for work wearing make-up, skimpy tops and high-heels and asked his colleagues to call him Susan. He even started to develop breasts because of his treatment"*. The copy was wrapped around a piece on comedian Jack Dee who was *"set to shock fans… by dressing up as a woman"*.

The **Daily Record**'s reputation for homophobia over the years has, of course, been legendary. An ordinary gay bar - in this case, London's Brief Encounter - was transformed into *"a notorious gay haunt"* in one report. Determined to get a laugh at any price, they reported *"complaints"* to the Scottish Crofters' Commission of rams chasing each other instead of ewes under the headline: *"Woolly woofters"*. The **Record** appeared delighted to describe the career of Sir Michael Hirst, the *"disgraced former Scottish Tory chairman… well and truly over"* after branding him a *"GAY shame Tory"*. And after a man was gang-raped at knifepoint by three men in Edinburgh, they took to picturing the street-sign near where the rape took place: Gayfield Square.

When Paisley MP Gordon McMasters gassed himself to death in his garage the **Daily Record** wrote that his enemies *"cast doubts on his sexuality…* and accused the **New Statesman** of muddying the MP's memory by alleging that Gordon McMasters was gay. The **Record**'s editorial opined: *"There are now three openly gay Labour MPs in the Commons… So where's the homophobia?"*

The **Record**'s agony aunt, Joan Burnie's approach to issues of sexuality was often marked by an undercurrent of conservatism and intolerance. One instance was the occasion that an army recruit caught his wife kissing a female, bringing back painful memories of his own mother's gay relationship. *"I put my arm through a glass door, which was just as well, because it stopped me from thumping them both"*, he confessed. Burnie replied *"I'd apologise to your wife as soon as possible. Explain why you went up in a blue light and then try to accept that you misinterpreted something which was wholly innocent"*. And if it wasn't... 'Innocent'? Did that excuse his action?

Her delegation of homosexuality to second-class status was frequently made apparent. An answer to a 16-year-old male who claimed he had stopped fantasising about men to focus on women was solidly endorsed for having *"managed to work everything out pretty accurately. It's not as if you actually ever had sexual relations with your own sex - you only thought about it. That is not unusual. Now you fancy girls..."*.

For a college boy harbouring *"big worries"* about his sexuality because he kept harking back to when he was 14 and, after a heavy drinking session, climbed in the sack and had a three-some with his mates. *"The trick is not to let it happen again..."* Burnie warned. *"What you have done unfortunately is to build this one daft night into something it wasn't. Allowing it to blight your life would be really stupid, wouldn't it? Look at your pals. They've probably forgotten all about it and now you must try to do the same... So stop worrying... And ask that girl you fancy out"*.

*"...Although I am not gay..."* one girl assured 'Old Mother Burnie', *"I have always wanted to know what it would be like to make love to another woman... but should I take precautions and, if so, what?"* Sensible enough question: shame about the answer! *"While I commend your insistence on safe sex, I don't think you need extend your sexuality further and include women in your repertoire of fun and games"*. Her advice oozed negatives: *"I'm not sure why you should bother turning this pretty common fantasy into reality... It could ruin a beautiful friendship... Of course, there are genuine bisexuals, but I don't believe you are one. You are just a bored young woman who fancies a little sexual tourism"*.

The advice for a young married woman who had fallen for a female friend and wrote asking where she could meet other bisexuals was: *"You're not free to go looking for singles, straight, gay or bisexual... And that, by the way, includes your friend. Leave her alone".*

An 18-year-old girl who had also fallen *"desperately"* in love with a female friend got little comfort too: *"It's a pash"*, scoffed Burnie. *"Everyone gets them at some point in their lives. There's no need to panic about your sexuality or to worry too much. It will pass. I don't think for a second she reciprocates your feelings. It's just wishful thinking on your part and for both your sakes, don't throw yourself at the woman".*

*"I castigate gay men (and women)... for going ahead with a straight marriage"*, she once moaned. But were society's prejudices pushing them into heterosexual marriage? Pah! *"No longer the case"*, she sniffed. It's *"no excuse"*. Many essentially gay men or women are torn between genuine love for their spouse and a desire to experiment with gay sexuality. 'Old Mother Burnie' displayed an element of impatience with one woman who had learnt of her husband's indiscretions. She claimed her *"whole relationship was built on a lie"*. Her husband, who had passed on a sexually transmitted infection to her, was described as *"little short of criminal"*.

'Old Mother Burnie' did not see the funny side of Elton John up on stage at Stonewall's Equality Show, backed by a team of dancers dressed as Boy Scouts. She launched a scathing attack on this *"bunch of amoral queers"* and asked: *"...What on earth is* (pop star Posh Spice) *doing cosying up to that pathetic old dancing queen Elton John and his kept man? She's a mother isn't she? So you might have thought she would have paused before she posed with a man who thinks it's a gas to present images little short of paedophilia on stage"*. Burnie - once thrown out of Brownies for dirty fingernails - was not amused. *"...Filth"!* she sniffed. Burnie thought the gay cause had been put back 20 years by Elton's *"two-fingered salute to decency"* and criticised *"others"* for not attacking this *"obscene behaviour"* because, apparently: *"It's not PC to criticise homosexuals for anything..."* Interestingly enough, a man dressed up as a schoolboy in striped blazer and cap on another stage to unveil a tilting train for Virgin was the very same man the **Daily Record** teamed up with to promote 'family values': Scottish entrepreneur, Brian Souter.

'Old Mother' Burnie's response to a woman who explained that she wanted a future with her HIV positive boyfriend despite him claiming he was frustrated by *"not being able to have a normal relationship"*, drinking heavily and telling his girlfriend *"sex wouldn't be a good idea, even with condoms"* was brusque: *"To be honest, I think you should walk away"*. The same advice was offered to a man who discovered his girlfriend had been using a lesbian chatline. Joan Burnie suggested: *"If she has genuine doubts about her sexuality, this isn't the way to go about resolving them… She shouldn't have done it… Maybe, in the circumstances, you should consider cutting your connection with her"*.

A High Court ruling in London making condoms available to prisoners had no affect in Scotland's prisons where gay sex is rife. Condoms are not easily available. A prisoner's letter was displayed on Burnie's page insisting that he was not gay, but had enjoyed gay sex nonetheless. *"It was just out of frustration…"* he apologised. Burnie reminded him: *"I hope you were careful and practised safe sex in prison"*. Perhaps she thought that meant the withdrawal method!

Promoting heterosexuality, another **Daily Record** columnist, Bob Shields hit out at Prince Edward before his marriage to Sophie Rees-Jones. *"There is no suggestion that The Geek shares the same bedroom as Sophie. But that's been Prince Edward's problem all along. We blokes have been crying for the suggestion that he loves tottie, takes a swally, watches Men Behaving Badly, drives his Porsche like a maniac and plays five-a-side every Wednesday against the butlers. But, no. Not for us a dashing, athletic, playboy, the Queen's youngest son who turns women pink with excitement and men green with envy. A Royal who could lead all us lads by example and show the world what it means to be a Great British Bloke… 'I'm no wimp"*, he insisted. *But the next time we saw him was in tights and frills, starring in It's A Knockout… It's just not normal. Most 34-year-old guys I know are giving it laldy every night, chasing anything with a skirt and a pulse. And that's just the married ones!"*

With the image of a boozy, pot-bellied nicotine-addict, Bob Shields was an unlikely character to be been chosen to cover the Gay Olympics in Amsterdam for the **Daily Record**, unless of course it was with the intention of poking fun at it. His most lasting impression of the event appeared to be what he learnt in a local bar and the back seat of a taxi. *"I'm no homophobic, but…"* he began, *"…my money is with the Dutchman at the wheel of car 1055. There's a time and a place for everything and two half-naked men, French kissing, at midday outside an ice cream parlour full of* *children is neither"*. The driver had apparently told him: *"We are very tolerant here… but we do not want to see them naked on our canal boats"*. His column was otherwise not short of a few mentions of busty blondes, rattling their jugs in the face of young readers. Take the time when he insisted *"sex is now all over our screens like a nasty sexually-transmitted rash"*. He was appalled to see on TV *"some old tart in her kinky threads"*, Zoe Ball in her Saturday morning show bending over *"in a skimpy top just to let us know her wobbly bits are still Alive and Kicking"*. So appalled, a large section of his page was taken over by a picture of Zoe's *"wobbly bits"* nestling in her *"skimpy top"*. And never mind that Scotland was in no position to lecture the Dutch on sex education, at the Gay Olympics he added: *"I'm all for safe sex as well… But blindly handing out Durex 'medals' with a condom inside to obviously under-age boys is trying to solve a problem while encouraging another one"*. In a local bar he chanced on a young *"teenager"* who reassured him that not everyone at this event was gay before Shields went off to watch the bodybuilding finals. He was satisfied there were *"no limp wrists here…"* but left asking: *"SHOULD this ever come to Scotland?"*

Bob Shields demands *"good, clean sex"* and once wrote: *"Put the filthy freaks back in their plastic macs in quiet corners of seedy cinemas where they belong"*. Of the Edinburgh Fringe Festival, he called it: *"CRUDE, LEWD AND NUDE… You're welcome to it…"* and grumbled how *"some time after 2am, the tables were cleared and the young Fringers and bingers boogied on down - or whatever it is they do these days"*. To illustrate his point, the **Daily Record** pictured The Naturals; a couple of performers parading down the Royal Mile in Edinburgh in nude bodies made of latex. Two stickers marked CENSORED covered them.

One of the **Record**'s most homophobic writers is Tom Brown. His summing up of the perfect marriage was one very similar to his own. *"…Really contented couples are a wife who thinks her man is an over-weight, untidy layabout… She feels superior and he gets to slump in the couch, having tea and biscuits and watching the footie. It's the recipe for the perfect marriage. Trust me, I know"*.

The **Daily Record** provided the old Boys' Brigadier and former religious affairs correspondent, Tom Brown with a regular platform for his opinion of homosexuality. He insisted, *"flaunt-*

*ing homosexuality and setting it up as a rôle model of acceptable behaviour is something I believe, most people are uncomfortable with... I know it's risking the tired old accusation of homophobia..."* but *"PRIVATE LIVES SHOULDN'T BE PUBLIC... There's a difference between tolerance and actively promoting it... While we've now got to accept homosexuality... flaunting homosexuality and setting it up as a model of acceptable public behaviour is something, I believe, most people are uncomfortable with. Yet is happening".* He was particularly perturbed by the activities of the MP Chris Smith's boyfriend: *"Dorian tells cosily how they cook dinner for each other... What are we to make of this muddled message the government are sending?"* (I don't know. That they cook for each other)? Cross-dressing left him completely cold. *"Blokes who dress like women are either mixed-up or think that gender-bending is funny. For the life of me I can't see the joke..."*

'Brigadier' Brown proudly advised: *"Yours truly is a militant feminist"* and *"all for helping women to burn their bras... But the demand for pay parity for Wimbledon tennis stars, whatever their gender – and lets face it, there is frequently some doubt – should be ruled out of court".* His argument slid downhill from there. *"Women's tennis may be easier on the eye... A pair of pretty young things in disco dresses, playing pit-a-pat across the net, is not the blood-and-thunder, gut-wrenching effort of a hard-fought five-setter you get in the men's tournament. The reason they get smaller purses is not because of the standard of tennis they serve up, which is usually boring – squeak, serve, squeal, volley, then bat it back and forth, until one makes a mistake or the other feels faint or has a tantrum. The attraction of the women's game is that it is babe tennis, in which the practitioners grow up to be the Page Three pin-ups of sport... Winners tend to be butch female Schwarzeneggers with more muscles in one thigh than most blokes have in their whole body... There is hardly a single sport in which women perform or entertain as well as men... Women's soccer is a pale imitation, as is women's golf. Women boxing and wrestling are an obscenity – and only sad, sick people would watch women's rugby. You will have to work out for yourself why there are no women motor-racing drivers. The reason is too sexist to mention – even for me...".*

The Trinity Group, owners of the **Daily Record** and **Sunday Mail**, denied discriminating against gays, but obstinately refused to accept personal ads from lesbians, gays, bisexuals and people of transgender. Many other Scottish newspapers impose a similar ban. They are not so particular when it comes to reporting men who are arrested seeking *other* means of finding partners, usually accompanied by names, addresses and even pictures. The high profile of gays in the Scottish media was certainly enough for reader, Anthony Faulkner from Wetzikon in Switzerland to write to the editor of **The Herald** to say that, *"the homosexual lobby has long wielded an influence out of all proportion to its numbers, especially in the media"*.

The **Sunday Mail** boasted a sexually repressive columnist called Gary Keown and packaged the overweight skinhead journalist as their *"voice of tomorrow"*. He berated women, or *"would-be men"* who *"slug pints, belch, drop their drawers at a stroke and pretend they understand football"*. He thought such women's behaviour *"vile"*. Then, in a complete *volte-face*, Keown congratulated them for entertaining him with *"one of life's great spectator sports. The drunker they are, the better..."* he belched, happy seeing *"two slappers pulling at each other's cheap perms... Mini skirts riding up flabby thighs..."* After seeing TV presenter Ulrka Jonsson *"guzzling a pint of lager like an unshaven navvy"* he had to confess it was *"sad to see a pretty girl making an exhibition of herself"*. Challenging Ulrika to join him and his mates in an *"ale-quaffing contest"* he said: *"We will happily pay her taxi to hospital – before banning her and her like from our pub for life... Why do it, ladies?"* he begged. *"Why do you refuse us an oasis of calm where we can get away from you for a while? Given the amount of pansies and downtrodden saps on the streets, your guerrilla tactics are having the desired effect"*. He was also pissed-off by women who *"take their hen nights into men's pubs just to cause offence"*. And of those that objected to men swearing: *"If you don't like bad language, then plank a bottle of gin in the cistern and drink behind the lace curtains like mum did"*. Otherwise, Gary McKeown was not entirely unpopular with all women. *"While wearing my kilt once, I had my backside BITTEN by an old boiler"*, he gasped.

With former editor Harry Reid's expressed interest in the Kirk, Scotland's bestselling broadsheet **The Herald** was also weighed down in favour of sexual conservatism with the likes of columnists John Macleod, Michael Fry and Stewart Lamont. Stewart Lamont knew as much about sexual politics as he did about acid house. And it showed. His piece on Michael Portillo's 'coming out' was bitter. Lamont scoffed that *"gay pride people"* (sic), were *"proud of everything that is gay, whether it be the sick types who lurk in toilets or the promiscuous pick-ups in gay bars which sadly are part of 'community' life. They want to be accepted just as they are. Sounds great..."* he bitched, until, goodness, me! What if 'straights' *"went looking for a date outside the ladies' loo"*? The majority of gays, of course, don't approve of men meeting each other in public toilets. Most men wouldn't boast about it. Lamont set about justifying Michael Portillo's hypocrisy: covering up his 'under-age' - as indeed it was given that the age of homosexual consent was 21 at the time - gay sexual exploits whilst supporting an unequal age of consent and preventing gays serving in the armed forces. *"It is... perfectly possible to have a liking for alcohol but to abstain from it"*, Lamont waffled. Not that Portillo had ever abstained from having gay sex until later in life, we are told! Lamont thought Portillo had the *"right"* to have his *"privacy respected"* since it was not as though he was *"out trawling Clapham Common at night"*. And, get this...! He thought, *"by opening politician's bedrooms' to the scrutiny of the public..."* we somehow release *"a demon"*. Then, (gasp...)! *"The whole of society becomes obsessed with deviant sex"*. Lamont's arguments were Victorian. About sweeping 'It' under the carpet and sticking to a prescribed moral code of fixed heterosexual values. *"Sexuality is a private matter"*, he reminded us. To be locked away *"...in the privacy of the bedroom of course, where it belongs"*. He went on to highlight those familiar stereotypes: Those *"who force the question of 'gay rights...'"* and those who *"attempt to promote homosexual lifestyles through Channel 4 television programmes"*. In a broadside against those who commented on gay lifestyles, he even went further, attacking those *"who bandy about the word 'community' as if they had a mandate from all the members of the minority they purport to represent..."*.

Charged with being anti-Catholic, **The Herald** was forced to defend itself in an editorial: *"The Herald is a pluralist paper that seeks to reflect the increasing diverse nature of Scotland. To do that job properly we hire columnists whose views are not necessarily those of the newspaper... It would be a dull newspaper indeed if it did not offer its readers the gamut of opinion on a wide range of topics... We are not tokenist. Our door is closed to no-one, either as a contributor or* *potential employee… We abhor bigotry and prejudice and criticise them when they rear their ugly heads…"* But when has **The Herald** ever sought to properly balance the string of religionists, homophobic and sexually repressed columnists that make up its opinion pages?

Homophobia was everywhere. *"What seems to be happening to my Glaswegian?"* begged Flora Davids from Hillhead in a letter to its editor. She complained about having to endure articles about a festival called Glasgay! *"Never in my life have I heard of such a ridiculous event. And the picture beside that story* (a couple of Scots soldier-boys necking) *almost put me off my breakfast. What is the world coming to in the 1990s? I would hope this is only a temporary fall in taste and the Glaswegian will return to its rightful place, not highlighting these ridiculous minority groups who don't deserve the time of day".*

But it was not just in the printed media Scotland's homophobia lurked. One of Scotland's most famous radio 'shockjocks' was Scottie McClue who had a regular phone-in programme on Scot FM. His reactionary opinions bought him a full page in Scottish editions of **The Sun** where he was able to blast *"hackit-faced lesbians"* and claim: *"The gay lobby are up in limp wrists about the fairy on top of the Christmas tree giving them a bad name. I suppose the lesbians will be moaning about sexism because the trees have balls and they don't. Mind you, looking at some of them I'm not too sure about that…".*

For his column, Scottie McClue penned this verse: -

*"My first true love wa' Bonnie Jean*
*But she turned into a lesbean*
*She had a body fit to please*
*Noo it's wasted in dungarees…*
*Aye bonnie Jean you were a dog anyway".*

His talent for verse had him indulging in more rhyming couplets like this ode to a single mum for his column in Scottish editions of **The Sun**: -

*"Wee sleekit whoorin' cadgin' bintie*
*Wi' yon wean ye've made a mintie.*
*And intai the bargain a free cooncil hoose*
*A' because yer pants were always loose*
*Aye and costing us a' a wad o' cash*
*Cos she drapped them in a flash*

> *But it disnae have to be that way*
> *Pull up yer knickers and there they stay*
> *If you don't agree wae me that's just tough*
> *It's yer ain fault fur getting up the duff".*

After two gay men took their lives following a police sur-veillance operation in a Stirling public convenience McClue wrote: *"I don't care what gays do as long as they don't scare the hors-es… I'm as tolerant as the next guy as long as he doesn't move in and call me Nancy".* Of the Gay & Lesbian Christian Movement he said: *"Gay Christians were those happy people… They WERE gay but gay in the jolly sense of the word. Not like that new lot who've hijacked the word. You know… them… God doesn't like gays. Sorry, but that's the truth. Why do you think he destroyed Sodom? He looked down from on high and said to himself: 'Right, that's it. I'm fed up explaining the concept of Adam and Eve to you lot, so cop this thun-derbolt'".*

Scottie McClue's contract was not renewed at Scot FM and soon after, Scottish editions of **The Sun** dropped his column. McClue left for England but was soon back on a station eager to attract a bigger audience: Paisley's QFM.

With homophobia rank in the Scottish press, small wonder the public frequently duck and dive round the delicate issue. The word 'gay' has never been met with universal popularity. The Gay Gordons is a popular traditional Scottish country-dance. That was until an Ayrshire school, St Joseph's Academy in Kilmarnock began considering it out of step with modern times. Staff renamed the dance the 'Happy Gordons', according to the press reports, so they could avoid the possibility of *"caus-ing embarrassment among pupils".* PE teacher Mr Dorian said: *"The word gay has a stigma, which we are removing from this dance".* A year later, Lindsay Clark, organiser of Gordon 2000, a millen-nium celebration taking place in the Aberdeenshire town of Huntly, birthplace of the Gordon family pointed out that the original old Scottish word was *'gey'* which had been changed over the years. **The Sun** and **Record** made a meal out of it. *"Dance is not O-Gay",* (**Sun**) and *"It's a gey silly row over Gay Gordons",* (**Record**). The **Record** reported: *"Scottish country dancers want to stifle sniggers - by renaming the Gay Gordons"* in *"a bid to distance the dance from the modern meaning of the word gay",* even though Ms Clark assured them that this was not the case at all. A gay ceilidh, a three-day event held at the Cummings Hotel in Inverness forced the **Sunday Mail** to report a *"startled Highlander"* who gasped: *"There were more kisses and hugs than the Oscars and BAFTA awards put together. I've never seen anything like it in my life"*.

There appears to be something about a man living with his mother that also sparks a hint of derision from journalists. Club entrepreneur Stefan King who made a significant contribution to Glasgow's club and pub scene with the award-winning Polo Lounge, Delmonicas, Club Archaos, and his five million pound investment transforming Glasgow's old High Court. His ventures are either outright gay or gay-friendly. When Stefan King faced allegations of racism after Asians claimed they had been turned away from Club Archaos, the **Daily Record** was quick to point out he was *"the millionaire power broker of Scotland's glitzy, raunchy club scene who still lives with his mother"*. The fact he might have been part of a close family, or just a caring son never entered the equation. It is not the first time the Scottish press have made somewhat uncomfortable references to a man living with his mother. In the **Scottish Sun**, Julian Danskin, the lawyer who made an erotic video in his office was described as: *"Balding bachelor Danskin – who lives with his mum"* and Glasgow's **Evening Times** noted of gay community activist, Brian McKenna, who also lived with his partner and claimed there was a campaign amongst colleagues to brand him a pædophile: *"Mr McKenna lives with his mother…"*

It is not always necessary to use the word 'gay' to denigrate its meaning, as occurred in the following example of a female police officer. Women leave their husbands every day to set up home with someone else but rarely qualify for a full page in the **Scottish Daily Mail** with bold headers and colour pictures. Not, of course, unless the wife is leaving him to set up home with *"a rugby-playing WPC"*. A woman with *"cropped black hair and legs that could kick-start a jumbo jet"*. The word lesbian is not mentioned once. They didn't have to. *"The tiny rural settlement of Mouswald in Dumfriesshire"* otherwise offering *"a safe and sleepy lifestyle…"* was now *"awash with rumour and scandal…"*.

The press often have great difficulty handling gay sexuality if it doesn't fall neatly into the handbag-swinging clichés that abound. The **Daily Record** once printed pictures of three soldiers who had been jailed for sex assaults on young recruits. One teenage rookie had been spread-eagled, half-naked across a table in a hotel bar in Split, Croatia. He was then assaulted with an empty beer bottle. Later, two other soldiers were assaulted in the same way. The soldiers dismissed this in the report as *"just drunken horseplay during an initiation ceremony... under stress after their posting to Bosnia..."* They all, of course *"denied the offences"*. Whatever else a trained soldier can handle, gay sex is clearly too shocking to contemplate.

In a similar story closer to home, the same paper carried a front-page headline describing: *"SEX SHAME OF CRACK PRISON WARDERS"*. The warders were on a weekend-long team effectiveness exercise at a Scots hotel when a male warder was *"indecently assaulted"* by a male colleague. Only the gay sex *"shame"* made the front page while *"drunkenness..."* getting involved in *"a couple of fights..."* and *"damaging a chalet door"* were delegated to small print on an inside page.

The effort to sweep away any mention of homosexuality was demonstrated again in the story of *"barracks swinger"*, George Muir, a 52-year-old caretaker of a Territorial Army centre in Dundee, who used Army mail to organise parties for *"women who enjoyed three-in-a-bed romps and husbands who shared their wives...* The **Daily Record** noted how Muir *"...Even used envelopes marked: 'On Her Majesty's Service' to arrange orgies"*. Unfortunately, his bosses shared the same narrow vision as the **Daily Record**, and he was sacked. Apparently, *"Major B P Gilfeather, the T A commanding officer, had told the Dundee tribunal the Army had feared terrorist infiltration"*. What was even more surprising was Muir's response who begged: *"There was no homosexual aspect to the threesomes...*

**The Glaswegian** claimed, *"gay kiss advert on bus sparks outrage..."* The *"explicit"* advert for Sisley revealed two sexy women leaning towards one another in what looked like a simulated kiss. But where exactly was the outrage? **The Glaswegian** didn't say. *"FirstGlasgow have received no complaints"*.

An advertisement for Richard Branson's Scots-made Virgin Vodka was described by the **Daily Record** as *"Branson's bender"*. It was supposed to *"shock viewers... showing two men snogging"*. Suitably shocked, the **Daily Record** wheeled in their favourite two church spokespeople. *"Scots Catholic Church spokesman Father Tom Connolly said the commercial was 'in bad taste'. The Rev Bill Wallace, of the Church of Scotland, branded it 'offensive'."*

For a down-market tabloid, you would expect the **Daily Star in Scotland** to have been fairly liberal over sexuality diversity. It carried its own problem page, edited by 'Uncle Percy'. *"I'm in deep doo-doo, Uncle Percy. Can you recommend a cure for Aids?"* wrote someone signing himself: *"Julian Fist, Pansy Cottage, Sodham"*. Uncle Percy replied: *"You must eat prunes, Julian. Prunes, prunes, prunes. Eat them for breakfast. Eat them for lunch. Eat them for dinner. Eat nothing else. They won't cure you of Aids, but they'll sure teach you what your back passage is meant to be used for"*.

Guidelines issued by the National Union of Journalists was intended to alleviate some of the misunderstandings and incorrect reporting that often accompanied stories featuring the subject of HIV or AIDS. It is important to know that AIDS is not an infection and cannot be 'caught'. Neither is it helpful to describe someone living with AIDS as a 'victim'. The **Daily Record**, reporting a predicted 10% increase in cases of AIDS amongst heterosexuals by 2000, wrote *"little change in the rate of drug users, gays or bisexual men catching AIDS"*, and the **Hamilton Advertiser** wrote *"AIDS claims four more victims"*. The story revealed: *" HIV infection in Lanarkshire has risen by four in the past 12 months...* This was also incorrect, since it was the diagnosis of AIDS that had risen, not HIV infection. In another report, the **Daily Record** wanted to point out why Scotland was *"on top of the sick list"*. One of the reasons given was that *"a third"* of HIV infections in Scotland in one year were *"from gay sex"*. No explanation was given to the fact that it would have been 'unsafe' sex.

Reflecting the ignorance surrounding the subject of HIV infection, the **Scottish Sun** printed a selection of letters on the subject of HIV-positive nurses working at hospitals. *"Now that this is out I wonder how many more infected nurses there are around the country. I would not wish for either me or my family to be treated by them..."* M Henry, Greenock. *"NHS chiefs in Wolverhampton have sunk lower than the Titanic..."* D Watson, Alford, Aberdeenshire. *"Surely patients deserve better..."* Peter Harris,

Redding, Falkirk. *"I was horrified to read that the NHS are allow-ing student nurses with HIV to continue their training. Although I do think that HIV carriers should be given job opportunities... It seems HIV is being welcomed with open arms".* K Millen, Brechin. *"People who are HIV positive should be banned from the medical pro-fession. I'm honest enough to admit that I would not want myself or my children to be treated by someone with the virus".* Jenny Thomson, Sighthill, Glasgow. *"It's spine chilling..."* J Dunne, Hamilton. Only one woman, Diane Mitchell from Aberdeenshire demonstrated any compassion.

Ephraim Hardcastle, a regular columnist in the **Scottish Daily Mail** demonstrated his belief that some terminal illneses were more worthy than others when he wrote: *"Elizabeth Taylor: A Musical Celebration takes place at the Albert Hall. She'll be sere-naded by singing stars with the proceeds – surprise, surprise – going to Aids charities. No one doubts that Miss Taylor, pictured, has a good heart, but why is it that she deems Aids – for which a mountain of charity cash has been raised – more worthy than far more deadly killers like heart disease and cancer? The old trout loves being a gay 'icon'."*

Aberdeen's **Press and Journal** raised a few eyebrows when their front page reported: *"HIV Risk... Oral sex can transmit viral infections involving HIV, the virus that causes Aids... At the start of the HIV epidemic, research concluded that the risk of catching Aids from oral sex was negligible".* But it still was! The report sent out a completely wrong message since the transmission of HIV orally was fairly miniscule, especially given the numbers of men and women across Scotland who enjoyed it. By far the greater rise in HIV infections across Scotland amongst gay men was through unprotected penetrative sex.

**The Glaswegian** reported how Milngavie Primary School had to send out a newsletter to parents explaining how its motto: *"Each Aids The Other"* was going to be changed. *"In view of the additional meaning of the word AIDS we are looking for a replacement motto",* it said.

It was quite misleading for this same paper to report: *"Gay men are being given condoms to have sex in Glasgow parks".* Those same men still risked violence, arrest and public condemnation. Health planners, with a duty of care, couldn't afford to be so judgmental. They recognised that large numbers of married and closeted gay men were frequenting *"well known gay haunts"*, as **The Glaswegian** put it, and targeted them with appropriate measures to protect them and their partners. The paper otherwise drew reader's attention to a similar campaign in Strathclyde Park *"slammed"* by church leaders *"who blasted the Lanarkshire plan as 'quite appalling and an affront to public decency..'. Critics said the move would encourage homosexual activity in the park, which currently has around 4.6 million visitors a year"*.

With a homophobic media, an unsympathetic church, a lack of protective legislation in Parliament, an ill-informed and often brutal police and a general public that was largely ignorant of sexual diversity, Scotland's lesbian, gay, bisexual and transgendered citizens remained particularly vulnerable. In 1995, captured on a closed-circuit television camera, William McGeoch was seen on the evening news in Scotland coming out of Bennets gay nightclub in Glasgow. Hugh Friel, (24) and Jason O'Donnell, (20) of Govanhill, pulled McGeoch to the ground and jumped up and down on him, beating him so badly he nearly drowned in his own blood. Diana Cotton QC of the Criminal Compensation Board ruled McGeoch should get nothing, partly because he had previous convictions. Police told the Board that McGeogh had started the aggro.

'Big-Man' is a well-used turn of phrase acknowledging respect for a fellow male in the macho city of Glasgow. 'How'r y'r dain' Big-Man?' No wonder there was such a hoo-ha when a hint of the colour pink was detected in Scotland's football colours. The football tops were well designed and featured two colours, one of which was only as pink as the sandstone of a Glasgow tenement, home to some of the hardest of the city's men. Two models of both sexes showed-off the new tops in the **Sunday Mail**. The girl's breasts were made to swell out of an unbuttoned top forcing the tabloid to comment: *"She looks the part, he looks a prat…"* The **Sunday Mail** photographed a builder, pointedly laughed at by his mates as he paraded up and down in the shirt: *"WHAT A SITE… builders blow the whistle on a pinko pal"*. The **Daily Record** sniggered over *"…Scotland's little pink number"* and *"…one of the worst strips ever"* before demanding: *"So who decided our boys would look pretty in pink?"* Doctoring a picture of the culprit they added: *"No* *wonder he's blushing"*, and sought the opinion of World Cup defender Colin Calderwood on the new 'away' jersey that the Scottish Football Association planned to *"unleash on the country's poor fans..."* Calderwood said: *"Even if it's horror pink... I can't imagine anyone daft enough to go up to Colin Hendry and call him a nancy boy!"* While **Record** columnist, Bob Shields spluttered: *"...It's bright pink!"* Decision-makers were *"attacked"* by former Scotland and Celtic star Alan 'Rambo' McInally who said: *"It's a case of going from bravehearts to brave tarts in one quick move. And I should know, I've been out with a few"*.

When Scotland's rugby team wore pink shirts in support of Imperial Cancer Research Fund's 'Think Pink' appeal, the **Daily Record** griped: *"the sight of the players flouncing around passing a pink balloon is hardly likely to strike terror into the heart of Jonah Lomu"*. Wearing pink was serious enough to warrant issuing a note of reassurance to its readers. *"But fans needn't worry about the team's image. Come the clash with New Zealand... they will be back in traditional and more macho blue"*.

The divisions that have existed between the Catholic and Protestant religions have frequently manifested themselves in the bigotry and hatred that sometimes boil over between Rangers and Celtic football clubs in Glasgow. Be it sectarian songs or murder, their conflicts are legendary. The **Scottish Sun** was able to show a level of Celtic Football Club's ability to combat prejudice by throwing Ivor Blackburn's difficult transgender status onto their sacrificial altar of "public interest". Pictured on its front page, the **Scottish Sun** told how the *"gender bender dad-of-two..."* a *"tattooed Celtic fan..."* from Forfar had *"been red-carded by his supporters club - after switching from a Bhoy into a girl"*. A spokesman for his local supporters' association confessed they had sent him a letter warning him *not* to turn up in clothes more befitting his intended gender status. *"We don't want repercussions... It's all very well having a laugh about it but after a few drinks these things can get out of hand"*.

For on-pitch, public displays of unashamed, man-on-man contact in the media, football deserves most of the credit, surpassing that of Scotland's leading gay magazines! Behind the gaol-scoring euphoria are pictures that only gay men carry forward into emotional reality. The *"first with the action"* **Sunday Mail** delivered yet another picture of Paul 'Gazza' Gascoigne

*"kissing team-mate Rino Gatusso after bagging two goals in Rangers'
7-0 win over Dunfermline"*. This was no idle peck, either. Gazza,
who is prone to crying, snogging and pulling the pants off his
fellow players, was right down the throat of Rino. *"Poor old
Gazza must be losing his grip. He was out with Sheryl at the weekend
but who did he decide to hug - Rangers pal Alan McLaren...! No,
Gazza... hug Shezza"*, the **Daily Record** implored, ignoring the
fact his estranged wife, Sheryl was pictured happily entangled
with Alan's wife, Jan McLaren.

On Morris dancers, the **Sunday Mail** warned: *"They look like
hanky-waving wimps with bells on..."* The tabloid tried to challenge this impression by supporting dancer Dougie McClone's
claim he was macho. *"The brawny Scot was knocked unconscious
by a six-foot fella waving two huge batons - and that was one of his
own Morris team...! But the robust Betsy is no pansy. Apart from the
risk of being knocked out cold by slap-dash dancers aiming for your
head, there's the threat of cracked knuckles, sprained wrists and bruis-
es galore"*.

In a piece on women boxing in Seattle, USA, the **Daily
Record** portrayed fighting as the exclusive preserve of men,
and anyone losing to a woman, a wimp! *"The guy never stood a
chance in a despicable battle of the sexes. Never mind that the male
'fighter' was such a wimp he kept landing low blows and lost on
points. The fact that it took place at all debases the former 'noble art'"*.

Shaking up Britain's Victorian sex laws was bound to bring
out the worst in the Scottish press. When it was suggested the
gay male offence of 'gross indecency' was destined for the
scrap heap, the **Daily Record** screamed: *"Gay men allowed to kiss
in public"*, a headline they conveniently dropped beneath a picture of a pursed-lipped Baroness Young who was leading a
Christian crusade in the House of Lords challenging sexual
reform. The **Record** brought on Stephen Green of Christian
Voice to claim the plans *"proof of the Government's obsession with
homosexual rights"*. Jim Sillars in the **Scottish Sun**, wrote: *"A
new policy floated by Jack Straw's Home Office for a change in the law
to permit sex acts in public, including public toilets, is an outrageous
offence to the values families try to instill in their children. Decorum
in its widest sense means more than just exercising good manners...
But this Government is so captured by the politically correct that they
are blind to the rising tide of anger among those trying to keep fami-*

*ly values, and civic standards, as a framework in which their children can grow old and develop... 'Do you support the abolition of Section 28, and are you in favour of open male sex in public toilets?'"* he bellowed. These were *"unavoidable questions calling for unavoidable answers that will sway many a vote"*, Sillars warned under the headline: *"Sex will bring Labour down"*. In fact, they landed themselves with a landslide victory at the very next election.

There was no shortage of sexually repressed 'spokespeople' to 'balance' a story that Victorian sexual offences laws were being reviewed. **The Scotsman** even went south of the border to revive a man so retrenched in his right-wing 'values' even the Tories forced him to drop any mention of them in his campaigns. Dr Adrian Rogers of Family Focus found Europe *"bringing down the social fabric of our society"*. The **Scottish Mail** used a man ousted by the electorate and brought back by the Scottish Tories to bolster their claim of *"widespread fears"*. Phil Gallie said: *"The way the ECHR* (European Court of Human Rights) *is being interpreted is unravelling the very moral fabric of our society"*. Whilst in England they quoted Tory MP Julian Brazier who told them this was *"another step towards the acceptance of the gay equality agenda"*.

One of Scotland's most notorious homophobic columnists, Gerald Warner fanned the flames of his own unnatural obsession in **Scotland on Sunday** and watched the world slide *"into moral anarchy"*. Former gay Tory Ivan Massow's defection to Labour because, Warner mocked, they were *"being beastly to homosexuals"* got right up his nose, crying: *"New Labour is now the party of homosexuality. That is its defining ethos"*. Wondering if anyone should have been surprised if *"...a cabinet in which homosexuals were represented at six times - six times! - their proportion in the general population would not promote a sodomite agenda"*. He leapt out of his chair to announce: *"...The next tranche of legislative degeneracy... Plans to allow homosexuals to engage in intimate behaviour in public, even in the presence of children, and to legalise 'cottaging' - homosexual activity in public lavatories. A father taking his small boys into a public convenience could find them confronted by one of Joe Orton's human 'pyramids', but would have no legal redress. Under New Labour, Britain is not so much a society as a sewer"*.

The incorporation of the Human Rights Act 1998 into

Scottish law would not protect gays having sex in public places. Whilst numerous laws have been unfairly used to prosecute gay men, (for example, Section 5 of the 1986 Public Order Act, which was introduced to curb football hooligans and used against two 19-year-old gay men who were arrested and charged with kissing each other in a London street in 1988), only gross indecency, part of the Sexual Offences Act 1956, applied exclusively to gay men and gay men only. It was interesting how none of the indignant papers noticed the point made in the Home Office Summary Report and Recommendations, Setting The Boundaries: *"A new public order offence to enable the law to deal with sexual behaviour that a person knew or should have known was likely to cause distress, alarm or offence to others in a public place"*. This hardly indicated an unqualified approval of gay sex in public places.

Along with many Conservative politicians and sections of the Church, the **Scottish Daily Mail** found itself in the unlikely position of making a case against the imposition of human rights in Britain. After running a front-page story on two *"dangerous Sikh terrorists"* who had been allowed to stay in Britain thanks to the European Convention on Human Rights, the **Scottish Mail**'s editorial used the story to attack gays when, at the same time, the European Court in Strasbourg found Britain in breach of Article Eight of the Convention, the right to respect private life after a man, known as 'ADT' was arrested for participating in an orgy. He was awarded £33,000: £11,000 to cover legal costs defending himself in England, £12,000 towards legal costs in Europe and £10,000 damages. The **Scottish Mail**'s editorial squealed: *"The compensation culture will flourish as never before. The legal aid bill will explode. The courts will be clogged. The bitter irony is that ever-increasing rights for minorities damage the rights of the wider public. People who don't want terrorists living in their midst? Or who feel queasy at the prospect of gay sex in public…? Who cares? After all, they're only the majority"*.

During a seminar on human rights at the Scottish Borders Council, one member demanded councillors over 65 should be forced to retire after accusing four of them of falling asleep.

The media made challenging homophobia extremely difficult. Academic Martin Plant was described in the **Scottish Daily Mail** as *"receiving £8,000 of taxpayers' cash to ask homosex-*

*uals how people treat them"*. It was, in actual fact, necessary research requested by Edinburgh City Council and the police on the subject of homophobia. Martin Plant was charged with *"bungling"* and Ann Allen of the Kirk's Board of Social Responsibility spoke out in the **Scottish Mail**: *"There are parishes in Edinburgh where there are concerns about the activities of gay people. These people should be surveyed too"*. She insisted: *"It was wrong to base the results solely on the experiences of homosexuals"*.

When a member of staff of a children's home took a 15-year-old to a gay club to help establish her sexuality, the sexually repressed media were virulent. Both the **Scottish Daily Mail** and **Daily Record** linked the story to a previous story involving another Edinburgh children's home where children had been involved in sexual abuse by former care workers Gordon Knott and Brian Maclenan. The **Scottish Daily Mail** ran the headline: *"CALL FOR PROBE OVER ALLEGED GAY CLUB VISITS WITH STAFF"*.

Ann Coltart, the Equality officer of the West of Scotland Freelance Branch of the National Union of Journalists wrote a sharply worded letter in the **West of Scotland Freelance News** expressing her alarm at the homophobia in the press she believed was helping to legitimise hostile attitudes towards people because of their sexuality. Putting forward a motion calling for equality, the branch turned it down. *"Even the macho NUM started supporting gay rights in 1985 (and its members have worse industrial problems to face than we have)"*, she fumed.

If the courts indulged in double standards regulating and legislating against sex, the media parodied their duplicity. When teacher John Paterson appeared before Falkirk Sheriff Court charged with indecent assault of four girls aged between 12 and 14, **The Herald** found his school rector who declared Paterson had an *"exemplary record"*. When, in the same paper a Scout assistant commissioner who took photographs of *"naked and partly-dressed teenage boys"* aged between 15 and 18, it was a *"perversion"* and no otherwise, *"exemplary record"* was found. Sheriff John McInnes went on to say Allan Ewan had caused *"considerable damage"* to the Scout movement. In the same week, far from being portrayed as a victim, Scottish editions of **The Sun** announced: *"Schoolboy Thomas Weldon is... a 14-year-old superdad"*.

The *"naked squaddie in dorm romps with posh schoolgirls, 14"* was also portrayed in a positive light. Scottish editions of **The Sun** drew reader's attention to the squadron's *"horny"* badge and mottoes: *"'I Rise Again With Greater Splendour' and 'Yield To None'"*. **The Sun** quoted one of the cadet's opinions of the girls: *"Some are incredibly good-looking and very well-developed and certainly look older. One of them took pictures of him. But I think they will be far too strong for Boots to process"*.

When a 33-year-old mother took a 13-year-old boy to the US and had sex with him, the judge was especially lenient. She was spared having her name, address and picture printed in the paper and was put on probation because the judge ruled their sexual relationship was consensual. At Nottingham Crown Court, Mr Justice Potts said: "I fully recognise and give weight to the fact that at all times the boy was a willing and active participant in what went on. I also proceed on the basis that at all times you and he… were extremely fond of each other… This is an exceptional case. This is not something that happens every day". The judge acknowledged the boy had not suffered long-term harm and added: "He's a mature and sensible young man who is capable of thinking for himself".

*"Pervert"* Kevin Drumgoole received no such slap on the back in **Scotland's Mirror** when he *"preyed on foreign boys"* visiting Edinburgh. The former swimming instructor *"would take them back to his flat, get them drunk and have his evil way"*. They were all *"youngsters too drunk to know what was going on"*. The *"youngsters"* were aged between 14 and 17. Kevin's defence counsel described him as "a rather pathetic, lonely, insecure type of person". He was jailed for 18 months. Meanwhile, in the same court, a former gym teacher, *"father of eight"*, George Brough, who abused two 15-year-old schoolgirls, walked free. **The Herald** reported that Lord Johnston told the court *"it would not serve the public interest to send him to prison"*. They learned how he had since become a pillar of the Catholic Church in Edinburgh and had undergone a 'spiritual conversion'. The priest accompanying him to court told the **Scottish Daily Mail**: *"If a man is genuinely ashamed of what he has done and has stopped sinning, but cannot find forgiveness in the Church of Christ, then where else can he go?"* Known only as Donna, one of his traumatised victims told the **Scottish Daily Mail**: *"Community service*

*doesn't even touch upon the pain he has put me through all these years".*

Demonstrating a commitment to religion in Scottish courts might reduce a prison term by years. 20-year-old David McPhail admitted shaking a two-month-old baby boy so severely, whilst his mother was out Christmas shopping, that the child suffered catastrophic injuries leaving him blind, deaf and unable to sit up. Doctors found extensive bleeding behind both eyes and an almost inch-long tear to the baby's brain. Judge Lord Caplan sentenced McPhail to three years probation after hearing how he had been taken in by a strict Christian drug and drinks dependency clinic. The right-wing Family and Youth Concern seized the opportunity in the **Scottish Daily Mail** to undermine progressive sex education. *"Sex education in schools is not enough... Schools are far too busy showing children how to put condoms on bananas rather then the things that really matter".*

In another case, William Williamson, a radio deejay on West Sound in Dumfries and a choirmaster who promoted Christian values on the air was suspended after allegations arose that he had made sexual advances to a 14-year-old while he was choirmaster at St John's Episcopalian Church in Moffat. He escaped prosecution by agreeing to have a form of psychiatric treatment known as 'diversion' therapy.

Throwing out of court consensual cross-generational sex between 15 and 33-year-old gay *guys* had the tabloids up in arms. 33-year-old Dean Stewart, a manager of Our Price records in East Kilbride was spared because a Sheriff claimed the youngster was happy to take part in what the **Daily Star of Scotland** called: *"his sick sex games".* Adding: *"The pervert... took advantage"* of the *"teenage boy..., abused him"* and *"performed sex acts on him".* Colette Douglas Home in the **Scottish Daily Mail** thought the lad could be *"damaged by a relationship he might later regret".* Many married gay men can testify to that!

Tom 'Brigadier' Brown dismissed a woman running off with a young boy as the *"stuff of schoolboy fantasies".* His! *"Especially if she wore black stockings",* he confessed.

When talented designer Versace was murdered, 'Brigadier' Brown didn't believe it qualified for international news coverage. In a piece crudely headed: *"THE DAY WE FORGOT OUR*

*PRIORITIES…"* he turned to trumpeting the death of a *"decent Catholic girl who fell for a Protestant boy"*, asking: *"Which death should have stunned us and stopped us in our tracks…? The slaughter of Bernadette should have made the Versace killing look insignificant. The dress designer's death was just another symptom of the seedy and dangerous 'gay' underworld"*. Bob Shields, also writing in the **Daily Record**, described Versace's sexuality as *"a little on the dodgy side"* and asked: *"What made a man surrounded by the most beautiful women on the planet gay?"*

When Agricultural minister, Nick Brown's gay sexuality was thrust into the public arena, the **Daily Record**'s Tom Brown displayed yet more double standards by declaring that the sexuality of politicians was not completely off limits. *"Neither should it be"* he stamped. Only months earlier he had insisted: *"Private lives shouldn't be public"*. 'Old Mother Burnie' reflected on *"…these sad and sordid little affairs"* before defending the press. It's *"not OUR hypocrisy, but theirs"*, she stated. *"…It was Number 10 which kicked a naked Nick Brown right out of the closet…"* But whether that was some rascal making a fast buck selling a story, or the Prime Minister, Tony Blair's own press secretary, Alistair Campbell, should that make any difference?

Dundee's **Courier & Advertiser** reported a *"six year sentence for alcoholic sex case priest… Docherty sent erotic love letters and Valentine cards to the youth to try to win him back when their relationship had ended…"* Mrs Justice Steel was reported saying: "To say that this case is sad and sordid is an understatement". In the same paper on the same day, a *"baptism attack priest"* was jailed for just 21 months for carrying out a sex attack on a 13-year-old girl shortly after her baptism. 57-year-old Father John Lloyd was cleared of four rape charges and seven further counts of indecent assault. In a separate case, a 68-year-old Kirk elder, Colin Stirling sexually molested a nine-year-old girl at his Sunday school. He was jailed for just three months.

One of the biggest and longest child-abuse investigations in Scotland led to two former care workers being jailed by Lord Bonomy for gross sexual abuse of youngsters in Edinburgh children's homes dating back to the 1970s. **The Herald** announced a *"day of reckoning for two child abusers"*, Gordon Knott for 16 years and Brian Maclennan for 11 years. Knott was convicted of one count of sodomy, two attempted, seven counts of indecency and keeping indecent pictures of children. Maclennan was convicted of unlawful sex with teenage girls and three indecency charges. Knott paid the heaviest penalty.

The **Scottish Daily Mail** focused on a *"pervert priest shielded by Church for 20 years"*. Jailed for three years, Father Desmond Lynagh *"violently abused teenagers in his care at Blairs College, Aberdeen, which trained youngsters for the priesthood"*. The **Scottish Daily Mail** said Lynagh *"molested two boys..."* and indulged in *"various indecent acts"* with his *"victims"*. He confessed in court to *"shamelessly indecent conduct"*. Hidden deep in the text was the astonishing fact that the *"boys... were aged 15 and 17 at the time"*. Each year there are many more teenage girls facing pregnancy or abortion through sexual encounters with older men. Few expect any mention in the Scottish media. The 'Sexfinder General', Father Tom Connolly sent his blessing to what the **Scottish Sun** called the *"paedophile priest"* after 57-year-old Lynagh planned to marry an unmarried 51-year-old Mary Docherty at a secret ceremony in Edinburgh. After the Catholic Church had spent years hiding his secret trysts with young lads, the 'Sexfinder General' added: *"The church is a church of forgiveness... We wish him every blessing and hope that he goes forward and learns from the sadness of his past"*.

Arresting men in expensive under-cover operations did nothing to curb men meeting in areas that became known as gay meeting places. 24 hours after police arrested 57-year-old Balloch farmer, William Rennie, his body was found floating in a loch. Following complaints from 'worried parents', Strathclyde Police rounded up 17 men in their five-day operation. With the help of the **Helensburgh Advertiser**, more men became aware of: *"Helensburgh's Kidston Park... toilets near Duck Bay Marina and... East End public toilets in Balloch"*. After more swoops, the local paper reported a further forty arrests!

The more society puts pressure on people to declare their heterosexuality, the less likely they will be able to express differences they might harbour about their sexuality; there will be more suicides; more marriages will be broken; more arrests for indecency. And more names will be tragically added to the growing list of Britain's shocking record of sexual pathology and crime in the shape of gay serial killers like Dennis Nilsen,

Michel Lupo, Colin Ireland and Peter Moore. The police and judiciary will be kept as busy as ever, filling the courts with victims of victims. And before former Prime Minister, John Major ever set the seeds for the growing hysteria over homosexual sex crime behind a religious-backed moral revolution, championing a sporting nation and setting up voluntary cadet teams in state schools, he should have considered that fewer men than ever would be prepared to take up the responsibility of looking after young boys.

# Chapter Six
## *Social Purity, Selling Sleaze and Getting Out Your Chopper*

*"What you gonna say, in private*
*You still want my love*
*We're in this together*
*But what you gonna do, in public*
*Say you were never in love*
*That you can't remember.*
*So discreet…"*
**Dusty Springfield**

Moral restraint, temperance, self-control and sobriety provide a smokescreen for prudery and sexual repression. The dignity afforded by the addition of manufactured laws defining, ruling and constraining an apparently rampant sexual desire confirm and mollify the sexually repressed.

As society changes, so do the space it offers for opportunities to sexually negotiate, explore and experiment. Now morally purged, today's private and municipal baths are no match for the sexual opportunities once provided by the Victorian mahogany and white-tiled public baths of yesteryear. It is now usual to be met with a battery of warning notices advising: 'costumes must be worn at all times'. The unhealthy practice of keeping them on in saunas and steam-rooms is now *de rigueur*. Closed circuit video surveillance cameras are installed to discourage sexual impropriety. Rows of changing-cubicles facing others in use are often deliberately closed off. More areas are designated 'family' changing areas and bathers are becoming more cautious as they try to wash themselves in their bathing-costumes. We have become a society with an almost paranoid fear of each other's bodies, shored up by restrictive regulation governing sexuality. In an attention-grabbing headline, the **Daily Record** found a *"Scouts chief in kid sex scandal"* at a swimming pool. The story revealed him, *"...allegedly spotted filming with a camcorder in the male changing room of a swimming pool. The 34-year-old computer operator now faces indecency charges"*. A hysterical worker at the pool warned the **Daily Record**: *"I just want parents to know that all their children are at risk... The problem with these modern pools is that there are more open changing rooms and less staff patrolling them. The only way to clamp down on this kind of thing is by fitting screens to the top and bottom of cubicles and security guards watching at all times"*.

Part of the reason we wear costumes at all in public swimming areas is through the efforts of organisations like the Association for Moral and Social Hygiene, the National Purity League and the National Vigilance Association. The latter, in an *"energetic legal crusade against vice in its hydra-headed form"*, declared itself in a *"hand-to-hand fight with the world, flesh and the devil"*. The task of morally policing outdoor bathing areas - frequently used by naked boys before the First World War - fell to Britain's first policewomen.

Nudity today is subject to more control and regulation than ever. Delivering repressed and narrow-minded views on sexuality are only compounded by the belief that the sight of something as natural as the human body is somehow 'unnecessary' and 'obscene.' Three sixth-formers were disciplined when they ran on stage naked at a charity concert in Edinburgh covered only by their guitars. The **Daily Record** was on hand to give voice to the outrage and describe how they had to be *"hustled off stage by horrified staff..."* Whipping away their guitars for a final 'Full Monty' in front of *"children as young as 11"* was not going to earn any points with the tabloid that soon unearthed a *"horrified"* parent to register disgust. *"People get arrested for less than what those boys did. They should be ashamed of themselves"*.

The **Daily Record** even expressed shock over the cover of Green Party frontman, David Icke's new book. *"Only a 'censored' peel-off sticker covers the... privates"* they gasped. A spokesperson for the Edinburgh-based bookshop, James Thin calmly told them it *"wasn't generally policy to censor"*; after all, he added: *"We do get a lot of book covers with naked men and women"*.

On the decision by a jury in London that Vincent Bethall had not caused a public nuisance by wandering around naked in public, the **Daily Record**'s agony aunt, 'Old Mother Burnie' grabbed a towel. *"...Not in front of me"*, she squealed. Basting her excuses in fat, she found just one more reason to be ashamed of your body: *"Most bodies are bodies unbeautiful, particularly male bodies. For one thing, 30 per cent are currently classed as obese and I would prefer they kept their excess baggage out of sight"*.

Under the heading: *"PUT AWAY YOUR CHOPPER"*, Ken Adams reported in the **Scottish News of the World**: *"Blushing Scots nudists have been left exposed after lumberjacks chopped down the trees, which hid their remote club"*. It was not just the inference that naturists should have been *"blushing"* at Sunnybroom Sun Club in Alford, Aberdeenshire but his inability to resist stereotypes. *"Passers-by can now glimpse naked members playing volleyball..."* Later, in another piece under the heading: *"Angry nudists get b-air warning"*, Adams compounded the suggestion of embarrassed nudists when he wrote: *"Red-faced naturists have reported an increase in low-flying planes above their colony"*.

The **Sunday Mail** assumed that *"stunned onlookers watched in disbelief..."* at the match at Tranent as a *"STREAKER ran on to the pitch"*. A cartoon rugby ball covered the offending part while the tabloid got back its breath. *"Incredibly, the team then let him take the CONVERSION KICK starkers to land them the points"*. He was dismissed as a *"madcap Englishman"* before the tabloid found a *"not-so-happy parent"* to scream: *"It was disgusting. I had to put my hands over my little girls' eyes. You don't expect to see that kind of thing in public at two o'clock in the morning, never mind two in the afternoon. He could have been arrested for indecency"*. Such prudery, of course, did not necessarily apply to naked women! Female revellers at Glasgow's 'T in the Park' pop festival were described as a *"Tease in the Park"* by the **Sunday Mail** who featured a picture of a couple of girls *"putting on a bra-ve face"* stripping down to their bras.

22-year-old *"cheeky"* Ayr United fan Gordon Benson was shown romping naked across the field in the **Scottish Sun** *"to show off his famous tackle"* as thousands watched after Rangers beat Ayr 7-0. An Ayr United logo was strategically placed by the **Scottish Sun** to hide it. *"I'm planning to become a serial streaker - the buzz is amazing"*, Gordon added shamelessly. His *"naughty"* escapade however, raised £50 for charity and a charge of breach of the peace.

Five streakers appeared at Cupar Sheriff Court after they stripped off at the Millennium Open Championship at St Andrews. Sheriff Patrick Davies told the three women and two men they had ruined the concentration of golfers and had the potential of triggering serious public disorder! They were fined between £100 and £200 each. In his column in the **Scottish Sun**, Bill Leckie moaned: *"If I walked through a crowded street in St Andrews and dropped my pants in front of women and kids, I wouldn't be a streaker. I'd be a pervert… So how come some tart who whips her kit off and runs across a golf course in St Andrews is hailed as a fun-loving exhibitionist and gets a fine that'll take ten lap-dances to pay off? Forget the £100 fine - if specky Jacqui loves nudity so much, give her 200 hours community service picking up dog poo naked on St Andrews beach in mid-November and see how much of a thrill it is then"*. The **Daily Record** collared Jacqui Salmond's mum for a story on the *"agony"* of being left *"too humiliated to leave the house"* and left *"seeking medical help"*. The piece declared: *"My Jacqui's shameless streak ruined our lives"*. Over family album snapshots of *"the little fallen angel"* the **Record** cooed over her past 'innocence': *"Jacqueline was the apple of her mother's eye as a sweet and well-behaved little girl. Family Christmases were treasured and her school days showed great promise for university and beyond"*.

Columnist Rikki Brown in the **Scottish Sun** hit out at the few prepared to go bollock-naked. *"Streakers are perverts and should be put on the sex offenders' register - I mean, that tackle-out bloke at Wimbledon could have been and probably was seen by kids"*. Eager to expose his own double standards, he added: *"Don't mind female streakers though. That's different because they don't have incredibly ugly dangly bits, but I just wish some of them would visit the Bikini Line Waxing Parlour prior to their impromptu kit-off"*.

To point out the harmful affects of smoking, the **Record** bravely used an illustration of a naked man. To spare its readers any embarrassment, most likely affected by a drop in the sperm count, they could only bring themselves to point to a round green blob marked *"penis"*.

A comedian at the Edinburgh Fringe Festival was led away handcuffed for saying *"penis"* in the street. As the police dragged him away, the public began chanting *"penis"*. Naughty David McSavage was given a good dressing down at the local Sheriff Court before being let off for good behaviour.

Sarah Wolstencroft was judging the Scottish heat of 'A Thong For Europe', a programme shown on Channel 5. The **Scottish Sun** decapitated the head of 'The Full Monty' star, Robert Carlyle and stuck it over stripper, Solid Gold's *"winning assets"* with the caption: *"You don't want to see what's under here"*.

Newsreader Simon Willis was out hillwalking when he fell in a burn and had to take off all his sopping wet clothes! The **Scottish News of the World** demanded an explanation and tried to contact him at BBC headquarters, but he was not available. They were forced to quote an insider who told them: *"...It's not quite what is expected of a presenter"*.

Scottish editions of **The Sun** reported that a security guard had been sacked after a secretary saw him through a window at Pringle's knitwear factory in Hawick *"with his hands in his lap"*. He insisted he had just been eating a banana.

In the headline: *"KID'S CAMP CONS SNEAK OFF TO HOTEL FOR NOOKIE"*, the prisoners working at a children's camp sneaked off for sex with their wives. The **Daily Record** warned: *"The pair have been shipped back to tougher prisons to pay the price after the Record blew the whistle on their saucy capers"*. Chief Inspector of Prisons, Clive Fairweather suggested that weekend sex sessions with partners and even homosexual lovers could reward drug-free prisoners. The **Scottish Daily Mail** evoked the 'Sexfinder General', Father Tom Connolly of the Catholic Church to assert: *"I always assumed that people were put in prison because they had done something wrong. It should not be a question of giving somebody sweeties because they've done something good"*.

Poor Jim McCabe of North Lanarkshire Council performed an *"outrageous"* act to the sound of Hot Chocolate's, 'You Sexy Thing'. Not quite entering into the party spirit, the **Daily Record** revealed: *"The stripper who dropped his trousers at a drunken Labour party was last night revealed as the man elected to clean up a sleaze-hit council"*. Someone squealed: *"You could see his boxer shorts. That was enough for me and I left. At any Christmas party people want to relax and have a few drinks..."* An extraordinary statement to make in an area where drink, not sex, had already cost so many lives.

Another *"embarrassing row"* erupted at North Lanarkshire Council after its director of education, Mike O'Neill had a sexy strip-o-gram called Vicki, dressed in a *"kinky cop outfit"* sent over to celebrate his 50th birthday. SNP councillor John Murphy, poor dear, was outraged. He was forced to ask the Chief Executive to launch an investigation, telling the **Scottish Sun**: *"We need to get to the root of these claims. I believe it is shocking that a council office was used for something like this"*.

The **Sunday Mail**'s clairvoyant, Margaret Solis was so badly affected by an *"indecent assault"* at Banus disco in Glasgow that she told Scottish editions of **The Sun**: *"I was off work for weeks because I was getting headaches and couldn't concentrate to do my clairvoyant work... It was 12 months before I plucked up the courage to leave my house and walk out alone"*. The tabloid revealed on its front page how Margaret *"slammed... to the floor"* a *"lesbian dirty dancer who groped her..."* and explained how: *"The pervert rubbed the psychic's breast and touched her between the legs - then hitched up her own skirt to reveal she had no panties on"*.

Strippers did not appear to amuse the prudish sister paper of The **Sun**, the **Scottish News of the World**, either. Jim Lawson wrote about a landlady of a pub in Keith, Morayshire who had lost her licence because a male stripper *"performed a sordid barside sex act with a 15-year-old girl"*. Oh, dear! But read on. The **Scottish News of the World** breathlessly revealed… *"Drinkers looked on in horror as the man peeled down to reveal he was wearing a pair of scanty **WOMEN'S** knickers. He then exposed himself to his stunned audience before engaging in simulated, (repeat: simulated) sex with the under-age girl"*. Playing on the old 'near children playing' paradigm, the tabloid declared: *"The disgusting scene took place at a private party in the boozer – which is situated yards from a kids' playpark"*. Police seized the video footage filmed by the landlord, including, they said, pictures of *"a male stripped to his underpants and, more surprisingly, to a pair of ladies' underwear underneath… Which was seen by our officers and deemed to be indecent…"* The tabloid reported: *"Chief Inspector Stewart said the way the bar was run amounted to undue public nuisance and a threat to public order and safety… He also said that Keith Grammar School and local church leaders had expressed concern…"* The **Scottish News of the World** held up a dignified picture of the crest of the burgh with a caption underneath boldly proclaiming: *"SCANDALISED: Keith"* before begging for more: *"DO you know about a sex scandal? Tell us by ringing 0141 420 5301. Don't* *worry about the cost, we'll call you back"*.

'Old Mother (Joan) Burnie' in the **Daily Record** had something to say about Marks & Spencer's new range of *"dirty knicks and undies in size 22"*, offering some sound advice to the mature and over-sized women who bought them. *"Sadly, there comes a time in every woman's life, no matter how she looked in her youth, when she has to admit – or be told – that her time for long hair, low necklines, short skirts AND sexy undies, is way behind her"*. Burnie claimed to be a *"sensible woman"* who preferred those *"old reliables"* like *"a plain, white shirt in cotton or linen, something cool and classic..."* and was appalled at the sight of *"wretched"* thongs, or *"low porn undies"*. A woman who didn't like her husband wearing *"skimpy light trunks"* soon won her support: *"Have you tried laughing out loud at him, or better still, taking photos and getting others to giggle at him? Either that, or tell him it's you or the trunks. There again, maybe you could bribe someone to lose his luggage"*.

Men have enjoyed women stripping or lap-dancing for them for many years, but the moment any women suggested doing it for themselves, the **Daily Record** soon busted the party. *"SLEAZIER THAN THE MALE... An Edinburgh gay bar strip show is pushing back the boundaries of good taste"*, they spluttered. The **Record**'s religious cronies were each wheeled out to register their disgust. Mrs Ann Allen told everybody how it was *"extremely sad... People would have to be pretty impoverished on a social and emotional level to go to these lengths for entertainment"*. In fact, some of the girls absolutely *love* to show off their bodies. Doing it in front of other women, for some of them, was an opportunity not to be missed! Of course, the 'Sexfinder General', was assured of a front seat. He told everyone in the **Record** how *"sad"* he was (and for once, had many agreeing with him). The **Record** had their nose put out of joint by an otherwise reliable *"douce Edinburgh matron"*, Edinburgh Tory councillor, Daphne Sleigh who gave it the thumbs up! The story was 'balanced' by a *"good liberal"*, Jean Rafferty who told them *"lap-dancing is one of the most vulgar methods of getting sexual satisfaction"*.

Glasgow's Licensing Board was determined to throw the rope of moral restraint round the neck of Glasgow's lap-dancers. Both Glasgow Sheriff Court and the Court of Session threw out the Licensing Board's efforts to refuse an entertainment licence for a club wanting to offer 'table-dancing'. (This is where the distance of a table separates dancer and customer). Not giving in so easily, the Board sought an opinion from Senior Counsel with a view to taking the matter before the House of Lords. The press reported one of the reasons the Licensing Board gave for refusing the licence, as *"the persons likely to resort to the premises"*. The Board, however, was forced to *"reconsider"* its position and dismissed estimated costs of £500,000 to defend their moral stance as *"grossly inflated"*. Truffles, the only lap-dancing bar in Glasgow at the time did permit topless girls, but no naked acts. Chairman of the Board, John Moynes thought it a sleazy show. He was not known for his liberal views and tried to insist, after its defeat at the Court of Session in June 1999 that the Board took responsible decisions and only acted in the public interest.

The **Sunday Mail** had tabloid-tubby Gary Keown wringing his hands over the *"sordid lap-dancing club for lesbians"*, suggesting that damage was likely to be done to the very fabric of our society. In what was probably the best advertising the Fly Bar could have hoped for, the **Scottish Daily Mail** declared it *"condemned"* by *"church leaders and family groups"*. After its first night, reporter Marion Scott's exclusive in the **Sunday Mail** reported that the show *"fell flat on its face"*. The header declared, *"Scots aren't fooled by tacky new lap-dancing club for lesbians"*. But why should they have been fooled? It was clearly advertised as a night out for gay girls. Or as the **Sunday Mail** chose to put it, a *"tattooed clientele"*.

Night club owner, Charles Geddes, 51 was charged with 'shameless indecency' and put on the sex offenders register for getting clubbers to flash for a free drink at his nightclub. Or, as the **Scottish Sun** put it: *"To expose themselves in front of dozens of stunned partygoers"*. RAF trainee Claire Taylor, 23 appeared anything but *"stunned"* and confidently told the court: *"I didn't really think twice about it"*. She told the **Press and Journal**: *"It didn't particularly shock me – that sort of thing doesn't – and I got a big cheer"*. Defence solicitor-advocate Ian Cruikshank tried to explain: *"It was maybe the first time Forres had seen it"*. Aberdeen's **Press and Journal** said: *"...Unemployed Forres landscaper, David Ferrier, 34, leapt up on stage and pranced in front of clubbers with his trousers around his ankles, exposing himself"*. The

**Scottish Sun** said: *"The women flashed their breasts and the 34-year-old man showed his manhood"*. **The Herald** added that one of the girls was 15 and pointed out the name of one of the cocktails on sale: *"Sex on the Beach"*. The judge decided the clubbers had all been subject to corruption and been persuaded to do something indecent. Geddes's conviction was eventually overturned on appeal.

In much less of a report and more a mirror of a reporter's own sexual attitudes, Vivienne Aitken at the **Daily Record** was subjected to *"brazen footage…"* and *"shameless scenes"* after watching a video made during a break-in of football star, Paul 'Gazza' Gascoigne's Scottish home by a group of kids who frolicked in his pool. One of the boys *"zooms in on the girls' bodies"*, she wrote. *"One brunette girl"* was apparently *"wearing only a skimpy white top and shorts…"* and *"trying to climb on top of Gazza's inflatable whale toy…"* Aitken watched another teenage girl *"getting hosed down in the pool"* and the *"gang trying out the sauna…"* She then sees a girl with *"black bra and flowery knickers showing through her soaking clothes…"* before she *"abandons all modesty and dives back into the pool, frolicking around with the toy whale"*.

It seems extraordinary that the **Sunday Mail** should want to go to such lengths to impose a Victorian morality on their wordly male readers. Referring to Edinburgh's famous red light district around Leith harbour, they claimed to have *"uncovered a tidal-wave of vice…"* outside the offices of ScotPEP, the Scottish Prostitutes Education Project which had *"received £82,000 of National Lottery cash…"* The revelation of a red-light area in Leith was unlikely to have been much of a surprise to its readers, but maybe their rather twee reporter was on a learning curve after discovering *"just how easy it is to pick up a vice girl…"* Of course, he did the 'right thing' and *"declined her offer"*. I wonder how many **Mail** readers would have interpreted that as having 'chickened-out'?

It was just a small step from sex to drugs. The **Daily Record** saw it as their moral duty to step in and save the Salvation Army from ruin. Apparently, they were *"selling fragrant oils smelling of CANNABIS… yards from a primary school"*. The **Daily Record** also announced a *"crackdown on an illegal sex drug… The found amyl nitrite, or 'poppers' were *"popular with gay men and

*Hell's Angels"* and announced that they *"have serious side effects and can be fatal"*. True! A few deaths had resulted from people drinking and not sniffing the widely-used legal substance. A spokesperson for the Royal Pharmaceutical Society, otherwise criticised by a judge for wasting so much public time and money for trying to get a prosecution, told the **Daily Record** exactly what they wanted to hear: 'Poppers' are *"on open sale where even children can get hold of it"*. Glasgow's **Evening Times** found them in Record Fayre, a shop in Glasgow's Trongate. *"ILLEGAL AND DEADLY... but this man is still selling poppers to kids... Paul Gordon... is about to feel the full force of the law descend on him after being exposed today by the* **Evening Times***"*.

It was supposed to be the **Daily Record'**s Old Mother Burnie's job to discuss sex. She was, after all, the agony aunt. Although no one would normally expect her to be particularly explicit in her advice, one letter appeared to have slipped through the net. On the subject of oral sex, one elderly woman asked: *"...What exactly does it involve?"* Usually circumspect when it came to questions on pleasures of the flesh, Burnie appeared to take a rush of the vapours and sniffed: *"I am afraid I cannot go into the gory details here"* before recommending the writer pick up a sex manual from her local library. Most public libraries in Scotland still didn't carry gay lifestyle magazines, or if they did, hid them behind the counter. There was certainly no erotica and if there was a sex manual, it certainly wouldn't have been on display.

For someone who enjoyed sex, it must be disappointing to see yourself described as leading a *"double life as a sordid photographer of young women"* as well as *"a self-styled pimp and former male escort..."* After studying psycho-sexuality, *"brazen"* Alan Forrester from Edinburgh set out to explore new ways of getting down to some hot babe action; advertising in the local newsagents for models to pose in front of his camera. Very upfront with callers, he had the misfortune to meet Shona. She told the **Daily Record** exactly what they wanted to hear about *"seedy... Forrester"*. She said: *"I thought the whole thing sounded sleazy and revolting. It's horrifying that some young girl might fall for this... Surely if you want models for that kind of thing you would advertise in those sleazy magazines"*. Two undercover **Daily Record** reporters were sent out to uncover his *"sick antics"*, apparently retching, as he pulled his car into the quiet cul-de-sac where he lived: *"Forrester likened his home to the scene of horror movie Psycho"*. Forrester must have wondered what to make of the pricked faces in the back seat of his car when he quipped: *"'Unfortunately my house looks like the Bates Motel'"*. He tried to explain: *"I don't force anybody to do anything they're not happy with... I can be very discreet. I know how important it is. None of my friends know anything about this..."* But they sure as hell did after his story appeared in the **Daily Record** under its new editor, Martin Clarke. *"Forrester went white and slumped in his car seat"* when the reporters confronted him and asked him *"to justify his 'perverted hobby..."*

Throughout his editorship, Martin Clarke, who previously edited the **Scottish Daily Mail**, plumbed new depths in prudery. The **Daily Record** pursed its lips to report: *"Ginger smut Evans plays it dirty"*. A list of DJ Chris Evan's sins appeared, including, hosting an *"Ann Summers sex party live on Virgin Radio, with smutty talk and a vulgar game involving a large pair of Y-fronts"*. But as the sales figures of the tabloid slid, some people began to wonder if readers really shared the **Daily Record**'s obvious disgust.

The **Daily Record** must have been grateful for the introduction of a spray *"to help nail two-timing husbands"*. The tabloid pointedly advised: *"it glows green if traces of sex are detected"*.

*"With its windows full of words like 'huge chests' and 'strippers', it looks like a strip joint. But in fact, these saucy slogans aren't promoting a peep show - they're selling furniture"*. Olympian Pine in Edinburgh had caught the attention of the **Daily Record** when it stuck up some imaginative posters in its windows. Edinburgh Conservative councillor Tom Ponton branded them *"ridiculous"* and *"sleazy"* saying: *"The council's planning department should enforce regulations to take them down... There's no need to parade sexual words around town like this. It's giving the wrong image of Edinburgh to visitors. It gives a sleazy impression of Edinburgh that we want to avoid. It's a big concern. Edinburgh is a beautiful city with lots to offer, but not this"*. Siglo's bar in Edinburgh was another target. A poster said: *"Big Jugs Well Hung... The Rev William Mackay, clerk to the public questions committee of the Free Church, said the posters were desensitising people to real sexual problems"*.

After the late Paula Yates' suicide, Lorna Frame in the **Daily Record** suggested her life of risk and danger had finally caught up with her. She added that her *"sexual history is decidedly distasteful. She boasted that she had oral sex with Bob Geldorf in the back of a taxi"* and, as if she were ever likely to have dropped it all for a mock-Tudor semi in Newton Mearns, wrote: *"She was never going to live a stable, suburban life"*.

The **Daily Record** declared *"the revelation rocked the population of 1316"* on the tiny Scottish island of Barra after a teacher ran up a £200 bill calling a chatline from his school in what was peculiarly described as a *"sex call shame"*. Although children had no access to the room and he paid the bill, he was chastised for his *"sleazy antics"*.

Behind the measured rhetoric was the Church. *"RANDY REV BANNED"*, the **Record** reported after *"a romeo minister..."* was banned from his Kirk *"until he has therapy to cure his philandering ways"*. Former hospital chaplain Douglas Stevenson was sacked after admitting *"an illicit affair with a single mother"*. The church court ruled, *"he must get help"*. The 39-year-old had also *"made unwanted approaches to nurses"*. The married cleric had used the computer *"at his family home to send sexually explicit e-mails"*.

The **Record**'s sister paper was also adept at prudery. The **Sunday Mail** teased readers with what a TV star liked most to do in her bed. *"Telly stunner Kirsty Young has revealed her secret bedtime passion"*. Under a full-length picture of the blonde presenter draped in black, the tabloid announced: *"She loves nothing better than snuggling up with... a HOT-WATER BOTTLE"*.

A sexy lingerie shop selling goods on the Internet became a target for the **Sunday Mail**. According to the tabloid, this former butcher's shop *"is the centre of world-wide sleaze empire... The kinky knickers-on-the-net business is being run from a shop in historic Fife, overlooking the ancient village cross"*. The **Sunday Mail** weaved the language of repression and indignation into what was probably a perfectly innocuous statement from the shop owner. *"Boss Graham Gilmour boasted that thousands of bored Scots businessmen were tuning in to his sordid Internet address..."* It is doubtful if the owner ever described his business as *"sordid"*, let alone dismissed his client-base as a bunch of *"bored"* businessmen.

The **Daily Record** discovered another *"sex shock in the mail"*. Apparently, *"kinky sex brochures"* had been thrust through letterboxes all over Scotland, advertising *"lesbian sex and three-in-a-bed romps"* along with contact ads for people with *"exotic sex habits"*. The **Daily Record** had to revive *"stunned mum, Jean of Shawlands, Glasgow"*, who explained that the envelope was actually opened by her 15-year-old son. Fortunately, no harm was done because, she said, *"he is a sensible lad"*.

That was nothing compared to the shock a couple of Edinburgh students gave the **Sunday Mail**! *"EXPOSED... Scotland's sex capital. Just when you thought it was safe to go out..."* the paper squealed in terror. The students had tried to organise a convention for people of all sexualities who enjoyed sex. The **Sunday Mail** saw it differently. *"A sinners' convention"* for *"bed-hopping sex cheats* (who) *are set to turn Edinburgh into Scotland's capital of sin"*.

A report in the **Scottish Daily Mail** revealed Reverend Stanley Bennie's weekly show on Isles FM, based in Stornoway was *"far too rude"*. How do we know? We don't. Because, as the paper explained: *"Some of the... examples, which referred to sexual practices and organs are too outrageous to repeat in a family newspaper"*. Anyone would have thought the banter between Bennie and his co-host Gordon Afrin had been utterly scandalous. Afrin had said: *"Here is a record we haven't played for a long, long, long time"*. Bennie replied, (look away if you don't think you can handle this): *"That's because it's horny"*. And worse! Bennie said: *"I like a nice cup of tea at night before I go to bed"*. And Mr Afrin replied in camp tones: *"I'll make sure you get a really nice cup of tea"*. The **Scottish Daily Mail** explained that Isles FM bosses had asked them to tone down before the tabloid found *"one shocked islander"* who told them: *"I was driving along listening to the show and I could not believe what I was hearing. Their comments are extremely risqué and it is not just me who complained. I spoke to a guy in a petrol station in Stornoway who was also disgusted"*.

The language the media uses to describe sex and sexuality is very important and is likely to have a profound affect on the attitudes of its readers. The **Sunday Mail** underlined religious-inspired attitudes to sex outside marriage when they described former Edinburgh football boss Gordon Bennett a *"sad execu-*

*tive... shamed... 54-year-old batchelor"* with *"vices"* and an *"addiction"*. All he did was use chatlines and visit sexy saunas!

It is a measure of Scotland's conservatism that organisers of a nude swim across Loch Ness had to call in English volunteers after locals were too shy to participate. And while campaigners walked naked amongst High Street shoppers on World Naturism Day in a number of cities, not one Scot participated in the summer event in 1999. There are only around 2,000 members of British Naturism in Scotland. The **Scottish News of the World** warned that a Helensburgh group had been *"infiltrated by weirdos and would-be wife-swappers"* and an Internet site to encourage newcomers attracted *"perverts asking for saucy photographs and couples looking for sex sessions"*.

If naturists evoked the ire of the Scottish media, sex workers and those seeking their trade would be in receipt of even greater vitriol. After picking up a sex worker, Robert Paterson became a man who could not be trusted. He was caught driving off to a café and ordering teas and burgers! The **Sunday Mail** gasped: *"He even locks up as the last man out at night"*. Paterson, a senior manager for the Royal Bank of Scotland was *"seedy... sleazy... balding..."* and *"a director of the Scottish Centre For Children With Motor Impairment"* (if that meant anything)!

After the sixth murder of a female sex worker in Glasgow, ex-Religious Affairs correspondent, Tom 'Brigadier' Brown thought he had some answers for the **Daily Record**. *"The common factor is that the victims have all been prostitutes, seedy whores who worked the streets of Glasgow"*. So, he called for a toughening up on the laws on prostitution. Otherwise, *"girls would think it has become a lawful, acceptable occupation. What next"*, he snorted, *"exams in how to be a successful tart?"* Brown was appalled *"they are given advice on how to minimise risk. Public money is spent on supporting them and coping with the sex hygiene problems they create... But the law tolerates them - even though they are the tip of a sick, sleazy, diseased sector of society... With HIV and hepatitis, they are a health menace, if nothing else"*. His comments appeared soon after Tracey Wylde's body had been found dumped in the river Clyde. *"Because they were 'on the game',"* he argued, *"the police say the public don't care... There was a communal shrug of the shoulders... There are better people than prostitutes to waste our sorrow on"*. 'Brigadier' Brown demanded men who sought out the services of sex workers *"publicly pilloried for it"* after he found *"areas of Glasgow and Edinburgh where no self-respecting citizen can go. Sights where the signs of heterosexual and homosexual activity are openly offensive... I certainly don't say they deserved to be slaughtered"*, he added, *"but it shouldn't have been made easy for them. ...They put no value on their own lives. ...These six prostitutes died because prostitution is tolerated. They went into a high-risk racket, knowing that if their drug habit didn't eventually kill them a 'client' might..."*

Brian Donnelly murdered Margo Lafferty on his nineteenth birthday in 1998 after he had been rejected by a female workmate. Margo was 27-years-old and only five-foot tall; he was six-foot three. After her head had been smashed against a wall, she was strangled. Her naked and beaten body was found next day. So were two condoms, one containing the semen of Brian Donnelly and the other the semen of David Payne, a convicted sex offender who had been jailed for holding up a woman at knifepoint. Brian Donnelly was convicted for murder in February 2000.

Soon after the death of a seventh girl working the streets of Glasgow 'Brigadier' Brown wrote: *"Why are the boys in blue so concerned about the women of the streets? I only ask because it seems Scotland's biggest force are patrolling the wrong beat - Whore Alley. Hookers are being molly-coddled by our police... Do tarts pay more council tax? Isn't protecting prostitutes a job for pimps? Are loose-living women, who choose to put themselves in harm's way, entitled to better protection than a decent wife..."* He wanted them *"off our streets"* and to find *"REAL work"*. He didn't want *"public money... spent on setting up a special whore-protection unit. Or issuing attack alarms to prostitutes"*, (despite one saving a sex worker from a particularly nasty attack within weeks of them being issued). *"Or offering them self-defence courses... By all means let's see more policemen on the streets. But NOT doing the job of pimps at our expense"*. One of the female sex workers interviewed on 'Frontline Scotland' disagreed: *"See, when the last lassie, Margo, got murdered, just like two weeks before it. The uniformed polis harassed us that much it was hard enough for us to look after ourselves looking aboot for where's the polis, nevver mind to all of a sudden try and look out for any other lassie"*. She also claimed she had been raped and said police warned her *"it goes with the job"*.

Professor Neil McKeganey, who had been involved in an extensive study of the Glasgow sex workers, said that the number of murders was not a very good measure of the amount of violence he had witnessed being performed against them every night. In one case, sex worker Diane Ledgerwood had her bag strap grabbed by two men, trapping her outside the van as they sped off. She was hauled 30 feet until the vehicle ran over her, breaking her pelvis in three places. David Weir, 17 and James Greenshields, both of Glasgow, were out 'for a laugh' and were sentenced to two years after admitting assault. DCI Nanette Pollock led a group of Street Liaison Officers. Their job was to offer a sympathetic ear to sex workers who were otherwise rounded up and arrested by her police colleagues. Pollock admitted her position was a *"confusing, cloudy issue"*.

Shortly before conservative editor Martin Clarke left the **Daily Record**, the tabloid launched a stinging attack on prostitution. They insisted: *"It is... insulting to single mothers who struggle to keep their families together by decent means"*. Over the Scottish Executive's plans to open a drop-in centre and accommodation for a small number of female sex workers in Glasgow's red-light district, the **Record** snapped: *"Instead of sending messages of tolerance and support to prostitutes, government ministers should be reminding them that their way of life is shameful, illegal and wrong"*. Their report was garnished with comments from spokespeople for the Church of Scotland's Board of Social Responsibility, the Catholic Church and the Conservative Party.

'Brigadier' Brown's views are echoed in history. With the introduction of the Street Offences Act of 1959, Dr A D Broughton MP remarked: *"It is better, I think, if we have a festering sore, to keep it covered and out of sight rather than have it exposed, a revolting sight to decent people and a possible cause of infection among the young"*.

During the First World War, the press launched a campaign to protect *"our unfortunate soldiers"* attacked by *"an enemy in our midst"*. Legislation was soon passed under the Defence of the Realm Act, 1918, whereby it became an offence for any woman with VD to have sex with a soldier. In an extension of the notorious Contagious Diseases Acts, established over a century ago, women could be detained for medical inspection and imprisoned for up to six months if necessary. Following hot on its heels, shocking revelations of child prostitution landed the **Pall Mall Gazette** record sales and led to the emergence of the National Vigilance Association and a quest to purify the nation of 'vice'. Joining forces with feminists - such a campaign was never at odds with their faith in religion and its Victorian ethic of sexual restraint - their actions helped establish the Criminal Law Amendment Act of 1885. This raised the age of consent of girls from 13 to 16 and made homosexuality a criminal act through Section 11, the so-called Labouchere Amendment.

Not until 1943 did any programme of education about sex-ually-transmitted diseases ever start in Britain. Even then, the press behaved prudishly and irresponsibly. Words like *"sex organs"*, and *"clap"* was cut. The **Daily Mirror** broke the mould and made a bid for a liberal readership, launching a poster campaign aimed at men. Most people approved. It was so effec-tive, in fact, incidences of venereal disease dropped.

A positive attitude to sex workers was attempted on an Aberdeen-based website which **The Herald** called a *"city vice guide on the Web"*. Recommending the best sex workers in Aberdeen and marking girls with up to three cartoon cats for looks, value and performance, 'The Mannie' wrote: *"This site has been created for the information of those who share my hobby - the enjoyment of the company of prostitutes... We have some lovely lassies here and with a relaxed police attitude, you can really relax and enjoy yourself. Here in Aberdeen there is an enormous choice, but for the poor old visitor (or even local), very little information. The site only contains information that I have personally checked out myself (damn hard work I can tell you)... I have to say that the majority of the street girls I've been with have been nice people who have given me a great deal of pleasure"*. Mrs Anne Allen told **The Herald** she felt it *"obviously gives information to anyone who cares to access it on purpose - or by accident... I think it further demeans the women who are involved in prostitution and it's really a very sad commentary on the person involved"*.

Clouded by a personal opinion, put under pressure by supe-riors or misinformed by outside sources, misrepresenting sexu-al issues in the media is commonplace. In response, press guidelines, the Press Complaints Commission (or in its former guise as the Press Complaints Council) have all proved useless in stemming some of the worst excesses. Commenting on AIDS, the Press Complaints Council allowed Ray Mills from **The Star** to say: *"The woofters have had a dreadful plague visited upon them... Since the perverts offend the laws of God and nature..."* They accepted a story in **The Sun** on *"pulpit poofs"* and permitted **The Star** to get away with headlines like: *"The poofter MPs'...* and *"up, up and a gay... Council's free flying lessons for poofs".* The Press Complaints Commission urged newspapers to *"avoid publishing details of a person's sexual orientation, unless it is directly relevant to the story".* That didn't stop them tearing into the sexuality of a Norfolk social worker who had a minor rôle in deciding a couple couldn't adopt, and adjudicating on a lesbian couple who left seven children in the care of a 16-year-old whilst on holiday. Neither did it protect the manager of former pop band Take That, whose lover died of AIDS, the gay solicitor defending a multiple-murderer, or the *"homo provo"* whose 'cottaging' habits appeared to disgust **The Sun** more than his sentence for his part in an IRA bombing.

A front-page news story in the **Scottish Daily Mail**: *"THE TRUE COST OF BROKEN FAMILIES"* made disturbing reading. It was a 1996 report on a long-term study into the behavioural development of 1,000 children in the west of Scotland by the Joseph Rowntree Foundation. The **Scottish Daily Mail** said, the Foundation, *"more commonly known for fostering the beliefs of the Left..., overwhelmingly confirmed... more starkly than ever that it is the children who suffer most from ever-rising rates of divorce, family break-up and single motherhood".* Hell-bent in its moral crusade for the nuclear family, the **Daily Mail** thought it had scored a massive goal. The story was spiked with selective quotes from an interview with researcher Helen Sweeting. The **Mail** condemned the Foundation for previously publishing *"a notorious report"* showing inequality in Britain greater than at any time since the war. A study, it remarked, had been used *"remorselessly by Labour and Left-wing politicians".* The **Mail** interpreted the Joseph Rowntree Foundation's findings as they saw fit. The editorial launched into a tirade of moral outrage against permissiveness: *"How pernicious were the permissive doctrines of the Sixties... Part of the same sad scene is the rampant divorce rate... Unless firm steps are taken soon to buttress the institution of marriage...",* they opined. Helen Sweeting, a social scientist at the Medical Sociology Unit in Glasgow, was not best pleased with the **Daily Mail**. Helen explained in the **Independent On Sunday**: *"Girls were most likely to end up taking drugs not when their parents divorced, but when their mother or father died - a result which… leads to the conclusion that the best thing that parents can do for their children (and themselves) is staying alive".*

As the **Scottish Sun**'s attempt to *"expose the bedtime secrets of randy Scots"* revealed, the press were not just sexually misrepresenting homosexuals. Whilst Scotland was shown to be far more liberal and adventurous in bed than anyone - or at least anyone at the **Scottish Sun** - had previously thought, the paper moralised on *"fornicating liar"* Bill Clinton and his affair with Monica Lewinsky. *"Maybe we Brits, even if we don't all go to church, have a clearer sense of right and wrong than our holier-than-thou trans-Atlantic cousins"* they insisted, before adding righteously: *"Doesn't anyone do the decent thing anymore? …Public figures who were caught out used to 'fall on their swords' and quit without making a fuss".* The **Scottish Sun** looked at others in this *"hall of shame"* including singer George Michael who had been arrested in a Los Angeles public convenience by an undercover cop. The **Scottish Sun**'s *"sizzling expose"* of the *"Sex Secrets of the Scots"* - by the same paper that once referred to a dildo as a *"plastic manhood"* - began by thumbing through the pages of successful **Scottish Contacts** magazine. *"…Every perverted request will be granted"*, it sniffed. There was a sense of deep shock as one sexual 'perversion' was listed after another. *"A granny in her 60s is pictured in stockings and suspenders begging for ANY man for sex… The leather-wearing masked perverts know no limits as they dish out pain in a bizarre sense of fun… There are also uniformed stern butlers, naughty maids, strict headmistresses and naughty school boys – even a bus driver! They will romp anywhere – trains, car parks, the country-side and one picture even shows a man writhing naked in a massive muddy puddle".* The story was wrapped round a shot of a nicely scrubbed male model wrapping his arms protectively round a pretty, blonde girl. Were readers supposed to be shocked by this or were they supposed to take the **Scottish Sun**'s advice and cut out the coupons for books containing *"free sex tips"* like **Esquire** magazine's 'Men On Sex?' **The Sun** advised, *"eight hundred men have been stripped* *bare (so to speak) and their views and feeling about sex candidly explored by top psychologists...*", which presumably, made it all legitimate! The feature contained interviews with fetishists, a lesbian and a transsexual. Women who were prepared to satisfy men's sexual needs figured prominently. *"And so to bed... Scottish women as you've never heard them talk before"*. While the **Scottish Sun** was attempting to sensationalise sex in Scotland, their diarist, Rikki Brown sniffed at the sight of a couple not being intimate in the privacy of their own home. *"Frankly it's embarrassing to watch and I wasn't the only one who thought this. ...They must have been about 15. Yes, I was young myself once but I didn't winch in public"*.

Amongst much else, the **Scottish Sun**'s weeklong exposé on the 'Sex Secrets of the Scots' *"uncovered"* the extraordinary fact that *"a quarter of Scots men think that curry is the ultimate aphrodisiac"*. But before the tabloid had finished trumpeting how Scotland was at last *"losing its sexual hang ups"*, they were *"on the trail of the sleazy video kings"*. Scots were supposedly *"stripping off their inhibitions sparking a huge boom in DIY porn"*. The tabloid condemned *"the main culprit... an elusive hardcore filming den based somewhere in Maryhill, Glasgow"*. The spotlight was turned on censorial Glasgow's Trading Standard's officers. After finding a studio in Glasgow's Paddy's Market, a spokesman declared: *"It was nothing more than a tacky room with a manky bed and sex toys everywhere... We were delighted to bust it. I'd much prefer going home and watching Disney videos with my kids..."*.

Showing topless girls on page three was no demonstration of how liberal the **Scottish Sun** was. The tabloid ran a story on *"scandal-hit"* Thurso High school in Caithness where a boy *"asks Miss for sex act"*. This was prudely described as *"pupil's lewd request to RE teacher"*. At the same school, police were called to investigate claims that two fourth-year boys had had a threesome with a 12-year-old girl, the 15-year-old embarrassed the teacher with an *"obscene comment"* and, much to the **Sun**'s chagrin, *"was suspended for just a week"*.

Although they have made enormous strides in the past century, the presentation of women in the media often falls far short of an ideal. The **Scottish Sun** referred to sport's presenter Hazel Irvine as an *"inquisitive wee lassie"* while **The Scotsman** found her *"bereft of makeup"*, observing, *"the pale face that grins out from under a Nordic mop blonde hair could belong to a 14-year-old. Which in a sense she still is. There is something of the eternal schoolgirl about Irvine, if not the eternal swot"*.

The **Daily Record** swiped tennis star *"Stefi Graf-Zeppelin... She says the arm wrestlers like Mary Pierce and Venus Williams will eventually take over from grace and finesse players, like Russia's unexploded sex grenade Anna Kournikova and that wee Swiss chocolate Martina Hingis. But what would thunder thighs Steffi know about grace and finesse. She used to roll over the pit pat girlies like a panzer... It must be time for her to retire and have some babies"*.

*"Scotland's best-loved agony aunt"*, as the **Daily Record** described 'Old Mother Burnie', was not generous to Professor Germaine Greer when she called her the *"big and bolshie Australian academic"*. She called her book, 'The Female Eunuch', *"over the top"* and suggested: *"The old girl's only doing it either because she wants a little sugar on her pension or craves her past fame as much as her passé feminism"*. Admonished for being *"predatory"*, Burnie bitched: *"If a man caught her usually passing fancy, it was Greer who did the asking - and plenty lined up to be asked. That was, after all, part of the message. A woman's right to choose, not only how to live her life but with whom she would live it. Her affairs were many while her one disastrous marriage lasted a fortnight"*. Meeeow! Having once described International Women's Day, *"patronising and awful"*, her views were unsurprising. Burnie echoed critics of the suffragettes in criticising 'The Female Eunuch' for preaching *"wholesale revolution"* instead of allowing women to *"progress upwards step by careful step"*. She clawed at the *"bunch of female chauvinist sows"* for *"hijacking everything which men once saw as theirs"* and wondered if men needed liberating from *"the monstrous regiment of women"* who have *"robbed them of their jobs..."*.

During the summer of 1999, Scotland's press was filled with a story the **Sunday Mail** described as *"Scotland's most famous lesbian trial"*. The **Scottish Daily Mail** nostalgically resorted to images of Radclyffe Hall's tragic 'inverts' when they reported how: *"A middle-aged gym mistress was yesterday accused of preying upon her younger female colleagues to satisfy her sexual cravings"*. The dastardly college head of sport and leisure, 41-year-old Mary Collins was promptly dismissed for gross misconduct.

The words of her 'victim' were tragically emboldened in the **Mail**: *"She told me I had a great body and she had to have me... She said it is only sex... She told me I'd be sacked"*. Whatever Karyn Loudon sought, she was a qualified lifeguard who took classes of gay swimmers, had gay friends and was devoted to her gay brother before he tragically died - it seems unlikely that 'Scotland's most famous lesbian trial' was it. The **Mail** reported how fellow lecturer Kirsty Ewing went for a drink at the gay-friendly Tron bar with Mary Collins intending to confront her over her treatment of Karyn before ending up at Mary's house - *"only to be pinned down and groped... She tried to kiss me"*, Kirsty gasped. The **Sunday Mail** made it quite clear that 29-year-old Karyn - or *"Miss Loudon"*, as they chose to describe her - was at one time *"confused about her own sexuality"*. The fact that the alleged the assault *"lasted 40 minutes"* surprised the **Sunday Mail**'s Melanie Reid who blasted: *"I mean, COME ON! Shrinking violets? Those two?"* Neatly skipping over the contribution the **Sunday Mail** had made to Scotland's *"buttoned-up"* society, she otherwise declared it: *"Lesbianism in small-town Scotland... A sad tale of people in turmoil about their own sexuality... It's a story of misunderstanding and malice. Of a buttoned-up society in which folk are so bad at asserting themselves or expressing themselves that they end up in court... With the rest of the world laughing at their expense"*. If Karyn Loudon wanted to be portrayed a sexual victim, she could have done no better than talk to the **Daily Record**'s reporter, Vivienne Aitken. She found Karyn, *"a whisper of the fun-loving girl she was 12 months ago... wringing a tissue in her hands"*, a victim of: *"lesbian sex abuse"*. The court case ended with a 'not proven' verdict and Mary Collins was compensated by her college to the tune of £15,000 for unfair dismissal.

Glasgow's 80-year-old gay poet laureate, Edwin Morgan, criticised Scotland's puritanical atmosphere for keeping him in the closet until the age of 70. But challenging a liberal agenda of equality, fair play and progressive legislation, conservative commentators used a moniker that would keep its currency for more than a decade: Political Correctness.

A favourite of **Scotland on Sunday** and the **Scottish Mail**, Conservative Gerald Warner regularly hammered home the evils of 'political correctness' to his readers. *"Is there no end to the*

*march of the politically correct?"* he begged in the **Scottish Mail**.
An eight-year-old girl, terrified of her fate in a dentist's waiting
room had been thrashed six times on her bare bottom by her
father, a teacher. He was reported by a member of the health
care staff and consequently lost his job. Warner thought the *"the
juggernaut of politically correct intervention implacably rolled over
him and his family"* and warned: *"The case has the fingerprints of
political correctness all over it. The unfortunate teacher is a pawn in
a much larger battle... It is spreading across the land like a virus.
Political correctness is the creed of a tiny, bigoted but determined
minority. Increasingly it is infecting the sane majority, sometimes
with catastrophic consequences for their lives and happiness.
Essentially, it is an inversion of the normal. Criminals are cosseted;
law-abiding citizens are criminalized... The belief that children
should be protected by Section 28 from homosexual propaganda is
branded as intolerance; those who reasonably argue for its retention
are demonised as homophobes"*.

When Edinburgh City Council's director of corporate services, David Hume suggested the Council attempted to monitor
employees on the grounds of gender, ethnicity and disability,
and, if it was at all possible, sexual orientation, the **Daily
Record** referred to it as the *"council's bid to be as politically correct
as possible..."* shrieking: *"WE WANT TO KNOW YOUR SEX
SECRETS"*. The **Scottish Daily Mail** found councillors who
were ready to admit that the Council had *"impinged on civil liberties"*. Tory councillor, Daphne Sleigh was, as usual, prepared
to put her name down and blasted: *"I don't think someone's sexual orientation is anyone's business. I'm sure some staff will be horrified..."* Phil Gallie was reported gasping: *"I think it's obscene"*. A
gay manual council labourer said in the **Daily Record**: *"...If my
colleagues found out I was gay, I'd never hear the end of it"*. A point
of view, that was, after all, what the Council wanted to address.
The **Daily Record**'s sister, the **Sunday Mail** added columnist
Gary Keown to the furore. He scorned the *"cancer of political correctness"* that left *"no future in remaining a fairly strait-laced, fam-
ily-conscious taxpayer with no criminal convictions... Sadly, it
means some guy with a faultless CV could lose out on a job to a less
talented individual, just because the boss is under pressure to have
more blacks... Convicted killer Winston Silcott should have been
strung up... And it is a disgrace that Scotland's football team now has*

*a Jamaican who hadn't even set foot in the country until last week".*
He begged, *"decent and clean-living people be given back their
rights".* This obviously excluded Edinburgh City Council, recommending *"the PC mob"* should be burned at the stake.
Turning his attention to Glasgow's Glasgay! festival, he
attacked it as a pointless waste of time. *"I really don't feel the need
to pull on a feather boa and liberate myself in a public park. Sadly, I
have no kids otherwise, I could feign some faith in the system by rop-
ing in a couple of sex pests as babysitters".*

*"So many unattached young women in Scotland are cheap tarts at
heart",* cried Gary Keown in the **Sunday Mail**, attacking *"single
mums"* or the *"jobless strumpets"* who were given *"the cream of
the council housing stock",* depriving the *"normal family"* and a
*"pensioner who has been waiting three months for a hip op..."* He
accused *"loose ladies"* who participated in *"drunken knee-trem-
blers behind the pub bins"* of knowing *"the NHS will cough up to
keep their low-brow lifestyle intact",* citing the handing out of
morning-after pills by Lothian Primary Care Trust to *"floozies".*
These were women he felt deserved to be made *"outcasts by
society... It's not pills these 'ladies' need... They should be clamping
them with chastity belts".* He advised: *"I DO understand, girls...
Should you fail to snare an unsuspecting chap with a baby or some
other kind of emotional blackmail, the benefits of becoming a fallen
woman are obvious".* This was just the excuse Gary Keown needed to bemoan the demise of the Oxo advert and the personifi-
cation of the *"normal family".* Who was going to replace them,
he cried? *"Maybe we'll get a gay couple and their test-tube twins".*

His opinion of women in a top-selling tabloid was decidedly suspect. Why would a chap go to an over-priced drinking
hole, he asked in his regular **Sunday Mail** column, *"if it wasn't
for the chance to pick up a slapper?"* He accused female graduates
of being *"the most shameless bunch of flirts this side of Bangkok"*
and branded women's rights campaigners: *"Horrendous... neu-
rotic bra-burners",* raising their heads and letting *"their bellies
rumble far too often to be taken seriously. If you're a man, they'll castrate you on the spot..."* he advised, denouncing Scottish
Women's Aid and Zero Tolerance as *"a menace".* Keown called
on them to *"Disband. Get a life and get something approaching a
sense of humour... Lighten up and stop getting your knickers in a
twist. If you do that, and you're halfway decent-looking, I might even*

*take one of you out sometime"*. Of Lorraine Mann, seeking to job-share a position as Member of the Scottish Parliament, he was equally scathing: *"What does she think being an MSP entails? Turning up two days a week, in between her coffee mornings and watching TV soaps? If she's so eager to jobshare, she should go and work at a fruit shop or hat stall"*.

The film 'Dogma', controversially dealing with aspects of Catholicism, had Gerald Cunningham writing to Aberdeen's **Press and Journal**, bemoaning the restraints put upon him by so-called 'political correctness'. *"No one would be allowed to insult and mock homosexuals and lesbians in the way we Catholics are so mocked and insulted in this film. Political correctness is the order of the day"*.

In a plea for men to *"rise up and make a stand - in every sense, including the naughtiest one"*, Ally Ross in the **Scottish Sun** was niggled by an *"overabundance of equal opportunities legislation"*. He wrote: *"One or two blokes I know even sneaked a look at the drawings of the Gerry Adams lookalike humping that ugly hippy bird, every which way, in The Joy of Sex book. And the moody cows are still not happy... Court papers reveal that 30-year-old Tina Bacon felt she wasn't getting porked enough... Deluged by feminist propaganda and right-on diktats from the Government's PC thought-police, males are increasingly treated like second-class citizens"*.

When Judy Owen challenged sexism in the workplace - which she claimed included bosses referring to women players as 'dykes and lesbians', and being told that ladies were not allowed to wear trousers - she took the bosses at the Professional Golfer's Association to court. The **Scottish Daily Mail** claimed the PGA was *"proud of its equal opportunities record – half its staff are female"*. An astonished Chief Executive Sandy Jones told the **Mail**: *"Just because we haven't got a written-down policy does not mean to say that we don't actively practise equal opportunities"*. When Judy arrived at the court, her 'work-mates' were waiting for her *"all wearing dresses and skirts to show their solidarity with their bosses"*. With echoes of 'Stepford Wives', one woman told the **Daily Record** how much they liked the *"happy atmosphere"* of where they worked.

After a gay group, calling itself Direct Action taped a military policeman suggesting gays should be shot; army chiefs banned Military Police from patrolling outside Edinburgh

Castle. The crackdown was ordered because top brass *"feared militant gay activists"* would launch a revenge attack on the Redcaps. According to the **Scottish Sun**, they were living in fear. An insider told the **Scottish Sun**: *"Somehow the gays also found out where the officer was living... Now he has received personal threats and his family are under army protection"*. Another Military Policeman added: *"They are terrified that the MP patrols and the gays might clash, and spark off a war... We are being made to look like big girls' blouses"*, the MP gushed. *"The bosses want to be seen to be very politically correct over the gays. So this lot who have promised to cause trouble can get away with it"*.

With gay sex still far more serious an offence than fighting, the **Scottish Sun**'s attention was once again in the corporals' mess at Edinburgh castle at 4am on a Saturday night after a *"sordid"* charity bash. On what most **Sun** readers would comfortably call a 'blow-job', Kenny McAlpine reported: *"A military policeman had a sex act performed on him by a gay pal at a boozy bash..."* Army chiefs launched a *"probe"* and the tabloid gasped: *"It's believed the man who performed the sex act is training to be a MINISTER"*. An Army insider spluttered: *"This is the craziest thing I have ever heard anyone doing in the Army... He just stood there and let this man perform a sex act in front of everyone. It's the talk of the place... There had been a lot to drink but this pair's behaviour just went way over the top. It wasn't just military policemen who were there, there was also civilian police. No one could believe what they were seeing. His colleagues grappled the guy from the floor and turfed him out"*. His moment of pleasure, witnessed - as the **Scottish Sun** described, by *"a dozen disgusted guests"* – had Ministry of Defence investigators concerned since the incident involved a civilian and Corporal Steven Daniels was promptly suspended. The *"insider"* told the tabloid: *"Most of the men didn't agree with it but put up with them. Then he rubs their noses in it and shames the army before he leaves"*.

'Old Mother Burnie' was forced to channel her disgust at a Scottish town in her **Daily Record** column. *"Nairn - Nairn! I ask you - is allegedly after a bloke to wear this year's gala Queen's robes and crown"*. Aberdeen's Press & Journal quoted the rector of the Academy who sensibly advised: *"Highland Regional Council operates an equal opportunities policy and we have a responsibility to implement that policy"*. But he left the broadsheet's editorial in a quandary. *"Either the gala organisers relent; bow to the tide of opinion, and ask for a king to be appointed, too. Or councillors decide to take a stand against political correctness; press on regardless and declare The People's Republic of Nairn for a week in July"*. The **Press & Journal** dug up some wag of a district council vice-convenor, Norman McCulloch to quip: *"Being politically correct is one thing, but this is going right over the top. So they want us to appoint a male queen as well?"* Fellow councillor, David Fraser could barely restrain himself: *"I think this is all a fairy story. I can hardly believe what I'm hearing"*.

When Justice Minister Jim Wallace said on Forth FM: *"There will be no bastards in the new Scotland"* he referred to new legislation giving unmarried fathers legal rights in Scotland and expunging the term 'illegitimate' from the vocabulary of family law. A **Daily Mail** reporter described it as *"politically correct"*, leaving the Mail to ask: *"...Is it needed?"*

After makers, Hasbro recognised their Sindy doll was a little girl's aspirational rôle model, fulfilling the dreams and adventures they had, including playing football, **The Herald** reported, *"Sindy the doll has turned politically correct and donned a football kit, albeit in pink..."*

# Chapter Seven
## *Rounding Up the Perverts, Self Hate and Moss Mattresses*

> *"I think I'm done with the sofa*
> *I think I'm done with the hall*
> *I think I'm done with the kitchen table, baby!*
> *Let's go outside (let's go outside) in the sunshine..."*
> **George Michael**

Ever since Charles Craddock invented the word 'homo-sexuality' – an inspired cocktail of Latin and Greek - generations of gays have poured over medical textbooks seeking explanations and cures for their burgeoning sexuality. Apart from electric-shock treatment and hypnosis, precious little has been on offer.

Stumbling on a niche market, Christian evangelists came up with 'conversion therapy'. Andrew Comiskey, a soft-spoken, jet-setting American with a book to sell, reckoned: "To be dominated by erotic and emotional feelings for the same sex is, for many people, not something that is a source of ease, or peace, in real life". If he hoped thousands of self-hating closet gays in Britain would clear the shelves of his book, he may well have been right! He certainly wasn't alone. Drag queen Candy first saw the light, kneeling at the foot of her waterbed. Now, with that vital heterosexual component of a wife - herself a former lesbian conversion-job called Ann - Candy introduced himself as John Paulk, set up Love In Action and declared himself to be "dedicated to helping people coming out of homosexuality". And when 26-year-old Simon Harvey filled his car with exhaust fumes leaving a suicide note explaining that as a gay Christian, he was "too filthy to live", his father, believing gay sexuality to be driven by little more than "impious thoughts", promptly tore it up and opened the doors of U-turn Anglia. He too became dedicated to curing the 'perverted'.

It wasn't all plain sailing in the ex-gay ministry business.

Chris Metcalf, a 'counsellor' at the True Freedom Trust who denied sexual encounters with converts, faced accusations from young men like Alec Kemp who claimed Metcalf had given him "a very sexual hug and was clearly aroused" and Drew Payne who said "he was rubbing his groin against mine".

With so much of gay sexuality still secret, those who brought it all out into the open were often deeply resented and accused of 'banging their drum'. Outrage!, a gay human rights group fronted by Peter Tatchell, became a regular target. Labelled 'Red Pete' by the tabloids, and a 'militant left-winger', Tatchell was in fact a Democratic Socialist. His picture was doctored by the **News of the World** to make him look grossly effeminate in lipstick and eyeliner. The **Sunday Times** once focused its attention on *"barking mad"* gay campaigner Peter Tatchell and *"his handful of supporters called Outrage!"* The half-page spread, by journalist Brian Deer, dismissed Tatchell as insane, his arguments little more than a reflection on *"how deep his own injuries go"*. The frank submission was made even more remarkable by Deer's confession within the feature to being gay himself! It was a surprising appraisal of Peter Tatchell, a lifelong pacifist who 'outed' a handful of bishops who had voted for anti-gay motions at a Church of England synod. None of the clergy subsequently denied it in public and David Jenkins, the former Bishop of Durham, even went as far as to describe the outing as "a perfectly reasonable and understandable tactic". Rupert Murdoch's press, which include the **Sunday Times** and **Sun** newspapers, harbour no such principles when they indiscriminately 'out' public figures to boost their readership. Even so, Deer chose to join the journo-mob, planting the jackboot of the British press firmly up Tatchell's backside. *"Obnoxious creep"* one newspaper described him. A *"terrorist"* squealed the **Daily Mail**; a *"fascist"*, barked the **Daily Express** and *"the most odious man in Britain"* seethed London's **Evening Standard**. As for the so-called 'gay friendly' newspapers, **The Guardian** thought him *"a hypocrite as well as an intimidator"* and **The Independent** found *"few less attractive characters in British public"*. Even London's former gay weekly, **Capital Gay**, joined the scrum, devoting a two-page spread to a readers' survey that asked: *"Peter Tatchell: Prince or Prat?"* before exposing a surprisingly lacklustre capital unanimously plumping for the latter!

After denouncing outing as a *"brutality that is literally fascistic"* and *"an act of fascist terrorism"*, Allan Massie warned in the **Daily Telegraph** that Peter Tatchell might be the target of an assassin which, he added, *"many might think quite an honourable part to play"*. Such a tacit 'invitation' to murder was helped when television news bulletins showed a close-up of Peter Tatchell's letter to the Bishop of Durham, Dr Hope, displaying his address and telephone number. As a result of such persistent vilification, Tatchell says: "Bricks have been thrown through my windows, swastikas painted on my front door, my locks have been jammed with super glue and nails, and rubbish has been dumped on the doorstep. I have received everything in the post from dog droppings to bullets, razor blades, white feathers, sexually sadistic diagrams, invitations to my own funeral and newspaper photographs of myself embellished with drawings of daggers in my throat and guns blowing out my brains. My phone has brought me a stream of obscene hate calls and death threats, including middle-of-the-night calls where the caller very calmly and quietly utters a single word associated with death, such as coffin or morgue, and hangs up. I have been punched and spat at in the street, threatened with knives and broken bottles on the Tube: I have had cans, wood, screwdrivers, fruit, coins, paint and stones hurled at me from passing cars".

Peter Tatchell conducted a peaceful, but widely reported action, interrupting the homophobic Archbishop of Canterbury's service to take the platform and condemn his stance on equality. Richard Littlejohn wrote in the **Scottish Sun** that he wanted to see lifelong pacifist and human rights campaigner, Peter Tatchell posted outside the Rangers football ground, *"handing out his leaflets at the Auld Firm derby at Ibrox on Sunday afternoon"*. He remarked that Tatchell *"should have been dragged from Canterbury Cathedral and clubbed like a baby seal"*.

Graeme Woolaston, an occasional contributor to **The Herald**, wrote to the broadsheet to express his opinion. *"As a contributor to The Herald from an openly gay perspective, on the occasions when it is relevant, can I make it clear to Herald readers that neither Peter Tatchell nor the wholly London-based Outrage! have any mandate whatsoever for their repeated claim to speak for the gay* *community. On the contrary, most gay men believe that the impact of Tatchell's grossly inflated ego, humourlessness, and total lack of personal charm has significantly held back progress towards greater acceptance of us in public life"*. Of course, Peter Tatchell has never claimed to speak for the gay community.

By the early nineties, there was at last one regular 'out' gay columnist writing for a national newspaper: but what a disappointment! John Lyttle in **The Independent** wrote in one of his columns: *"Actually, I hate gay men. Loathe them..."* after claiming someone squeezed his bum in a crowded gay bar.

Unfortunately, it is only a deep sense of shame that closeted gays bring with them after being 'outed'. Over 40 years ago, Peter Wildeblood, former diplomatic correspondent for the intensely homophobic **Daily Mail**, served time for 'homosexual offences' as a result of the notorious Lord Montagu scandal in the fifties. He wrote: *"I am no more proud of my condition than I would be of having a glass eye or a harelip"*. He went on to give evidence to a Departmental Committee set up by the Government on the subject!

When the gay sexuality of playwright John Osborne was revealed after his death by his lover, so too were accusations that Osborne had mocked the "clamouring AIDS lobby", supported Section 28 and condemned equal rights campaigns by "fairies" and "poofs". Gay Russian playwright Nikolai Gogol went one better. At the age of 42, his sense of shame led him to starve himself to death.

Posthumously blowing the lid off the closets of such men as the head of the American FBI, J Edgar Hoover and Senator McCarthy's right-hand man, the late Roy Cohn, likewise revealed two men who had ruthlessly persecuted gays throughout the fifties.

It can be equally baffling why so many MP's in the House of Commons, allegedly gay or bisexual, should want to vote against an equal age of consent. Such a paradox - a thorn in the foot of gay emancipation - has a morbid parallel: some of the world's worst serial killers of gays were themselves gay: Fraserburgh-born Dennis Nilsen, Jeffrey Dahmer and Michael Lupo, to name a few. Behind the repression of sexuality follows pathology and crime. In September of 1995, 21-year-old fishpacker, Daniel Harding went out for a drink with his soon-to-be married neighbour, Allan Williamson, and murdered him on Broadsea Shore, near Fraserburgh. He was charged with repeatedly striking his alleged victim with rocks and pieces of wood, stripping him naked, cutting him with a knife and - as **The Courier** in Dundee delicately put it - *"performing other acts on him"*. Harding hurled his friend over a 30-foot cliff, stripped him naked and, as the **Daily Record** said: *"Carried out a vile sex act"*.

There is little to recommend hiding or repressing sexuality, yet it should come as no surprise to find, at the heart of sexual repression, the Church. Despite an appalling record of massacres, murders, burnings, torture, rape, pillage and homosexual persecution over the centuries, Christianity still maintains an effective foothold within the gay movement. In fact, the Lesbian and Gay Christian Movement has been for many years the largest gay membership organisation in the UK.

Another gay membership organisation in the UK - originally set up in the early seventies - the Gay Outdoor Club boasts groups throughout Scotland, including Glasgow, Edinburgh, Inverness and the Borders. It has a full calendar of events, which include swimming, cycling, windsurfing, badminton, rock-climbing, caving, canoeing, hill-walking, hostelling and camping weekend events across the country. There are a high proportion of professional men within its membership. Organised walks have attracted businessmen, company directors and even a Tory MP. Many are sensitive to public exposure. One teacher privately expressed his a fear of "young people being openly recruited to the club". Another teacher from the Midlands told me he feared if that happened he would have to leave the club. A few years later, he was 'outed' at his school following a serious blackmail attempt by a young man he had met. Fortunately, he had the school's support during the ordeal. Former Glasgow organiser Douglas Bingham claimed opposition had been voiced in the past to any affiliation of the Gay Outdoor Club with the Scottish Youth Hostel Association. "I've been a member for almost 20 years since I was 19. I was at a GOC meeting when this was discussed and I was disappointed", he said.

Threats to politicise the club by involving the Gay Outdoor Club in campaigns for gay equality were met with a barrage of protest in its newsletter. *"I go out with GOC to get away from all the political crap"*, snapped one committee member. *"I for one am not prepared to man the barricades every time some issue or other crops up and certainly prefer to walk up a small hill in northern Britain rather than march in London on some demo..."* wrote another angry member. *"Do we want some sort of frivolous group to organise 'pink picnics?'"* added yet another in exasperation.

The inclusion of young people in the Gay Outdoor Club hasn't always been met with universal approval. *"There are enough screaming queens on the scene without GOC becoming Priscilla, Queen of the Pennines"*, wrote one disgusted member. Another suggested *"we should be trying to attract the thousands of totally closeted gays within organisations such as the Ramblers Association, rather than letting GOC degenerate to a level that may attract youngsters with no sports interests out of the gay clubs"*. Yet another was more forthright: *"If you want an outdoor club for the out under 25's... Why not start one? But don't call it GOC"*.

When a 16-year-old gay youth turned up at a weeklong Hogmanay bash at the start of 1997 organised by the Gay Outdoor Club outside Stirling, he walked into the epicentre of a shock-wave of hysteria that was still sweeping the country in the wake of Thomas Hamilton's massacre of a classroom of kids in nearby Dunblane. One man holding a sensitive government position panicked and promptly booked in at a nearby hotel. Another spent the night in his van before driving home. A small group, including a doctor and a couple of teachers, gathered in the lounge to decide the fate of the tearful youth before he was sent packing shortly before midnight. Said one man: "I'm sorry for him, but this is all too close to Dunblane". The youth later turned up at an organised gay badminton group in Glasgow. The leader, a gay teacher, was forced to abandon the group, citing his presence as one of the reasons.

The Gay Outdoor Club's behaviour is certainly not unique. Lesbian group KENRIC and Catholic group QUEST have also been forced to take on board cautious and conservative views expressed by its members, many of whom live in isolation outside city conurbations. These organisations are not - of course - political, yet, paradoxically, are part of gay movement directly affected by the weight of global discrimination meted out to them.

According to the **Scottish Daily Mail**, theatre impresario, Cameron Mackintosh was *"miffed"* about his name being added to a list defending Sir Ian McKellen's right as a gay man to receive a knighthood. (Apparently, he never read the covering letter). Cameron - who once ranked number 81 of Britain's richest people, owns 12,000 acres in Mallaig on the west coast of Scotland, donated £10,000 to the Conservative Party and has lived with his boyfriend for almost 20 years - smugly told the **Scottish Daily Mail**: *"Why does one owe it to the gay population to come out? It's nobody's business but mine. And I certainly resent the suggestion that I am any kind of gay rights campaigner. I am the exact opposite. I just want to be as integrated as any human being".* To help him on his way, the **Scottish Daily Mail** pictured him hugging, not his boyfriend, but Ruthie Henshall, a star in his production of 'Les Miserables'.

Research in both Italy and the US has uncovered evidence of homophobia being linked to the suppression of homosexuality. Living on the Hebridean Isle of Harris, John Macleod - the son of a minister of the Free Presbyterian Church, Professor Donald Macleod - is a **Herald** columnist with a reprehensible record of homophobia. Just 12 weeks after the brutal murder of Michael Doran in Glasgow's Queen's Park and in response to comedian Michael Barrymore's spectacular admission that he was gay, Macleod focused on *"forbidden desires"*, describing gays as *"unnatural… dangerous…"* and *"evil"*. He linked homosexuality to *"promiscuity, instability, neurosis, substance abuse, suicide, untold depths of degradation, misery, self-loathing"* and declared gays *"simply not equipped to live"*. This was apparently *"borne out by study upon study"*. (Omitting to say, of course, that those discredited studies were both conducted and funded by right-wing American Christian groups). The tramp of Jesus-in-jackboots across the pages of a newspaper not shy of muscular Christianity didn't stop there. Macleod praised closets who were persuaded that the expression of homosexuality was *"absolutely and in all circumstances wrong"* with the pronouncement that *"…theirs, in the end, is lasting fame and glory. Theirs is the Kingdom of Heaven…"* After warning that the outcome of Michael Barrymore's behaviour would end *"in the next world if not in this, in his utter destruction"*, he fumed that the comedian's *"spectacular declaration forces our attention, yet again, to homosexu-*

*ality. The gay lobby can scarcely believe their luck. A new star has joined their ranks and not a stereotypical flounce, like Larry Grayson; not a barbed lounge-lizard like Noel Coward; not such a glorious pansy as Julian Clary; not even such a manifest lump of evil as the late Derek Jarman, but a popular, straight-acting, wholesome family entertainer. And the gay lobby will make the most of it".* John Macleod even suggested after MP Ron Davies was caught on Clapham Common, that perhaps the gossip would cease *"only if Ron Davies were obligingly to kill himself".* Over Peter Mandelson's 'outing' on BBC's 'Newsnight', he suggested: *"I suspect... the incident caused him dreadful private pain",* then added, *"he has not obligingly killed himself".* And of gays in the Government...? *"Many, of course, hold sincerely that the presence of open homosexuals in Government is the end of civilisation as we know it, and a judgement on the land. The merits of that I leave aside".* For at least two years, **The Herald**'s contribution to World AIDS Day was suspect. John Macleod wrote: *"It has fallen to me to write a column for World Aids Day..."* In doing so, he turned on some of AIDS' more prolific victims: *"Wicked men like ...Derek Jarman"* and *"...the absurd Liberace".* Focusing on the Mbuma Mission Hospital in Zimbabwe, run by the Free Presbyterian Church of Scotland, he claimed: *"The storm in Africa rages on. The storm in the West, now abates".* And introduced people living with AIDS in Africa as *"the facts of Aids in the real world..."*

There were cracks in the wall. Writing in **The Herald** on the Synod Reports of the Free Presbyterian Church, John Macleod's ramblings developed into something verging on homoeroticism. *"For once it was not the usual litany of negativism against... homosexuality..."* With the concept of Hell a central tenet of his belief, he added: *"The section on morals, though caught my eye. It addresses the issue of post-modernism as one of the colourfully styled 'Devil's beans' - a lure, among New Age superstition and humanist optimism, whereby sinners 'are led to the place where happiness never enters... Post modernism fascinates me because, for near a year, I have struggled with it. Last summer - it happened a few weeks after a notorious family crisis -* (his father was accused of molesting women in his Church) *my entire world-view, built over 30 years, and founded largely upon the tenets of Evangelicalism, collapsed. Suddenly... It was a glorious day and I rose to a strange buzzing. The buzzing was* *that of a strimmer, a man cutting grass. It was a youth I knew well, a man who had scarcely darkened the door of a church in his life... but someone... in our acquaintance very good for me... We lounged on the grass to talk. But a switch threw in my mind then, a switch yet to throw back; within an hour I had begun demolishing ugly little trees in my garden... I found myself hacking and sawing for the next few days, thinking the same words: 'nothing makes sense. Nothing makes sense...' It still doesn't".* John Macleod was soon forced to plug the gap. *"The Bible to me is an absolute. In all my conflicts I have yet to be convinced of any inaccuracy, inconsistency, or contradiction on the pages of the Book".*

John Macleod's torment was his own expression of homosexuality struggling beneath the weight of his religious upbringing. When challenged, he e-mailed me: *"I will come out in my own time and in my own way and on my own terms and not at the behest of the likes of you".* He offered some insight into the difficult path he had to take in 'coming out' to himself as a gay man in **The Herald** when he remarked crossly: *"Hell was a swearword. Now, so help us, Hell is a joke".* In his feature, *"mocking the reality of Hell",* he was outraged over naming a TV programme 'Neighbours From Hell' and a glossy advertisement in the press for a 4 x 4 vehicle that showed *"the beast at the bottom of Bedean nam Beann with the friendly slogan: 'Stick it where the hell you like'... This spoofing of a central tenet in Christian faith is offensive, ignorant and dangerous",* he remarked crossly.

He offered the following apology for publication in **ScotsGay**, a magazine he was *"doubtful if the majority – even a plurality – of Scotland's gay population read..."* His apology came with the caveat: *"Out me if you choose. I will deal with you in The Herald... I will share with all Scotland how the self-appointed princes of the 'gay community' behave".* His statement read: *"Thanks for drawing my attention to a column I wrote in The Herald in September 1995, following the 'outing' of Michael Barrymore, in which I wrote of homosexuality in violent and hysterical terms and - which seems especially to have left abiding hurt and anger - used the phrase 'gays are simply not equipped to live'. Four years feels like a lifetime ago now, and I have travelled much in my intellectual and emotional life. Many have followed my journeying through my weekly column and it will be apparent my attitudes have changed in many respects. I unequivocally apologise for the offensive and absurd comments in that* *column and in others of similar vein: I think there were comparable beauties in December 1991 and May 1993. I hope anyone hurt by these - and I am thinking especially of young people in isolated, rural and perhaps unco guid Scottish communities - will forgive me. I have always written what I believe to be true; and I have never been ashamed to put my name to any article, written truly in a specific time and place. For this authenticity I do not apologise".*

While this apology was being prepared for publication in **ScotsGay**, he turned on *"militant gay activists"* in his column using the words: *"thugs of Scotland"*.

Away from Scotland and some of its retrenched sexual values, in Amsterdam, a huge billboard was erected to promote the production of Mark Ravenhill's internationally acclaimed play, Shopping and Fucking. When the same play appeared at the Citizen's Theatre in Glasgow, more discrete signs appeared advertising only Shopping and F***ing. At the same time, in a prominent display along Glasgow's Buchanan Street, few could escape the cheeky juxtaposition – or as Peter Hitchens put it in the **Daily Mail**: *"a slyly misspelt obscenity… an arrogant assault on gentleness and decency"* - of letters abbreviating the fashion store, French Connection UK, FCUK. This fell far short of Amsterdam's posters, two years before when the gay club, iT promoted its d'mix night on posters round the city depicting a naked heterosexual couple on roller-skates apparently performing anal intercourse. The city burghers didn't loose any sleep and its residents lived to see another day. FCUK may have got away with it to a point, but five years later, in 2001, the Advertising Standards Authority accused the clothes chain of bringing advertising into disrepute when they produced posters advertising their website address: fcukinkybugger.com in shops where children could see them. The ASA claimed their ads brought about the highest amount of complaints that year, a measly 136.

Amsterdam has always been markedly more liberal than British cities. Alongside the Homomonument, erected in the centre of the city to honour the gay men and women who lost their lives in wars, there is a bridge over the Keizersgracht. It was re-named Niek Engelschmann Bridge after the founder of the Dutch gay emancipation organisation, COC. Not until the end of 2000 was any plaque dedicated to gays erected in the UK on a public toilet in north London in honour of the first public act of gay defiance against police harassment. The honouring of gay men and women who gave their lives in two World wars for a freedom that was never theirs have always been met with derision by much of the British press and all leading Scottish gay rights campaigner Ian Dunn received after his death was a press obituary. When Scottish Catholic leader Cardinal Thomas Winning died in the summer of 2001, he had compared gays to German Nazi bombers, called homosexuality a 'perversion' and 'a disorder that had to be dealt with'. He lay in state in an open coffin before representatives from government, church and even the royal family attended his funeral amidst acres of nauseatingly sycophantic press coverage which included a contribution from John Macleod who wrote: *"It was brave of him to take on the gay lobby, one of the nastiest out, over the Section 28 debate…"*

All too often, when the city of Glasgow took a step toward becoming a liberal, progressive European capital it was hampered by the dictates of well-organised religionists, an inhibited media and moribund Labour councillors, as the banning of an exhibition of erotica clearly demonstrated. But has Glasgow ever been the moral, pure and sanctimonious city its media, churches and some of its civic leaders would have the citizens believe? True, only seven years ago, a MORI poll found a startling 36% of Scots baying for homosexuality to be made a criminal offence. And whereas 74% of the UK supported an equal age of consent in a Harris poll, only a meagre 9% of Scots could stomach it. Some comfort can be gleaned from the fact that what Scots say or do in public is often quite different to what they do in private! Grahame Miller, writing in **Gay Times** tried to explain this conservativism as *"symptomatic of an endemic Scottish malaise that stems ultimately from our status as a subject nation and our consequent lack of self-confidence"*. But lack of self-confidence could hardly explain Divally's. In the shadow of St Enoch's shopping centre, Divally's was an unusual socio-sexual construct. A Glasgow cinema-cum-pub where men leant up against the bar talking in voices hard enough to grate cheese, sometimes slipping through a back door to watch 'straight' erotica. It was also a place where a number of gay and bisexual men I spoke to claimed they easily enjoyed many a brief sexual experience. The police have raided the club on a number of occasions.

And sex on the streets? For years, Glasgow City Council dismissed any suggestion the city had any problem with sex workers whilst they supported a virulent police campaign to rid its streets of them. Not until after hundreds of arrests, repeated convictions and the murder of seven female sex workers was one of its councillors, John Moyne forced to admit in front of reporters that he "may have been wrong". Since then, in a curious dichotomy, and in what was been described as "a step forward", police were employed to both protect *and* arrest sex workers at the same time. Such behaviour would have surprised the eminent eighteenth century Scottish lawyer and writer, James Boswell who simply enjoyed sex with 'whores' in the open.

The plush, warm, darkened atmosphere of picture-houses was once the favourite place for a kiss and cuddle away from the grim reality of the Glasgow tenements. Green's Playhouse in Glasgow was once the biggest, fitted with two-seater cinema seats, encouraging a little more than a close embrace. In the thirties, the Glasgow's street gangs used to turn out the gas lamps in the tenement close and enjoy the classic 'knee trembler' up against the tiled walls. Frequently under the noses of the tenants and police who usually turned a blind eye. Gay sex is still frequently performed in private, outdoors. This is not quite the contradiction it first seems. As in any other major cities of the world, there are parks and open spaces where men cruise, seeking sexual contact with other men. One of the reasons that sex in 'public places' occurs is because - particularly in the instance of gay or bisexual men - there is no privacy in the marital home. Or because being seen with strange men might evoke suspicion from family, friends or neighbours in a close-knit community. In his book, 'Erotics and Politics', sociologist, Tim Edwards says: *"Public sex is paradoxically only public to the extent that it is not practised at home".* He adds: *"Local councils and police authorities deploy prison-like restrictions on these activities. The history of cottaging (and cruising) is, in fact, one of increasing sexual regulation whilst sexual activity has constantly widened and spread further into other areas".*

When researching a history of gay sex, it is not the positive aspects of picnics, nude swims, beach parties, forming of lasting relationships or brief sexual encounters on gay beaches or open spaces that is found. In law, gay lifestyles are represented as acts of criminal behaviour recorded in press cuttings for posterity. They are manifest in reports of moral policing, arrests, censure and condemnation from a media only too willing to endorse the censorial denunciation of chaste and reproachful religious leaders. And of course, there are reports of brutal attacks and murders. Gays occasionally have sex in the sand dunes of gay beaches in much the same way as anyone else. When exposed in a negative way by the media, gay sexuality is tainted by the notion that it is somehow more dirty; sinful; disgusting - and perverted. Heterosexuality is treated altogether differently as **Auto Trader** magazine's TV advert neatly demonstrated. A car parked up on a deserted beach, its windows misted, rocking furiously, in an otherwise positive portrayal of so-called 'sex in public'.

In modern, progressive, liberal cities like Amsterdam, reaction against sex in open spaces from religionists, editors, the police or public is not nearly so vociferous as it is here. Unlike Britain, the history of tolerance in the Netherlands is backed by legislation. A Dutch MP faced prosecution after suggesting homosexuals were no better than thieves and the Prime Minister Wim Kok even challenged the homophobic comments of a religious leader on television. Without such legislation to curb incitement to hatred, minorities are vulnerable to attack.

If someone wanted to make it compulsory to wear bathing costumes on a Dutch beach, special permission would have to be sought. Families usually congregate nearest parked cars and amenities as on British beaches, but most women sunbathe and swim topless. In Britain, they would face arrest. Neither is the public faced with a battery of warning signs when approaching a nudist area. It often integrates quite naturally, further along the beach. Gay beaches usually tag on at the end! Amsterdam's main gay beach is at Zandvoort with other beaches at Bergen Aan Zee and Scheveningen. During the summer in Amsterdam, trains are packed with day-trippers heading for the coast. They are not all heading out for ice creams and donkey-rides! Many gay men are drawn by the exciting prospect of sex in the dunes. It is not moral police or heterosexuals straying off the beaten track that constitute a problem for them, but a particular thistle used to keep the dunes together. For those who had the misfortune to encounter it, one enterprising sales-person occasionally trawls the beach selling tweezers!

Glasgow boasts three gay beaches within easy reach of the city, at Prestwick, Irvine and Stevenston. Ten years ago, the beach at Gailes, near Irvine was one of the most popular gay beaches in Scotland. That was before the summer of 1991 when a **Sun** photographer eagerly snapped a recalcitrant young, mar-ried police officer with his trousers round his ankles. He was put under investigation and suspended from duty. The result was an increase in moral policing and an attempt to wipe out nudism along this lonely stretch of the Ayrshire coast.

Prohibitive attitudes to sex *al fresco* are underpinned in Scotland by the media, police and a moribund church trying to define and regulate a code of behaviour that outlaws sex out-side marriage. The police and local authorities apply authori-tarian constraints, marshalling the population into practices conforming to the political and social ideologies of the day. But the wearing of costumes on beaches has not always been so rig-orously imposed. At the turn of the century, bathing naked was commonplace and a subject that inspired artists in the late nine-teenth century, like Henry Scott Tuke. His pictures of boys bathing would raise a storm of protest in today's moral climate. There was also the internationally acclaimed impressionist painter, Seurat who's painting 'Bathing at Asnières' perfectly captured boys swimming in the shimmering heat of a hot sum-mer's afternoon on the banks of the Seine. While the National Vigilance Association busily mapped out 'moral danger zones' like beaches, the Social Purity and Hygiene Movement set out to cover the nation's 'shame'. Before women were allowed to join the police force, several thousand women patrols, initially set up by the National Union of Women's Workers and funded by the police, patrolled parks and open spaces, initially to 'guide young and foolish girls' and save men from 'women of evil reputation'. One volunteer was described as being so dis-turbed by the activities she witnessed on a park bench at night that she had them boarded up. By 1918 Sir Leonard Dunning, Inspector of Constabulary was calling them the 'true guardians of the State in public morals'. Glasgow's billboards have been awash with one uniformed female officer chasing a group of naked boys with a stick along a stretch of the Serpentine in London's Hyde Park, advertising the popular Scottish soft drink, Irn Bru. More recently, Scottish editions of **The Sun** were declaring: *"Sex ban at lovers' lane"* after angry residents at Miller's Knowe, near Hawick wanted the road leading to a secluded spot blocked to stop *"saucy goings-on"*. A particularly astute Hawick councillor, Tom Hogg warned: *"When couples go up there at night they are not going up to gaze at the stars"*.

Iain Hector Ross in his Highland View in the **Scottish Daily Express** did a piece on a car park and picnic site above North Kessock which doubles as a gay cruising area and a place where the public go to observe the dolphins in the Moray Firth. *"It's the Highland constabulary in the middle I feel sorry for"*, he confessed, since they *"find themselves in the rather awkward position of trying to maintain a balanced approach to both groups while trying very hard to keep them out of each other's way…"* Detailing the *"balanced approach"* he reported: *"The police have apparently taken to plain-clothes, undercover observation of the site, disguising themselves on alternate shifts as either Black Isle farmers or dolphins-loving environmentalists, just to be fair to both sides"*.

If windbreaks were solely erected for breaking wind, then the long stretch of sand and secluded dunes near the Garnock estuary at Irvine would be fortified with flapping canvases as far as the eye could see. But the windbreak never was just about breaking wind: it is the family fortress, pitched to hide our 'shame' and do away with the inconvenience of having to wrestle with undergarments behind a small towel. Apart from Cleat's Shore, near Lagg on the Isle of Arran, Ardeer, near Stevenston is the only official naturist beach in Scotland - perhaps this is also why there are few windbreaks on Ardeer! Speaking volumes about Scottish attitudes to nudity, Ardeer is difficult to reach, strewn with broken concrete and backs onto a former ICI explosives manufacturing plant. As far as the quality of the water goes, with partially treated sewage gushing out of a long outfall pipe, it fails to meet even EC minimum standards. No one is very sure when it first got its reputation as a gay beach. I spoke to one of its oldest regulars, a man in his eighties who, while not exactly identifying himself as gay, remembered the beach at Ardeer in the thirties. He said, at the time, there had been an arrest on the beach of a couple of people bathing nude. He claimed the local sheriff reprimanded the police for not having something better to do. In a bid for privacy, regulars construct their own 'windbreaks' and individual enclosures from driftwood they find strewn along the beach. From some of the men who come here every summer there can be heard such antique expressions like 'he's on', to mark someone's gay proclivities.

In Britain during the 19th century, most villages and towns staged carnivals. Glasgow had the Glasgow Fair. If the sun was shining, many of its citizens flocked to the beaches in Ayrshire. The drinking, dancing, eating, fighting and sex provided a useful respite from the daily grind and they were celebrated throughout Scotland. Robbie Fishman, a Shetland Islander described these rituals to a University of Essex interviewer. "People dancing into the small hours after carding of wool and 'flatchies' (straw pellets) were spread out on the ground so that they could spend the night. This was a signal for the boys to come in". Wakes' weeks in the north and Whitsun in the south of England provided great opportunities for sexual encounters. The Victorians linked these events with immorality and succeeded in establishing sex segregation on many beaches used for bathing. The establishment of the Social Purity Movement paraded sexual repression with moral certainty, sexual prudery and Christian zeal. As fascism asserted itself across Europe, this led to an unashamed desire for racially 'pure' stock and a faith in science to deliver the ideal by interfering in sex lives.

Brighton housed high-class courtesans and prostitutes since Regency times, but during the inter-war years, with the development of transport and the ability of single men to afford holidays, Blackpool became the seaside sex capital of the UK. Secret doors linked hostel rooms that permitted sex to take place throughout the night. The sex that took place on the beach became a national scandal. In 1937, Mass Observation employed 23 investigators to do an anthropological study of beach sex at Blackpool. In a half an hour before midnight, they found 232 cases of petting; 120 cases of sitting down and embracing; 42 cases of standing up and embracing; 46 cases of lying on sand and embracing; 25 cases of sitting and kissing; nine cases of necking in cars; three cases of standing and kissing and seven cases of girls sitting on men's knees. After lines of observers had systematically beaten the sand dunes, one observer remarked: "When we began work in Blackpool we expected to see copulation everywhere: What we found was petting, feeling and masturbating one another". The research revealed very few cases of copulation, (only three), paralleling the sex that takes places on Britain's gay beaches and cruising areas today, which also amounts to little more than oral sex and mutual masturbation in most cases. Masturbation alone would have been enough to bring outrage in its time. Professor G Stanley Hall, once the world's leading authority on adolescence, described masturbation in 1911 as an "insidious disease", the "scourge of the human race" and "an influence that seems to spring from the Prince of Darkness". Today's commentators are, if nothing else, consistent with the past. In 2000, so-called "leading commentator" Gerald Warner attacked the Labour administration in **Scotland on Sunday** for introducing legislation that would treat gays equally: *"Christ has been supplanted by Mammon and every other horned beast... This country has sunk to unprecedented depths of barbarism and degeneracy"*.

On the gay beach at Prestwick, bulldozers have chomped into the sand dunes where men regularly sunbathe in hollows peppered by spent aircraft fuel from the aeroplanes taking-off and landing at Prestwick Airport. The notorious evangelical businessman, Brian Souter who launched a £2million crusade against 'gay sex lessons', once owned the airport. Prestwick pays the price for being within such easy reach of Glasgow being the most famous of gay beaches. Precious resources are ploughed into the regular moral policing of this stretch of beach in an area renowned for its conservatism, both politically and morally.

The **Daily Record**'s disapproval of *al fresco* sex stretched far beyond just moral indignation. Important sexual health work has been consistently challenged and discredited. The tabloid pounced on *"tacky"* magazine **Spurt!**, *"promoting sex in public"* and offering *"advice on how to pick up straight men"* to make its moral point. They made much of the annual £135,000 funding for Gay Men's Health and called on two ladies whose disapproval of gay sex was renown. First Daphne Sleigh, Tory group leader on Edinburgh council who asked: *"What has this got to do* *with men's health?"* She objected to the *"promotion"* of homosexuality and called **Spurt!** *"disgusting"*. Ann Allen, convenor the Church of Scotland's Board of Social Responsibility who is famous for promoting her evangelical views where and how she liked insisted **Spurt!** was *"advocating... sex where you like it and how you like it"*. The reasons and social history behind gay men meeting on Edinburgh's Calton Hill were brushed aside to wave a moral finger at the pursuit of sex. So too were the victims of appalling violence at this cruising area, including a Japanese tourist almost kicked to death in 1997.

The **Edinburgh Evening News** wrapped men cruising in the city in a headline labelled: *"DEATH OF DECENCY"*, calling the New Calton Cemetery *"a haunt for gay lovers"*. Few 'gay lovers' ever go there but it was still labelled a *"haunt"*. Finding it *"awash"* with, amongst other things, *"hypodermic needles"* the report then revealed not only gay men used it. The **News** found a 72-year-old woman overlooking the area to comment on *"that filth"* and Tory councillor Daphne Sleigh once again to bemoan the fact that the cemetery was *"frankly a no-go area after dark for most people"*. Why *"most"* people would want to go wandering around a graveyard at night anyway wasn't explained.

Preparing to build a new town on the outskirts of the Dutch city of Utrecht, provisions were made for an area where men could cruise to meet men. The ensuing controversy appeared not so much as to whether men could meet for sex but if society could actually construct such a space!

Another article in Edinburgh's **Evening News** featured the Royal Commonwealth Pool. Reporter Claire Gardner appeared to have reeled in horror at news that the sauna had *"become a pick-up joint"* for gay men. With a very pinched expression, one employee of the Dalkeith Road pool found the *"goings on"* so unspeakable he demanded anonymity before revealing how more and more gay men were using the sauna to pick up partners. *"To do it in a place where dads bring their kids at weekend is not fair to anyone... it's not fair on youngsters to be subjected in such a crass manner to gay sex"*, the employee added. *"They had a condom machine delivered earlier this week and we were told it was to be put up outside the male sauna to cater for the gay community needs... It's disgusting..."*, he said before reminding reporters he was not *"particularly homophobic"*. The **Evening News** checked out his story with Edinburgh Leisure but a representative told them there were no plans to install a condom machine outside the sauna. But never mind. The **Evening News** turned to Tory council leader Daphne Sleigh who told them: *"I'm surprised that management at the swimming pool are allowing this to go on. There should be more supervision... It should be dealt with at the highest level"*. Along with gymnasiums, saunas have been a place were gay men have met long before heterosexuals chose a quiet corner of an Asda car park. It is precisely because it is not labelled 'gay' that makes the sauna so popular with men wanting gay sex. Sex is, of course, a very healthy exercise, but how many actually end up in a sexual encounter on the premises depends on the availability of safe, private areas and the extent of moral policing. Men will always take chances, but considering the numbers of men interested in gay sex using the Commonwealth Pool sauna, there had been comparatively few incidences where police had been called. The Commonwealth swimming pool promotes moral policing to curb the slightest hint of sexual frisson and delivers a battery of warnings signs that advises of everything from 'family' changing areas to recommending showering in costumes. The showers have had an official marching up and down, inspecting them every few minutes. Not even in Victorian times were there such scenes of moral paranoia.

After the unbridled publicity offered by Edinburgh's **Evening News**, the **Scottish News of the World** sent its investigators to catch out the *"seedier side"* of the *"pool pervs"*. In his *"exclusive"*, David Taylor unconvincingly claimed, *"gay lovers were meeting there for sex sessions during their work breaks"*. And because so many men seeking gay sex were using the sauna, instead of chucking in the towel and holding gay sessions, the Commonwealth Pool ordered sauna users to cover up after they caught – in the words of the saintly **Scottish News of the World** - two men *"getting to know each other rather too well"*. The investigators were confronted by the unpardonable sight of men *"still walking around in the nude and getting changed without closing the curtains of their cubicles"*. A pool spokesman tried to reassure reporters that most of their sauna users were *"respectable people"*. These were presumably the ones forced to sweat it out in polyester swimsuits! The Commonwealth Pool was left fidgeting awkwardly behind a towel and the tabloid advised; *"the ban on nudity has also been extended to the swimming pool changing area"*. One sauna user complained on a public posting on Usenet that he witnessed a sign that read: No Nude Showering! He said he questioned this at the front desk since he found it helpful to shower in the nude but was told that this was necessary because "society is full of perverts and homosexuals".

There are other open spaces in Scotland where gay men have traditionally gathered. Outside Edinburgh, on Scotland's east coast, lies the beach at Aberlady. Here, those who have survived the hike across the Nature Reserve, can turn and watch the sun set breathtakingly behind the hills of Fife across the waters of the Firth of Forth. Many bathers who come here are gay and few it appears bother much with swimwear when they sunbathe in the dunes.

In the summer of 1996, two wardens, hiding in a dune, equipped with powerful binoculars, phoned the police after they spotted three male bathers naked in the water. A lone police officer, exhausted from his long walk in the heat across the reserve admonished the bathers for their 'unacceptable' behaviour. Despite assurances of 'several complaints', there had, in fact, on this occasion been only one warning from the wardens who were under pressure from the local council to stamp out nudity on the beach. As the police officer and wardens made their way back across the sands, dozens more gay bathers emerged from the dunes, completely naked, and leapt into the water.

John Wallace, a landscape manager for East Lothian Council, explained: "It is not officially a nudist beach. The majority of people who use this beach are not gay. They are families. Mums and kiddies have been frightened by what they've seen. We have had dozens of complaints, which is why the wardens were sent down there. I don't understand why they have to stand and cavort in the dunes. They've taken over. I personally find it very intimidating". A spokesperson for East Lothian Council told the **Scottish Daily Express** that the nature reserve was *"popular with parents and children"*, adding: *"You can imagine how embarrassed bird watchers might be if they spot a nudist through the binoculars. We urge sun bathers to stay covered up"*.

The **Scottish Daily Mail** gasped: *"Homosexuals are flocking to a popular Scottish bird sanctuary to bare their all".* (Or, *"getting their TWITCHERS OUT"* as the **Daily Star of Scotland** put it). *"But now furious birdwatchers have written to the police and council asking them to shoo off the unwanted visitors".* (The council had been *"inundated"* with letters and had *"scores of calls"* according to the **Scottish Daily Express**, which was somewhat surprising considering there was a local postal strike at the time). **The Herald**'s Diary sighed: *"East Lothian has always been seen as a safe spot to which to escape - no nonsense, old-fashioned standards, a short back and sides approach to life. Alas, no longer...".*

After its listing in an European naturist magazine, Alistair Robertson in the **Scottish Daily Mail** was concerned over *"busloads of European nudists"* turning up at Tentsmuir Forest and Kinsholdy Beach in Fife. *"Could it be that as the area is jointly run by Scottish Natural Heritage the magazine has misunderstood the use of the word natural?"*

Moral surveillance of 'gay' beaches has famously operated right across the country. Holkham is a peaceful and unspoilt stretch off the north Norfolk coast owned by Lord Coke of Holkham Hall. A moral backlash was sparked in 1991 after the press were alerted to warden Ron Harold's campaign when he promised he would 'clean up' the popular gay nudist beach. Harold was an employee of English Nature, an organisation ostensibly set up to promote conservation. He declared he would seek a citizen's arrest on anyone he found cavorting together in the dunes and woods. He began his campaign in earnest, marching up and down the beach, combing it for offenders, armed with binoculars, walking-talkie and a co-operative side-kick. His campaign encountered some opposition when around a hundred naturists lined up to taunt him as he trained his eyeglasses on a couple he had spotted entering the woods flanking the dunes, demanding they came out and face arrest. A number of others got together to smuggle the pair unseen to the safety of their car.

After some five arrests in 1991, Ron Harold erected new signs across the beach prohibiting nudism in the dunes above the high watermark!

Ron Harold was not always completely successful. In July of 1992, he caught a young gay couple of 17 and 21 in the dunes

and attempted another citizen's arrest. The couple was forced
to march the 25-minute walk across the sand to the main gate
in front of Harold's Land Rover. While he fumbled with the
gate's lock, the couple took a chance, leapt over the fence and
escaped.

Holkham beach is close to Sandringham and has always
been popular with the Royal Family who occasionally make
visits to their beach hut set back from the dunes. It was particularly popular with the Queen Mother whose own entourage,
using the beach back in the thirties, were rumoured to have
been responsible for establishing this stretch of sand as a gay
beach.

Further south along the coast, at Waxham - despite nine separate petitions in protest - the parish council joined the backlash
by banning nudism on its own stretch of seafront. In neighbouring Lincolnshire, on a little-known gay beach on the
Saltfleet dunes near Theddlethorpe, the local newspaper spoke
to Inspector Rod Bell of Louth police. He said that anyone who
exposed himself or indulged visibly in "lewd acts" would face
the full rigour of the law and warned that anyone caught naked
would be prosecuted and named and shamed in the local
newspaper.

Double standards are usually exposed in reports of public
sex involving heterosexual couples. A businessman filmed having sex with a woman on a north Fife beach by a man who
attempted to blackmail him was *"described as AB to protect his
identity"* in the **Scottish News of the World**. Such sensitivity
would rarely be offered to gay offenders. The **Scottish News of
the World** also dispensed with any moral criticism of what the
couple had been doing and concentrated on the *"sicko"* who
had attempted to film and blackmail them while they were
*"making love"*. The tabloid reported how Sheriff Johan Newall
had told the *"pervert"* that the offences were so serious he had
no option but to jail him. After a gay magazine feature
appeared on the subject of sex outdoors the **Scottish News of
the World** attacked it for having *"promoted"* Strathclyde Park as
*"a pick-up place for gays"*. That didn't stop them showing a
naked couple with their genitals pressed up against each other
in a report headed: *"SCOTLAND LAID BARE"*, which revealed
Scotland's *"top 10 spots to fling off your clothes"*.

The **Daily Record** is itself no stranger to double standards in attitudes to public sex. In the *"Scottish Office sex session"* the tabloid remained light-hearted over security guards who *"got an eyeful"* catching a *"passionate"* couple on their surveillance cameras. The paper stopped short of actually naming the couple, something they wouldn't have hesitated to do had the couple been gay, and light-heartedly reported how *"stills of the passionate pair later did the rounds in the Scottish Office"*.

The **Scottish Sun**'s sister paper, the **Scottish News of the World** printed what they enthusiastically described as *"Scotland's biggest Sex Survey"*. The first two words indicated where the Sunday tabloid would be going with this one. *"Sexmad Scots..."* they screeched. *"Our randy readers have had an average of seven sexual partners each"*. Here, for the titillation of readers, was a *"red-hot catalogue of thrills, frolics and fantasies..."*, but journalists David Leslie and Graham McKendry morally wrestled with the information landing on their desk. *"Torrid... Shocking... Worrying... An earth-shuddering 41 per cent of Scots have torrid bonking sessions between four and seven times a week... A shocking 47 per cent admitted they had been unfaithful and cheated on their partners... Foxy fillies also get turned on by the thought of having sex in public. And they just love sex toys, eating food off their partner's body, bondage and men in uniforms! Red blooded males, meanwhile, go for sexy lingerie, blue movies, three-in-a-bed sex and wife-swapping!"* The present-day reality, when *"a worrying 30 per cent of young Scots said they lost their virginity when they were aged between 13 and 15"*, was described as the survey's *"darker side"*. Despite the **Scottish News of the World**'s disgust at *"public sex"* by men on Scotland's gay beaches, the 'survey' contained an *"amazing confession"* revealing *"every steamy detail"* of *"leggy Lorna Gordon and hunky Liam Sullivan"* taking a swim *"...naked below the waist and making love in the water"*. There was no hint of the moral finger-wagging otherwise peculiar to this paper, just a posed colour photo-shot of the *"horny pair"*. In fact, the **Scottish News of the World** was forced to confess: *"Having sex outdoors is a massive turn on for randy Scots, according to one in three of the readers who responded to our sizzling survey"*. Any mention of gay sex in the survey was conveniently brushed under their nylon foamed-backed carpet.

The **Scottish Sun** gratuitously printed: *"YOUR SEX CON-*

FESSIONS", boasting: *"Sun readers do it in their cars... not to mention lay-bys, cinemas, swimming pools, department stores, hospitals... and even at the Ideal Home Show!"* They claimed to have been *"flooded"* with confessions. *"It seems Sun readers just LOVE to sex-periment"*, they chortled. Ann, a barmaid from Dumbarton revealed the *"staff bonding"* that went on every night at the bar she worked after closing. Caroline, who worked in a tearoom at a garden centre had her new manager *"naked in the main display fountain watched by two fairies and several gnomes"*. Rita *"ended up doing it as the sun went down behind the sand dunes. It was great sex!"* Tamara said: *"I absolutely love having sex outdoors. Last summer my husband and I made love naked in the undergrowth outside Hadleigh Castle near Southend. We were in the bushes while all these tourists and visitors were walking by just a few feet away. It really turned me on"*. Brian sneaked off with an 18-year-old to have sex in a field. *"We didn't realise there was a taxi rank about 200 yards behind the field until we suddenly heard cheers and shouts. Four or five cabbies were watching us. I'm not shy so I carried on anyway. The sex was excellent with no strings attached and I just walked away. It was the best sex ever"*. Nothing much in the way of condemnation there either!

Sex in public, like sex in magazines, newspapers, television or films rarely fails to evoke the ire of moral watchdogs, but why? According to the **Scottish Sun**, the most common fantasy amongst Scots in their survey was *"sex with a stranger in a public place"*. They revealed *"one in five Scots have had sex on a beach, in a park, in woods... and 50 per cent of Scots have had sex in a car"*. Most of the moral indignation attached to sexual liaisons that took place outdoors was reserved almost exclusively for gay men.

If seeking gay sex on an isolated stretch of beach can evoke moral indignation, that is nothing compared to what men who seek other men in public conveniences can bring. Behind the **Daily Record**'s reference to a *"Sex-shame workman"* was 60-year-old Michael Cummings, brought up in less than enlightened times, who died throwing himself off the Forth Road Bridge less than a week after being arrested in a public toilet in Stirling with another man. The **Daily Record** dismissed it as a *"sordid encounter"*. The public toilet evolved as a vehicle for initiating sexual and emotional liaisons between men, partly because of just the sort of heterosexual breast-beating championed by the likes of the **Daily Record**. The Internet is increasingly replacing this sort of activity in the new millennium.

Apart from the compounded isolation of a gay teenager exploring his sexuality during his school holidays, the police operation involving hidden cameras on a public convenience in Stirling produced 11 arrests and five attempts at suicide, two of which were successful. The men's names, addresses and pictures were printed in the **Stirling Observer**. On BBC's 'Frontline Scotland', convicted criminal 'Big Mags' Haney, from Stirling's Raploch housing estate warned she was off to a local gay cruising area *"to chase all the gays and prostitutes. If you've got to do a clean-up campaign, you may as well do it right"*. 'Brigadier' Brown in the **Daily Record** used his column to remark: *"The civil rights squad are squawking again… Here in Scotland, they're even moaning about the rights of homosexuals to pander to their sad, seedy perversions in a public place… Local people had complained about a public facility - close to a school - being turned into a gay bordello. **More disgusting and disturbing was the fact that a 14-year-old boy had been involved in whatever went on in these toilets… Come on! The line has to be drawn somewhere. And if sickos and sensationalists don't know where to draw it, then society must"**.* Of the suicides, Brown was dismissive. *"Unfortunate - but neither the police or society are to blame…"* Ignoring the plight of the gay youngster, driven to explore his burgeoning sexuality underground, he praised the police. *"I feel sorry for the copper who had to watch these sleazy videos. It's a dirty job, but somebody has to do it, for all our sakes"*. Exercising his opinion on the whole subject of gay cruising, he wrote: *"Near where I live is Strathclyde Country Park, but I wouldn't dream of taking a walk there or allowing children to play there in the evening, because it has become a notorious haunt for open-air homosexuals"*. Strathclyde Park has probably been a 'haunt' for the sort of 'open-air' homosexual the 'Brigadier' feared for much longer than even he had imagined.

Public conveniences, or 'cottages' have struggled to offer gay men a place of refuge for sexual negotiation since Victorian times. In 1916, on the subject of young rent boys gathering round the 'meat rack' outside the public conveniences in London's Piccadilly Circus, the Bishop of London said: "They are the villain more mischievous than German spies who lie in wait to stain the chivalry of our boys, poison their minds and undermine their characters... Shooting is not good enough for them". 'Cottages' are often at their busiest when straight-identified men call in on the way home from work, sometimes referred to as 'happy hour'. While rude-boy graffiti on toilet walls has kept everyone aware of sexual diversity through the worst of two centuries of sexual repression, Joe Orton, George Michael and a catalogue of police arrests and surveillance operations have helped keep the local 'cottage' fresh in everyone else's mind too. Scotland probably has one of the world's highest rates of suicides of men arrested in swoops on public toilets. Toilets usefully serve as a place for men to make contact with other men under the pretext of relieving themselves. Moral policing can be performed with the aid of hidden cameras, routine surveillance or the employment of a full-time cleaner keeping watch behind net curtains.

The **Dumfries and Galloway Standard** called time on the toilets in Castledykes Park with the headline: *"RID OUR PARK OF PERVERTS!"* after they found visitors to Castledykes Park were being *"put off - thanks to flashers and homosexuals"*. Reporter Doug Archibald reported indignantly: *"Indecent acts take place on a daily basis in the 'repugnant' gents' toilets..."* and declared them a *"nationally known meeting place for perverts"*. He attempted to explain to worried readers that *"males from the 'cottaging' fraternity"* were *"men who hang about toilets to commit indecent acts with each other"*. A Dumfries councillor, ex-policeman, Tom Holmes wanted to ensure the matter was fairly debated, so announced talks were to be held *"between himself, police and council officials"*. He wanted the installation of CCTV cameras in an action *"similar to those carried out in Stirling..."* and the recording of all cars *"entering or leaving"* the park. He wanted the public reassured by police pro-activity; the Procurator Fiscal to back the police when reports were sent to them; the eventual closure of the park convenience and park users to be encouraged to take down car registration numbers and hand them to the police. It was reported how messages constantly had to be scrubbed off the convenience walls *"which the homosexuals leave for each other"*. Tom Holmes told the **Dumfries and Galloway Standard**: *"Castledykes must be protected by those in* *authority so that it can be enjoyed by the public and made full use of especially by children"*. Holmes got the police to carry out *"a survey"* over the following weeks. Rumours soon circulated of a yellow van with mirrored windows parked near the gay cruising area before twenty men were *"spoken to"* and one was reported to the Procurator Fiscal. The **Dumfries and Galloway Standard** gushed with emotion: *"Castledykes is described as one of the most picturesque parks in south west Scotland because of its children's adventure playground…"*

In another open-and-shut case of moral policing, Ian Hill had a shock when he groped a stranger he thought had winked at him. The object of his attentions was an undercover policeman with an unfortunate facial twitch. Hill, a 48-year-old farmer, was promptly arrested.

If the rounding-up of gay men became too commonplace to satisfy the tastes of the sensation-seeking public, the **Scottish Sun** must have been delighted to report how: *"Park PC cops a feel of flasher's snake"*. A four-foot Boa was found in the pocket of Thomas Stevenson, 21, in Ardochoille Park in Stevenston, Ayrshire. Stevenson was described in the tabloids as a *"pervert… flasher"*, and *"weirdo"*. He was arrested, charged and pleaded guilty to recklessly concealing reptiles, resisting arrest, attempted theft - he had previously attempted to break into a neighbour's garage - and shameless indecency. He was even placed on the sex offenders' register.

Over a discovery police made at one public convenience, Sergeant John Riggans warned in the **Largs & Millport Weekly News**: *"We need to talk to everyone at the toilets… Innocent individuals who require to use the toilet facilities will be caught up in all this"*. He was reported having rounded up *"a number of males dressed as females in these toilets and brought them into the police office"*. The **News** said: *"A 50-year-old local man was charged with breach of the peace after police discovered him parked at South Bay toilets in mini-skirt, padded bra, fishnet tights and a wig"*. Sergeant Riggans claimed; *"adverts have been appearing in gay magazines telling people to go to Fairlie"*. The names of these 'gay magazines' were not forthcoming, but the Sergeant insisted: *"There is an 'underground network' of homosexuals in the area… The police have been monitoring the public toilets for the past four months… If we see a particular car that is positioned nearby the toilets on several* *occasions, we will take note of it and track these people down".* The **Largs & Millport Weekly News** helpfully added, *"both public toilets… are situated at the foot of School Brae on the Main Street and at the south bay car park".*

When pop singer, George Michael was caught *inflagranti delicto* in a Hollywood public convenience by an undercover cop, Scotland's notepad wasn't missing from the worldwide media swoop. *"GEORGE'S SHAME",* squealed the **Scottish Mirror.** Very few papers could bring themselves to examine the issue of 'cottaging' beyond what some papers delicately referred to as *"pleasuring"* oneself while George Michael was accused of making 'cottaging' fashionable. Most men, keen to divorce emotions from the physical act, would beg to differ. For them, toilets was not a fashion accessory, but a place to communicate in a way that would be forbidden in their home environment. The media tried to conjure, in the minds of its readers, a hot afternoon in the park with hordes of 'innocent' children, bursting in on George Michael while he was attempting to pin a half-naked cop helplessly up against the wall. But there was nothing for the public to have stumbled on; just a complicated sequence of manoeuvres and signals ensuring sex was carried out with consent and privacy. No one would have ever needed to have been shocked and disgusted had not the moral police and finger-wagging media made this private act so entirely public. George Michael later produced a triumphant fingers-up at his arrest by pretty-police with the release of a chart-topping video based on the event to back his new single, 'Outside'. The **Daily Record** labelled the video *"outrageous"* because *"one scene shows two actors playing Los Angeles policeman kissing"* and another depicted *"gay and lesbian sex".* They accused George Michael of *"poking fun at the scandal"* and added, *"some people believe* (the video) *glamorises open air sex".*

By Christmas of 1999, religionists were helping lift Cliff Richards' Millennium Prayer to number one in the British pop charts by buying up stocks and giving them away to churches. George Michael called it a vile exploitation. The **Daily Record** turned on the *"sleaze-hit star"* in fury. At a time when the homophobic Section 28 campaign raged throughout Scotland, they declared: *"…When it comes to music, like everything else, the majority is always right… If Cliff is a 'vile exploiter,' what are you*

*George?"* The **Daily Record** listed all the hits where George
Michael was supposed to have *"plumbed the depths"*, in his
videos. They dragged in 'Sexfinder General' Monsignor Tom
Connolly who praised Sir Cliff as *"an icon of goodness, a wonderful guy"*. Yvonne White, co-ordinator of the Cliff Richard Fan
Club in Glasgow said: *"George Michael has been involved in so
many scandals that the Lord's Prayer probably makes him squirm
with guilt"*. 'Old Mother Burnie' passed judgement on *"vile"*
George Michael's *"other record... the personal one which affronts
common decency"*, chastising him for *"imposing his own lewd
lifestyle on young fans"* and castigating him for *"committing an
illegal, homosexual act in a park's public loo"*. She reprimanded
him for *"exploiting something far more offensive than religion"*
before the **Record** asked readers to phone them and register a
vote: *"Do you agree with George Michael or Cliff Richard?"* Cliff
Richards' subsequent victory was hardly surprising.

This would not be the **Daily Record**'s first or last use of a
public convenience. After reporting a property boom in
Edinburgh, the tabloid innocently advised: *"Now the toilets - all
in central areas - are being touted as potential cottages..."*

This was not the only high profile arrest involving gay sex
to hold the pages of the nation's newspapers at this time. There
was also a matter of a *"lapse of judgement"* on the part of the former Welsh secretary, Ron Davies's choice of partners. Quite
apart from narrowly missing what could have been a severe
beating, cruising London's Clapham Common in the autumn of
1998, he also sided with a Labour party courting middle
England and a wife who declared they shared a sexless marriage. Even though the event had taken place in the dead of
night, the **Daily Record** used some comments from obliging
mothers who could help them squeeze children into the story.
One said: *"I regularly walk my children along there and see cars
parked up... It's not right my children should have to witness it"*.
Then another remarked: *"My husband told me that he once heard
loud groans from the cubicles"*. *"Local resident George White"*,
whose own 'cludgie' appeared to need regular maintenance,
quipped: *"On the few occasions I have been in there, there were a lot
of men loitering around looking idle"*.

The case of Ron Davies had an affect on attitudes over gay
men cruising in some of Glasgow's parks and open spaces. The

**Scottish News of the World** quoted Pauline Thompson of Scottish Parents Against Child Abuse who said: *"Children could be robbed of their innocence if exposed to flagrant sexual activity in the park"*. Over reports of men meeting in Strathclyde Park, Richard Lyle, SNP group leader for North Lanarkshire Council declared: *"I shall be raising the matter at council and police level. I don't want to see the park becoming another Clapham Common"*. The **Daily Record** shrugged: *"prosecutions for gross indecency are rare"*. There were 283 prosecutions for gross indecency in 1996, although not all of them were for arrests in parks, this hardly implied a rarity. Despite six years of falling recorded crime figures, in 1998, crimes of indecency in Scotland rose to their highest level in 26 years with a 39% rise in cases of lewd and libidinous behaviour.

'Old Mother' Burnie offered Ron Davies little sympathy in the **Daily Record**: *"Why shamed minister only has himself to blame..."*, the header snapped. She opined: *"To most of us such behaviour is as incomprehensible as it is shameful and disgusting"*. This was the *"darker side of homosexuality..."* and the *"shadowy side of sex... The only decent thing Ron Davies has done is to resign immediately..."* This was fuelled by psychotherapist Alan Wise who contributed by suggesting in the **Daily Record** that the sole reason men 'cottage' was because they enjoyed an *"element of danger"*. There were, of course, some notable exceptions to this rule as her response to a 'straight' 18-year-old girl, preferring the moss to her mattress, clearly demonstrated: *"...It's what YOU feel that counts. ...Stick to the great outdoors..."* she advised in a moment of bra-burning recklessness. In a letter from a 'straight' couple caught getting down to it, full on, in a public park the writer pleaded: *"...Suddenly we went from snogging to full sex ...I couldn't help myself"*. A woman raised the alarm and the couple were caught by a park ranger who promised he would forget the incident if he was slipped a tenner. Burnie's comments were devoid of the sort of moral judgement reserved for Ron Davies: *"It sounds a bit like a scam to me. Did he attempt to show you any ID? He could have been trying it on to get a tenner"*.

There is nothing new about the moral indignation following men cruising for sex. One observer recorded how in 1781 'Mollies' would sit along park benches in a gay cruising area in London and pat the backs of their hands. If you followed them,

they would weave a white handkerchief through the skirt of
their coat and wave it. In the eighteenth century at 'Sodomite's
Walk', an area of drained marshland at Moorfields in London,
police paid *agent provocateurs* to entrap men. In the sixties,
tabloids followed men wandering round London's Hampstead
Heath wearing *"white polo-necks"*.

The press frequently refer to Kelvingrove Park in Glasgow
as a *"notorious gay haunt"*. The response from the local authorities has been to trim back the bushes, causing the private activity to become more public, before it moves to dense shrubbery
elsewhere in the park. There is a very high risk of violence
attached to cruising. Alan, a caller on BBC Radio Scotland's
'Speakeasy' programme, said he had been attacked four times
in Kelvingrove Park. "The attitudes and the moral backlash I
got from the police was as bad as the attack itself", he said.
Another caller, Stephen, said after he had been attacked, all the
police wanted to know was what he had been doing there. He
claimed they took no action, and left him with the impression
that it was entirely his own fault. Two years ago, Robert Jarvis,
Chief Superintendent of Strathclyde Police told **The Herald**:
*"We are not aware of an identified problem of gay people being
assaulted"*. Strathclyde Police eventually changed its policing
tactics to take account of the violence many gays faced. During
the ensuing debate over repeal of Section 28, the law banning
the so-called 'promotion' of homosexuality in schools, an editorial in the **Big Issue in Scotland** declared: *"While researching
this issue, we spoke to one 15-year-old who'd had his first gay sexual
experiences in Glasgow's Kelvingrove Park. He couldn't think of anywhere else to go to find out about who he was. What have we come to
when we'd prefer to see young Scots seeking guidance about their sexuality in the middle of the night in a public park rather than in their
schools?"*

There were other areas in Glasgow where men met for sex.
A mix of heath and woodland, Cathkin Braes offer panoramic
views to the north of the Campsies, Kilpatrick Hills, Ben
Lomond and as far as Ben Ledi. At night, men cruise up and
down Cathkin Road in cars, pulling in at any one of the numerous lay-bys. There is sometimes a coded display of flashing
lights at night to signal intent. John, a middle-aged gay man
told me: "In summer, there are occasional disturbances from

youths from nearby Castlemilk. No one calls the police. The police sometimes pull up and wait before questioning you when you return to your car. They can be quite aggressive. They want to know everything. What you're doing here. Where you live and where you work". Another man in his early forties was more sympathetic of the police. "There was a mugging by youths from nearby Castlemilk. Four of them jumped a man; took his wallet and ripped off his watch. After the police were called on a mobile, they arrived on the scene in minutes with a police helicopter circling over the Braes. The police didn't question men what they were doing here at all". Another man claimed plain-clothed police carrying batons and torches interrupted his 'cruising' in the dead of night. He claimed they jumped out from behind bushes after he left his car and questioned him. There have been numerous incidents of assault, violence and vandalism at Cathkin Braes, often occurring in full view of others. Mounds of broken glass from smashed windscreens lay at the side of the road in a lay-by where men have left their cars. Some of the violent incidences in the past have been quite serious. One bisexual man fled after a woman coaxed him into the bushes followed by two men carrying batons. Four years ago a man was hospitalised after an assault, and, in another incident, a man suffered a heart attack after being jumped on by youths.

Strathclyde Park is an area where gay and bisexual men meet outside Glasgow in Lanarkshire. Jack Irvine, a leading campaigner against gay equality in Scotland, noticed, in his **Scottish Mirror** column, that *"the waspish columnist Tom Morton, referring to Bellshill as a gay cruising area, described it as 'MacClapham Common'."* Strathclyde Park was the site of a Roman Military Bathhouse. Soldiers would undress together in a room before moving into progressively hotter steam rooms, scraping off the dirt from each other before finally plunging into a cold bath. In the bathhouse, gay sex would have been commonplace. The emperor Elagabalus was said to have sent out emissaries all over the Empire to seek out men 'hung like mules'. Petronius wrote that in one public bath, a crowd gathered round a well-hung male and applauded! With its close proximity to a fairground and the towns of Motherwell and Hamilton, Strathclyde Park is a dangerous place for gay or bisexual men to walk. Reports of youths ambushing cars have been reported in the gay press. James, a middle-aged man told me: "I received 25 stitches to my head after I was beaten up. He ran off with my watch, which was worth about £20. I was too afraid to go to the police and told my family I'd been involved in a car accident". Park wardens sometimes trudge through the undergrowth while plain-clothes and uniformed police pull into the car park to question people or take car numbers. Local councillors have refused the distribution of condoms and safer sex information by health workers. Many of the men who would have benefited do not necessarily identify themselves as gay and don't have access to dedicated safer sex information. On London's Hampstead Heath, condoms are available from glow-in-the-dark boxes attached to trees and one summer, TV and cabaret star; Amy Lamé was hired to entertain late-night cruisers from a temporary stage.

Queen's Park on the south side of the city offers panoramic views over the city of Glasgow. On warm summer afternoons, people lay reading, talking or picnicking on the grassy slopes. It has also been the scene of some brutal attacks of gay men. On 2 June 1995 there was the murder of Michael Doran by a teenage gang on a 'queerbashing' rampage. His fate was tragically similar to that of John Cremin who was murdered in Queen's Park on 6 April 1960. This led to the last hanging in Scotland of Anthony Miller at Barlinnie prison on 22 December 1960. Miller, the youngest man in Scotland to have been executed in the 20th Century was only 19-years-old. Together with his accomplice, 16-year-old James Denovan - who was detained indefinitely after being found guilty of non-capital murder - acted as a decoy, luring men from the public toilets. Young James led John Cremin past Anthony Miller who pretended he was drunk before creeping up behind them and hitting John Cremin over the head with a flat piece of wood. John Cremin, his skull fractured and head bleeding, collapsed to the ground and later died of massive haemorrhaging. They robbed John Cremin of his bankbook, a wallet, a knife and £67.

Methods by which lesbians, gays, bisexuals and people of transgender have chosen to meet others for sex, friendship, partnership and lasting relationships are just as diverse, changeable and unpredictable as everyone else's. Over the years, the gay bar has stood out as the most obvious and conventional place to meet other gays. That is if a person seeking a same-sex partner is comfortable enough with their sexuality to socialise in one. Most major cities and towns have one. Mother Clap was the landlady of a popular gay bar or 'Molly House' in Covent Garden in London before she was raided by peace officers (the police of the day). At the trial, a spokesman for the Society for the Reformation of Manners said he "found between 40 and 50 men making love to one another, as they called it. Sometimes they would sit in one another's laps, kissing in a lewd manner and using their hands indecently". Three of the regulars were hanged for their behaviour. Mother Clap was found guilty of running a disorderly house, pilloried, fined and thrown into prison for two years.

Another method of meeting partners, although not so accepted in Scotland, is through personal advertisements or 'lonely hearts' advertisements. Whilst newspapers are quick to print names and addresses of men caught using more unorthodox methods of meeting, when gay men seek partners using personal ads in the same way as heterosexuals, barriers often come down. A sensational report in the **Sunday Mail** led to a crackdown on personal ads from lesbians, gays, bisexuals and people of transgender in newspapers. The advertising paper, the **Scottish Supermart**, the focus of the **Sunday Mail**'s attention, promptly banned them and has since refused to enter into any dialogue over the matter. Without encouraging the 'g' word, **The Herald** and Glasgow's **Evening Times** allow a section entitled *"Just Friends"* where gays advertise for partners. The **Scottish News of the World** has had Women Seeking Men; Men Seeking Men; Women Seeking Women and Friends & Sports Partners. Graham Leach, the general manager of the **Hamilton Advertiser**, (part of Scottish Universal Newspapers, bought by the Trinity Group in 1992), was unmoved by claims of the newspaper's own discriminatory policies. Leach insisted gays were refused permission to advertise for partners, not because they were discriminated against, but for 'commercial decisions'. His advertising manager, Ian McQueen, explained it was down to a 'shortage of space', but admitted it could be construed as discrimination. Leach later confessed "that there was not a category within the paper for anyone falling outside of heterosexuality". Trinity plc, which owns the **Daily Record** and **Sunday Mail**, defies progressive equality legislation and bans gays from advertising for partners in both these newspapers.

The arrival of chatlines with premium-rate 0898 prefixes in the eighties offered new opportunities for sexual exploration and was particularly welcomed by married men. However, their use quickly provoked government censorship. The media fuelled a public outcry over their use by children as families were outraged over massive, unexplained telephone bills. However, children were sometimes just the scapegoat for sexual indiscretion within the family unit. In any case, a provision for blocking the use of premium rate numbers was soon provided by British Telecom. The re-election of John Major's Conservative Government brought about a swift crackdown. OFTEL insisted users had to register to use premium-rate numbers bringing about a new breed of benign, non-sexual chatlines. Opening warnings demonstrated a caution that took some years to relax: *"Be warned! Attempting to say anything other than your first name or maybe where you come from could result in you having to do this again".* Forced by user's demands, TV and press advertisements and cheaper calls, the missing sexual ingredient soon returned to telephone chatlines.

Before the development of the Internet, only the walls of public conveniences offered such freedom for communicating uncensored sexual messages and images. The growth of the Internet soon overtook an impotent press. In fact, it did more than that. It sparked a sexual revolution. Internet rooms were becoming filled with married men and women seeking sexual encounters of all kinds. New sexual experiences, never available before were brought into the living room by just a click of a mouse. It was found almost 80 per cent of requests made to search engines were of a sexual nature. Whilst the press continued to malign this potential for sexual freedom, a growing movement demanded further censorship against Internet Service Providers and a steady growth of prosecutions against individuals followed. A widespread debate in the UK press over child pornography was inevitable, even though much of the criminal material originated from overseas. Newspaper readers were left with a feeling that most of the terrible crimes against children were occurring on their own doorstep.

Unsurprisingly, many felt a sense of duty to combat these crimes by enacting simple solutions on their own accord. *"...It's just not good enough to wring your hands or weep over the abuses suffered by anonymous children in unidentifiable settings"*, begged **The Scotsman**'s Linda Watson-Brown in one of her regular anti-porn campaign features.

# Chapter Eight
## *Red Frock, Red Top and Red Shoes*

*"Don't need this legislation*
*You don't need this score.*
*Don't need this fascist groove*
*Just to show pornography the door.*

*Don't mean to be too precious,*
*I don't mean to be uptight,*
*But tell me iron lady,*
*Are we moving to the right?*
*No Clause 28"*
**Boy George**

On 29 October 1999, in what was supposed to have been a low key affair, Minister for Communities Wendy Alexander, Labour MSP for Paisley North, told a gathering at Glasgow University that it was time for Section 28 of the Local Government Act (Section 2a in Scotland) to go. As a devolved issue, the fledgling regional assembly, the Scottish Executive, led by the late First Minister Donald Dewar, planned to repeal Section 2a in its consultation document The Ethical Standards in Public Life (Scotland) Bill which was launched in November 1999, based on the principles set out by the Nolan committee. Riding on the back of a wave of optimism for a new, progressive Scotland in Europe, Communities Minister Wendy Alexander said: "We believe that legislation is unjust, reactionary and has no place in the Scotland of tomorrow". She hadn't reckoned on the backlash from organised religion and moral conservatives.

Gerald Warner's attacks on Wendy Alexander were personal and damning. He blasted: *"Where are the visionaries to lead us out of the Wendy House?"* He rounded on the *"wee pretendy parliament..."* and asked: *"Why are we ruled by a gang of cooncillors and fat women from social work departments?"* He suggested Wendy Alexander *"interprets her portfolio as trampling upon the*

*wishes of the community. As she stood at the lectern, shrilling, pout-*
*ing and finger-wagging (two fingers would have sufficed to convey*
*her message to the despised Scottish public), she personified the arro-*
*gance and hubris that characterises the Scottish Executive...*
*Alexander is living testimony to the unwisdom of abolishing the*
*ducking-stool".*

Section 28, (or Section 2a as it was properly known in
Scotland) had been introduced by Margaret Thatcher in the
eighties to legislate against local authorities—not schools—to
prevent them from'promoting' homosexuality as 'pretended
family relationship'. It rode on the back of the largely right-
wing press fuelling public anger over a trend they labelled
'political correctness' in 'loony left' councils. They exaggerated
stories of black lesbian self-defence groups, vilified 'proselytis-
ing' homosexuals and printed wildly exaggerated stories of gay
sex being taught in schools. At her victory speech at the Tory
Party Conference, Thatcher declared to rapturous applause:
"Children, who should be taught to respect traditional moral
values, are being taught they have the unalienable right to be
gay".

Edited by Martin Clarke, the otherwise Labour-supporting
**Daily Record**, who had not been told of this impending
announcement to repeal Section 2a, fired a warning shot across
his pages: *"GAY SEX LESSONS FOR SCOTS SCHOOLS"*. *'Old*
*Mother Burnie'* was bewildered and wrote how she couldn't
quite grasp how the repeal of Section 2a would eliminate bullying; insisting MSPs had far more urgent business to deal
with! *"It's not as if homosexuality is something which dare not speak*
*its name in schools"*, she scoffed. *"Playground jibes about dykes*
*went over my head at 13...! God knows adolescence is confusing*
*enough without 'Sir' or 'Miss' standing up in class and urging every-*
*one to come out and be glad to be gay"*. She was afraid teachers
would promote it as a *"better alternative than the boring old het-*
*erosexual lifestyle... Besides, as Michael Portillo and a thousand pub-*
*lic school-boys can testify, sexual preferences can change... We have*
*enough straight teachers preying on their young pupils without the*
*gays joining in"*.

'Brigadier' Brown was spoiling for a fight. *"Who are the first*
*people you would want to help? Children? The shivering old folk?*
*Poor families? The homeless? Homosexuals? How did they get prior-*

*ity...? How come an insidious minority with a perverse agenda com-
mands the attention of a new minister...? We were not told about a
hidden policy to expose our children to harmful propaganda".*

Throwing itself at the feet of the campaign to retain Section
2a, the **Daily Record**'s editorial begged its readers to write to
the First Minister Donald Dewar. *"Write to him, fax him, e-mail
him and tell him exactly what you think about his plans. To make it
easier, we've printed a ready-made letter you can cut out, sign and
send".* They were joined by, amongst others, the **Scottish Sun**,
the **Scottish Daily Mail**, the **Daily Telegraph** and **Scotland on
Sunday**.

Alan Cochrane, writing for Scottish editions of the right-
wing **Daily Telegraph** challenged Wendy Alexander to support
her *"ridiculous claims... Where is her evidence that Section 28
encourages intolerance...? Next take her claim that Section 28 pre-
vents teachers from counselling the victims of 'homophobic' bullying
and ask her: how so? Give us one example of a teacher who could not
help the victim of such bullying because he or she feared being thrown
in jail because of this piece of legislation".* Without one good reason
why Section 2a should have remained, Cochrane mocked
Wendy Alexander's performance as *"laughable... Sanctimonious
arrogance... Inflicting a new morality upon us".*

The **Scottish Daily Mail** used a picture of Wendy Alexander
with a ferocious gait under the headline: *"Minister faces a backlash on plan for gay lessons in schools"* while Gerald Warner
begged: *"What's so wrong about protecting our children from moral
corruption?"*

Coverage of the repeal of Section 2a with such headlines as
*"ANTI-GAY LAW"* were as offensive to gays as 'ANTI-JEW
LAW' would have been to the Jewish community in Nazi
Germany. The vile rhetoric and shameful publicity orchestrated
by the religious right, moral campaigners and certain sections
of the press should never have been allowed to go as far as it
did. Indeed, if Scotland had been the Netherlands, the newspapers would've most likely been covering the arrest of a few
tabloid editors, religious leaders and a handful of other individuals instead.

The anti-repeal campaigners were soon joined by the late
Cardinal Thomas Winning, or 'Red Tom' as he was sometimes
known because of his frock. Peppering his comments with tired

clichés like 'political correctness' exposed a seasoned agitator, he refused to support those who wanted the Church to move on and allow priests to marry and in May 1997, evoked controversy by offering to pay pregnant women to have their babies. For any gay person wanting to follow the teachings of the Catholic Church, Winning was at great pains to explain the "joy and peace in living the virtue of chastity". He expressed the opinion that homosexuality was a personality disorder and even compared gays to German and Italian Nazi bombers. In the thick of the Section 2a debate, at the Orbiston Neighbourhood Centre in Bellshill, Glasgow, he was filmed publicly labelling homosexuality a perversion. The views of the Catholic Church on the subject of homosexuality are found in The Catechism of the Catholic Church. It draws a clear distinction between what are called 'homosexual tendencies' and 'homosexual acts'. Homosexuals are required to lead a chaste life, controlling themselves through prayer and self-mastery in order to find the only 'freedom' that really matters: Freedom from sin. In the recruitment of teachers, sports coaches, foster carers and the military, Winning believed discrimination against gays was "not unjust". He also described homosexuality as "a disorder... that's got to be... dealt with". On the repeal of Section 28, he told the press: "I worry that any repeal will be presented by the so-called 'gay-rights' lobby as victory in their battle to have the disorder that is homosexuality placed on the same footing as marriage and family life. We have already seen this tactic used before. Before the election we were told that all legislation would be given the 'family test' – namely, would a given policy benefit the family? If not, it would have no place on the new government's agenda. Yet... the families of Britain were left to come to terms with the idea that predatory male homosexuals would be able to indulge in dangerous, immoral acts with their 16-year-old sons, while our legislators washed their hands of the whole issue, proclaiming it to be a question of freedom and equality". Of the predatory ways of heterosexual men indulging in dangerous, immoral acts with their 16-year old daughters, Winning said nothing. To illustrate the pitfalls of the 'disorder' called homosexuality, he relied on discredited statistics used by far-right American Christian groups advising that the repeal of Section 2a would reduce the life expectancy of children. Using the populist tactics of the political right, he expressed certainty that people did not want "their council tax used to fund facilities for gay and lesbians which they do not enjoy for their own children". Winning declared the repeal would leave adolescents in a "fog of confusion" over their sexuality before suggesting: "Now is the time for reflection, not for knee-jerk reactions", but his knee-jerk reaction was exactly what Scotland got.

Cardinal Winning had at his disposal the best press manipulators. His spokesman Ronnie Convery once faced a barrage of questions about Opus Dei, a right-wing faction that pledges to "contribute to the evangelisation of every sphere of society" and operates within the Roman Catholic Church. Opus Dei was formed in 1928 by a Nazi-sympathiser, Jose Maria Escriva Albas. Its 80,000 members include priests and influential figures in both the media and government. Cardinal Winning had been reported stating his admiration for Opus Dei and Ronnie Convery admitted on the programme that he had once been a member himself. Convery denied that Cardinal Winning was at odds with the majority of Catholics and said: "It puts us in conflict with what you might call the forces of political correctness; it puts us in conflict with what you might call the siren voices of liberalism". The 'Sexfinder General' Monsignor Tom Connolly had said: "Opus Dei is a fully approved part of the Catholic Church. It has the full support of the Vatican and enjoys excellent relations with the Cardinal, who values the dedication and loyalty of its members. To describe it as a 'sect' or suggest it is somehow sinister is wilful distortion. It is also an insult to Cardinal Winning to suggest that he is under the influence of any 'group'." Many of the Pope's recent announcements have been sourced to Opus Dei; he made their top man a bishop and invited members to meetings. Some Church insiders claimed the Opus Dei faction had secured access to the Cardinal and criticised the Church leadership for allowing it to build a closeted power-base in Scotland.

On the morning of Friday, 14 January 2000, Scotland awoke to the news that a former bus-driver-turned-business-tycoon, Brian Souter - famous for his penchant for red shoes - had pledged to bankroll the Scottish School Boards' campaign to prevent the repeal of Section 2a. Brian Souter – or 'Soapy' as he was sometimes referred to in the press – was a prominent member of the evangelical Church of the Nazarene based in Kansas, USA and one of Scotland's richest men. *"Why can I not give £500,000 to help protect children?"* Souter begged. He courted Jack Irvine, the boss of PR firm Media House after spotting his column in the **Scottish Mirror** expressing outrage over an equal age of consent: *"A pretty young boy of 16 can't vote for his local MP, but he can now be buggered by him... So equality is the key, is it? In that case, shouldn't 16-year-olds get the vote, be eligible to become, say, policemen? No? Why not? Because they're not mature enough. But they are deemed mature enough to be bum chums for sleazy old pervs"*.

The day after Brian Souter pledged £1million to his 'Keep the Clause' campaign, a doctor working in cancer research was badly beaten outside an Edinburgh gay bar. In an open letter to **The Scotsman**, he wrote: *"I was hit from behind with a baseball bat and I lost consciousness for several minutes. Whilst unconscious I was viciously assaulted by several people and suffered fractures to the bones of my face and lost several teeth. I have also been left unable to remember much about the events surrounding the attack..."*.

The campaign to 'Keep the Clause' was joined by the **Daily Record**'s main tabloid rival in Scotland, the **Scottish Sun**, edited by Bruce Waddell. He delivered in a popular tabloid newspaper what was nothing short of a sermon, thinly disguised as an editorial: *"God put his own son in a household with a mum and dad... We are the ones who are today grateful to Brian Souter, the raiding of his charitable fund, and the righteous stirring of sensible Scots everywhere. To use a Biblical term, the thought of removing Section 28 is an abomination. To use another, the idea deserves the same fate as Sodom and Gomorrah"*. The **Scottish Sun**'s editorial smugly outlined the plight of gays: *"They have followed the call of their genes and by and large have forfeited the joy of children... Are we homophobic to reflect this? Not at all"*. The **Scottish Sun** revealed how Souter had been *"offered backing by political groups in America, British trade unions and a number of 'disillusioned' Labour MPs and MSPs"*. The government connection was not surprising. The Christian Right had a well-established strategy of developing lobbying skills, placing young Christians as researchers with MSPs, hoping they would become politicians or civil servants to shape policy from a Christian standpoint.

The Christian Institute and CARE both operated in this way within the Houses of Commons and Lords. With around 20,000 members, the Evangelical Alliance already had its own lobbyist in place in the Scottish Executive. His name was Jeremy Balfour and he told **Scotland on Sunday**: *"I suspect the only advantage we have (over other people) is that Christians are slightly better informed than the bulk of society and have a better understanding of how politics works"*. The **Daily Record** insisted: *"All Mr Souter is doing is evening up the odds a little for the silent majority"*.

There was a rash of contradictory public opinion surveys. The **Daily Record** got Scottish Opinion to call 940 people and screamed the result from its front page: *"2:1 AGAINST GAY LESSONS... Forget all the posturing from the politically correct classes. Forget all the po-faced lectures from ministers who think they know better than you do. Forget all the insidious propaganda that tries to portray Brian Souter – and anyone else who opposes its repeal – as a gay basher. Scotland does NOT want to allow the teaching of gay sex in our schools"*. Jack Irvine, the former **Scottish Mirror** columnist who now headed PR firm Media House smelled victory. *"...We will except no wishy-washy compromise. We regard this as a fight to the death..."* he told **The Scotsman**.

At a press conference organised by 'Keep the Clause' and fronted by the Scottish School Boards' Association, David Macauley proudly trotted out their list of celebrity supporters: SNP MSP Fergus Ewing; the Optical Express chief executive, David Moulsdale; the former SNP MP, Jim Sillars; the Scottish Muslim leader, Bashir Maan; the convener of the Scots Asians for Independence, Bashir Ahmed; celebrity chef Nick Nairn; Jim Kerr from the band Simple Minds; motor trader Arnold Clark; hairdresser Taylor Ferguson and Kwik-Fit boss Sir Tom Farmer. It took just a few words from the mouth of the Scottish political editor of the **Mirror** to have the whole circus tent crashing down round everyone's ears. "Nick Nairn supports the government". David Macauley sat down abruptly. Within hours, Jim Kerr, Nick Nairn, Arnold Clark, Taylor Ferguson and Sir Tom Farmer all publicly distanced themselves from the campaign. Jack Irvine's efforts had descended into farce.

Each day the **Daily Record** dutifully applauded the efforts of 'Keep the Clause', filling their pages with its propaganda. Eventually it warned: *"Next week it will step up a gear with a* *national TV ad and poster campaign. Parents and focus groups are already being asked about their views on Section 28. Their responses will be added to the ad campaign and the comments printed on dozens of billboards across the country"*. Tim Hopkins of the Equality Network told **The Herald**: *"We have heard that the words 'Keep the Clause' are being used as a form of abuse against young people, who are having it shouted after them in playgrounds and on the street. What is happening in this country right now is truly frightening"*. With 'KEEP THE CLAUSE' billboards staring from almost everywhere you looked, the police expressed their disquiet by admitting violence against gays was on the increase.

Terry Sanderson, **Gay Times**'s 'MediaWatch' columnist wrote: *"As the religious Right has found... It is very easy to create the image of the sinister homo. There is no law to stop you saying whatever you want about gay people, however nasty and defamatory. Other minorities may have protection against hate mongering. We have none. All that is needed is the money to disseminate the propaganda, and a few newspapers willing to frighten the punters, and the referendum is in the bag. And each time a referendum on a gay issue is lost, equality is pushed further from our grasp and our public image irreparably damaged. Those citizens who had previously been of an indifferent live-and-let-live frame of mind suddenly find themselves taking an active anti-gay stance. They have become convinced - often by malevolent and dishonest advertising - that their children are at risk or that society is about to be damaged in some way by homosexuals. Tolerance rarely figures in these campaigns. Souter's cohort, Cardinal Winning, was pushing his own nasty agenda throughout all this, and was a willing accomplice in these weeks of consistent distortion, exaggeration and scare-mongering. The Daily Record, too, became the organ of hostility, using its power to promulgate a totally one-sided version of the debate"*.

By March 2000, the **Scottish Mail**'s headlines spelt out a sinister new twist in the campaign to prevent the repeal of Section 2a in Scotland: *"LET'S PUT IT TO THE VOTE... £1m private cash for Scottish referendum over Section 28..."* It appeared 23 co-sponsors had put their names forward to pay for the ballot, the costs - £950,000 before VAT - was to be split between the backers with Souter underwriting the total. Many of those putting their names forward as sponsors of the referendum were part of Scotland's Entrepreneur Exchange network, and at least four of them winners of the top entrepreneur award sponsored by **The Herald**. They were Scotland's richest man, Tom Hunter; former Kwik-Fit boss, Sir Tom Farmer; the Church of Scotland's Anne Allen; Brian Souter and his wife Betty; Scotland's richest woman, Brian Souter's sister, Ann Gloag, whose wealth was once estimated to be more than the Queen's; **Scottish Sun** columnist and former MP, Jim Sillars; former retailer, Gerald Weisfeld; Optical Express owner, David Mousdale; Pat and Alex Grant of refrigeration company, Norfrost who has a gay son by her first marriage; former director of Rangers Football Club, Hugh Adam; Fife landowner, John Cameron; hotel chain boss, Donald Macdonald; chief executive of Scotland the Brand, George Russell; Sir David McNee, formerly Chief Constable of Strathclyde Police and Commissioner of the Metropolitan Police from 1977 to 1983 when Conservative leader Margaret Thatcher was Prime Minister; SNP MSP Fergus Ewing; Lord MacKay of Clashfern, a retired former Lord Chancellor and former member of Prime Minister, Margaret Thatcher's Cabinet; David McLetchie, leader of the Scottish Conservatives; Andrew Welsh, a chairman of the powerful audit committee of the Scottish parliament; Bill Hughes, once the Treasurer and Deputy Chairman of the Scottish Conservative Party, a key figure in the Scottish division of the CBI and an elder in the Church of Scotland; Neil Hood, Professor of Business Policy, director of Strathclyde University's International Business Unit and advisor to Scottish Enterprise and Vali Hussein, vice-principal of the Islamic Academy of Scotland.

After the Electoral Reform Society's Ballot Services's refused to conduct the so-called 'referendum', the **Scottish Sun** reported: "*Stagecoach boss Brian Souter last night accused a gay clique within Labour of trying to wreck plans for a referendum on Section 28*". Echoing the Nazi treatment of Jews in the thirties when there were references to powerful Jewish cliques influencing government and of Jewish trickery, the **Scottish Sun** referred to "*gay dirty tricks*". The **Daily Record** reported: "*Tycoon Brian Souter accused the Government and the gay lobby of sabotaging the plan for the referendum…*".

Gordon Currie's report in the **Scottish Daily Mail** showed the tabloid ever more strident: "*Gay law mob stage protest outside Souter's church… Gay activists and far left campaigners yesterday* *staged a protest outside the church where Stagecoach millionaire Brian Souter worships. The mob waved placards and chanted homosexual propaganda as churchgoers arrived..."* **The Herald** correctly referred to *"protesters"* and *"campaigners"* and showed a wide discrepancy over numbers attending the protest with the **Scottish Mail** declaring a *"50-strong mob"* and **The Herald** recording *"around a dozen members of the Perth and Dundee branches of the Scottish Sociality Party..."* The **Mail** also wrote: *"Banner-waving members of the Scottish Socialist Party marched on the church with gay rights leaders... The 50-strong mob thrust leaflets into the hands of worshippers"*. But no *"gay rights leaders"* were in attendance! The peaceful demonstration was organised by the local Scottish Socialist Party. At a similar demonstration in Edinburgh, under a picture of marchers under a banner waved by the Scottish Socialist Party, even the **Scottish Sun** was forced to declare: *"Peaceful Scots praised by cops"*. Brian's brother Rev David Souter who was at the church in Perth was given space in the **Daily Record** to address Tim Hopkin's group: *"We ask Scrap the Section to restrict their future demonstrations to activities involving adults to avoid situations where children could be intimidated"*.

On 21 April, Brian Souter's sister, Ann Gloag joined what the **Daily Record** called a *"pram protest"* of *"concerned mothers"* with their *"children at the front"* marching up to the Scottish Executive on the Mound. Unfortunately, being Good Friday, the Scottish Executive was closed. Ann Gloag begged: *"I don't usually do this kind of thing so I'm like many of the people here. They are mothers and grandmothers with their children and grandchildren. These aren't the demonstrating type but they feel so strongly that they are willing to march. We chose Good Friday because it is a day when families are together"*. Wearing Keep the Clause slogans and carrying placards, Gloag pushed her daughter Pam's one-year-old son Ross Macmillan in a buggy while his older sister Ashleigh, five, walked alongside.

After the results of Souter's 'referendum' which produced no conclusive results, the **Scottish Daily Express**'s front page featured a strained expression on Souter's face and asked: *"HAPPY NOW, MR SOUTER?"* The **Express** believed *"each vote Mr Souter secured for his Keep the Clause campaign has cost him £2 of his personal fortune... He has spent £500,000 on his advertising*

*trailer campaign, more than £1million on staging the poll and anoth-
er £500,000 on newspaper adverts"*. Their editorial was defiant.
*"We make our opinions on such matters clear at the ballot box, not
some millionaire's whim... That, Mr Souter, is how we do things in
this country. And, if you still don't like it, the answer is clear, stand
as an MSP next time round and see how many people support you -
when it really counts"*.

All the same, the religionists made the Executive dance. In
November 1999 ministers insisted guidelines on sex education
were adequate to protect children and would not need to be
reviewed, but later, with the help of the McCabe committee,
they were. In February 2000, ministers insisted there would be
no replacement to Section 2a, yet, by the following month, one
was tabled. In April, ministers were insisting the new guidelines would not be made legally binding, but by May, guidance
was statutory. Despite insistences that 'marriage' would not be
included in guidelines, that is exactly what happened.

The **Daily Record** warned: *"If they think it will now be plain
sailing from here until the next election, they can forget it. The real
weapon deployed against all politicians will not be a bus tycoon's
poster campaign, referendum or any private initiative. It will be a
sound trouncing at the polls by a disillusioned electorate. It should
have been kiss-and-make-up, but the government want forget-and-
shut-up. The Scottish people will not forget - and we won't be shut
up"*. But they were. By the time of the General Election in the
summer of 2001 the Conservative Party, the only Party to support retention of Section 2a, faced a massive defeat in Scotland
winning just one seat in the House of Commons!

On Wednesday, 21 June 2000, the public gallery in the
Scottish Executive was fairly quiet, most of the seats were
empty and no 'Keep the Clause' demonstrators were in sight.
At 6.23pm, during the debate on the Ethical Standards in Public
Life Bill, Section 2a, was sent on its way by a majority vote of 99
to 17, with just two abstentions. The whole Tory group voted
against repeal. Wendy Alexander said: "Repeal is not and never
has been about the promotion of homosexuality in our schools.
Nor is repeal about 'political correctness' or even marriage. It is
about building a tolerant Scotland". There was a spontaneous
round of applause from almost everyone in the chamber.

# Index